Picture Perfect Dictionary 2

Language and Content Consultants

Sarah Bingaman • Rosa Montes Kahoe
Bob Tintle • Everette J. Williams

About the Consultants

Sarah Bingaman
ESL Teacher, Kindergarten–Grade 6
Holmes Elementary School
Oak Park School District 97
Oak Park, Illinois

Rosa Montes Kahoe
Grade 6 Teacher
Ysleta Elementary School
Ysleta Independent School District
El Paso, Texas

Bob Tintle
Science Teacher
Robert Louis Stevenson School
Pebble Beach, California

Everette J. Williams
Bilingual Teacher, Grades 2–3
Fletcher Drive Elementary School
Los Angeles Unified School District
Los Angeles, California

Credits

Hampton-Brown
Editorial: Lisa Baehr, Mary Borgia, Fredrick Ignacio, Sheron Long, Sarita Chávez Silverman
Art/Design: Jeri Gibson, Ray Godfrey
Production: Cathy Blake, Andrea Carter, Curtis Spitler
Permissions: Barbara Mathewson

Brown Publishing Network, Inc.
Editorial: Elinor Chamas, Jean MacFarland
Art/Design: Jennifer Angell, Trelawney Goodell, Diana Maloney, Kathy Reynolds, Joan Williams
Photo Research: Libby Taft, Nina Whitney
Production: Cheryle D'Amelio, Anthony Fisher, Kathy Meisl, Kathleen Spahn

Acknowledgments

Every effort has been made to secure permission, but if any omissions have been made, please let us know. **author, autobiography:** p. 8 Photograph from Hau Kola, Hello Friend. Copyright © 1994 by Paul Goble. Photography copyright © 1994 by Gerry Perrin. Reprinted with permission of Richard C. Owen Publishing, Inc., Katonah, NY. **biography:** p. 13 Photo courtesy of NASA. **character, characteristic, cheerful:** p.19 PICTURES COPYRIGHT 1953 BY GARTH WILLIAMS, RENEWED 1981 BY GARTH WILLIAMS. Used by permission of HarperCollins Publishers. **chapter:** p. 19 TEXT COPYRIGHT 1932 BY LAURA INGALLS WILDER; COPYRIGHT RENEWED 1960 BY ROGER L. MACBRIDE. PICTURES COPYRIGHT 1953 BY GARTH WILLIAMS; RENEWED 1981 BY GARTH WILLIAMS. Used by permission of HarperCollins Publishers. **encyclopedia:** p. 31 From THE WORLD BOOK ENCYCLOPEDIA. (c) World Book, Inc. By permission of the publisher. **fact:** p. 36 From THE WORLD BOOK ENCYCLOPEDIA. (c) World Book, Inc. By permission of the publisher. **fiction:** p. 38 COPYRIGHT 1945 BY E. B. WHITE. TEXT COPYRIGHT RENEWED © 1973 BY E. B. WHITE. ILLUSTRATIONS COPYRIGHT RENEWED © 1973 BY GARTH WILLIAMS. Used by permission of HarperCollins Publishers. **great:** p. 46 COPYRIGHT 1952 BY E.B. WHITE; renewed © 1980 BY E. B. WHITE. ILLUSTRATIONS COPYRIGHT RENEWED © 1980 BY GARTH WILLIAMS. Used by permission of HarperCollins Publishers. **legend:** p. 60 From LEGEND OF THE BLUEBONNET by Tomie de Paola. Copyright © 1983 by Tomie dePaola. Used by permission of G. P. Putnam's Sons, a division of Penguin Putnam Inc. **magazine** (cover format only): p. 63 Reprinted from the May 1998 issue of Ranger Rick magazine, with the permission of the publisher, the National Wildlife Federation. Copyright 1998 by the National Wildlife Federation. **magazine** (photo only): p. 63 Photo © Rich Kirchner.

Acknowledgments continue on page 160.

Hampton-Brown
P.O. Box 223220
Carmel, California 93922
(800) 333-3510

Printed in the United States of America.

0-7362-0183-1
99 00 01 02 03 04 05 06 07 10 9 8 7 6 5 4 3

Contents

Special Expanded Entries

• More to See! • More to Learn!

Aa

accept
verb

You **accept** something when you take it.

trophy

*Luis was happy to **accept** the trophy for his team.*

act
verb

You **act** when you have a role in a play.

actor

*The students **act** in the school play.*

addition
noun

You use **addition** to add numbers together.

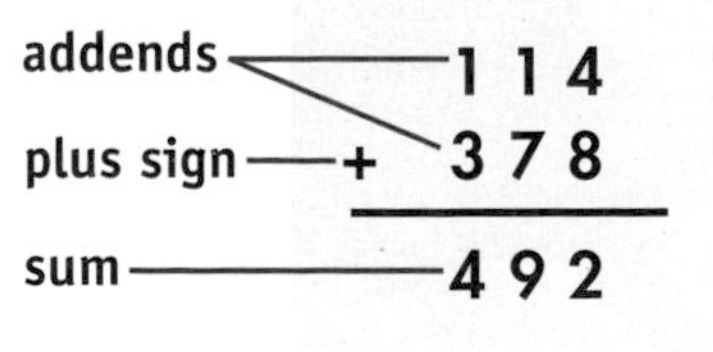

address
noun

An **address** tells the place where someone lives or works.

return address
envelope
stamp

S.J.Tarr
15 West Street
Fairbanks, AK
99712

Ian Kusugak, President
Nunivak Computers
100 May Avenue
Anchorage, AK 99501

address

adjective
noun

An **adjective** is a word that describes something.

*Big and green are **adjectives** that describe this turtle.*

adverb
noun

An **adverb** is a word that tells how, when, or where.

*Slowly is an **adverb** that tells how this turtle walks.*

advertise
verb

When you **advertise** something, you are trying to sell it.

ad

*A company made this ad to **advertise** toothpaste.*

agree
verb

People **agree** when they have the same idea about something.

*These kids **agree**—they all think this is a cute bunny!*

agriculture
noun

Agriculture is the science and business of farming.

See also: *farm* and *fertile*, page 37

growing crops

harvesting crops

raising cattle

always
adverb

Always means every time.

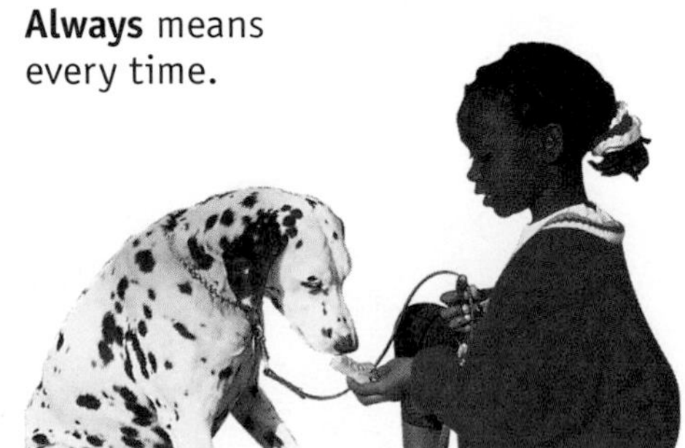

*After our walk, I **always** give my dog a treat.*

American

noun

An **American** is a person who is born in the United States, lives there permanently, or becomes a citizen.

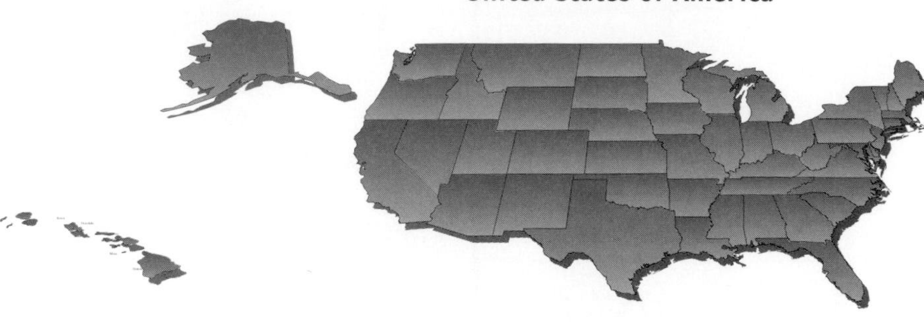

*These people are all **Americans**.*

ancestor

noun

Your **ancestors** are people from your family who lived a long time ago.

*This family has an old picture of their **ancestors**.*

animal

noun

An **animal** is a living being that moves and breathes. There are many kinds of animals. These include mammals, birds, fish, reptiles, and amphibians.

See also: ***arachnid*, page 8; *bird*, page 13; *insect*, page 52; *invertebrate*, page 54; *vertebrate*, page 114**

Mammals

Mammals usually have hair or fur and a backbone. A baby mammal is born alive from its mother's body. It drinks milk from its mother.

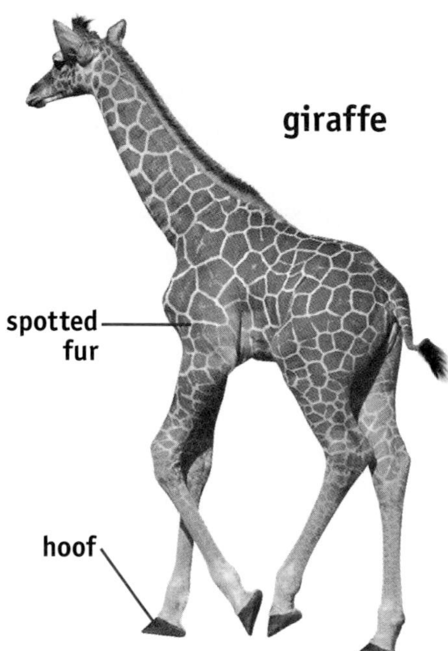

Fish

Fish live in the water. They have gills to breathe underwater. Most kinds of fish are covered with scales. Others, like sharks, have thick skin.

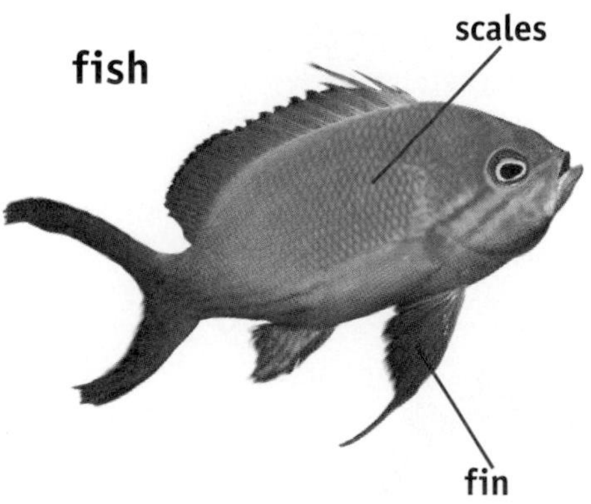

Birds

Birds have wings, and they are the only animals with feathers. Baby birds hatch from eggs. Their parents feed them and protect them until they can fly.

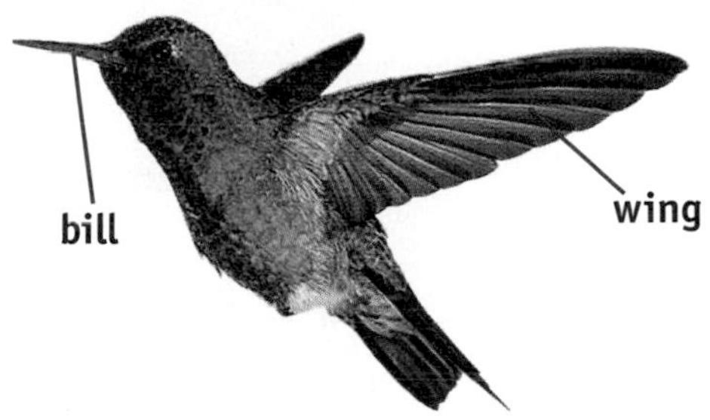

Reptiles

Reptiles have dry, scaly skin. Most reptiles live on land and lay their eggs on land. Some live in the water, but they must come up above the water to breathe air.

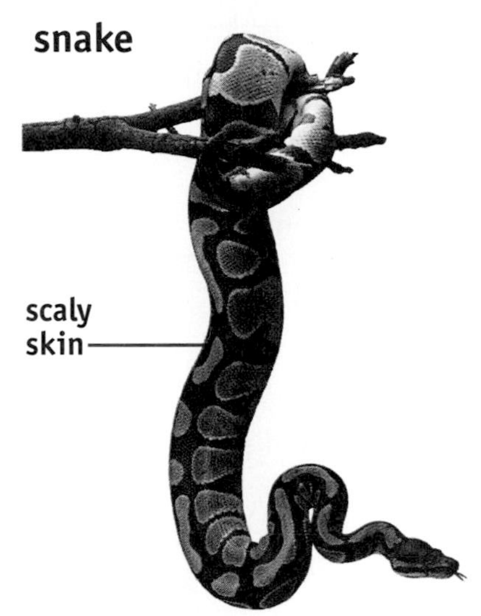

Amphibians

Amphibians have smooth, moist skin. They usually spend part of their life in water and part on land. Baby amphibians are born under water. Most amphibians breathe through gills, like fish do, until they develop lungs.

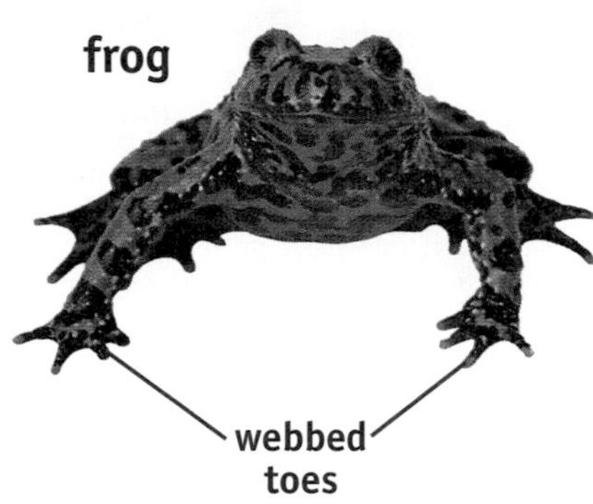

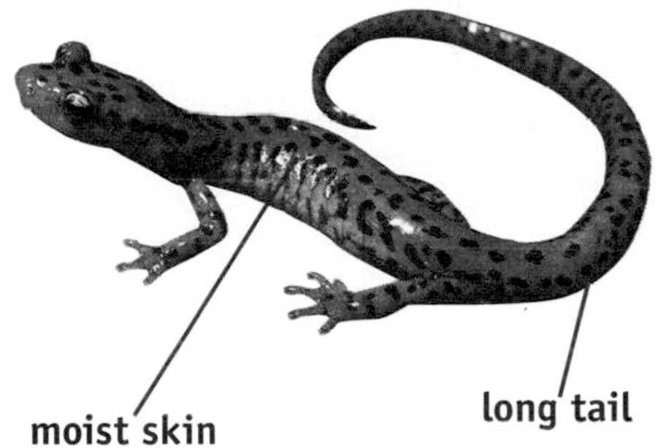

How do animals adapt to where they live?

Dolphins come up above the water to breathe air through their blowholes.

Flamingos put their heads upside down in the water. They use their special bills to scoop up food.

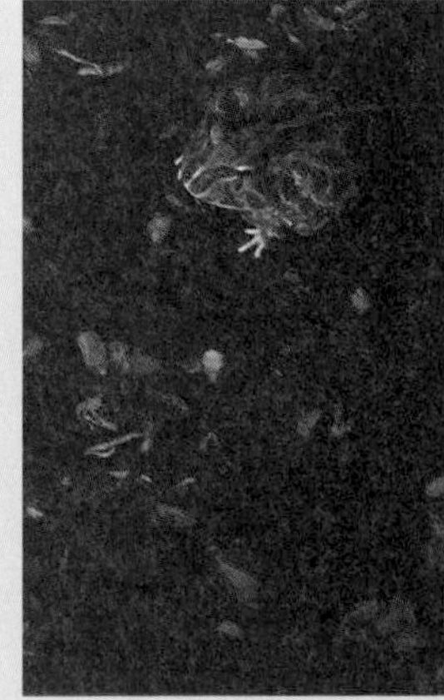

Some frogs have skin that helps them hide from their enemies.

Sea turtles use flipper-shaped feet like the oars of a boat. They swim quickly through the water.

annual
adjective

When an activity is **annual**, it happens every year, usually at the same time.

*Independence Day is an **annual** holiday, celebrated every fourth of July.*

answer
❶ *noun*

An **answer** is a reply to a question. It can be spoken or written.

*The student knows the **answer** to the question.*

❷ *verb*

You **answer** when you respond to something you hear or see.

*I **answer** the telephone when I hear it ring.*

arachnid
noun

An **arachnid** is an animal with eight legs.

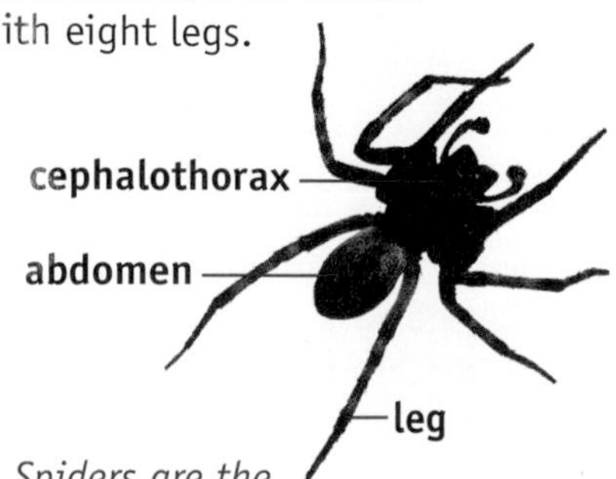

*Spiders are the most common **arachnids**.*

area
noun

In math, **area** is the size of a flat surface measured in square units.

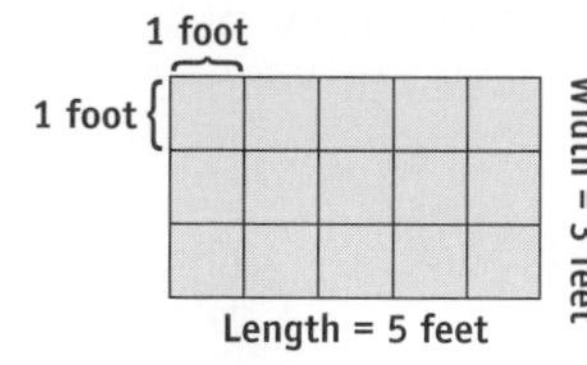

Area = length x width
= 5 ft. x 3 ft.
= 15 square feet

artist
noun

An **artist** is a person who dances, paints, or works in any of the other fine arts.

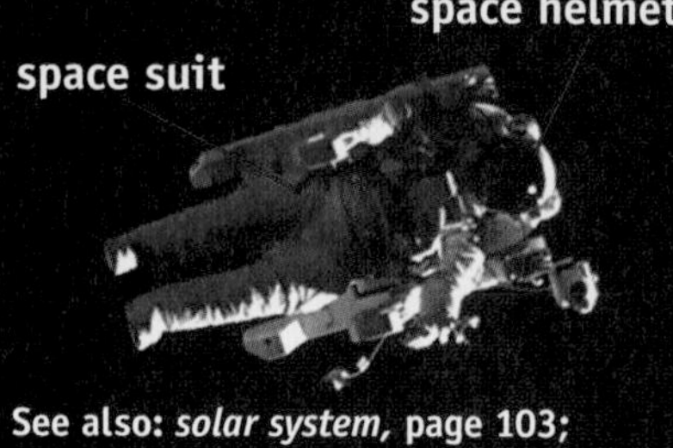

astronaut
noun

An astronaut is a person who travels to outer space in a spacecraft.

See also: *solar system*, page 103; *spacecraft*, page 104

author
noun

An **author** writes stories, poems, or books.

*Paul Goble is the **author** of stories from Native American cultures.*

autobiography
noun

An **autobiography** is the story of a person's life, written by that person.

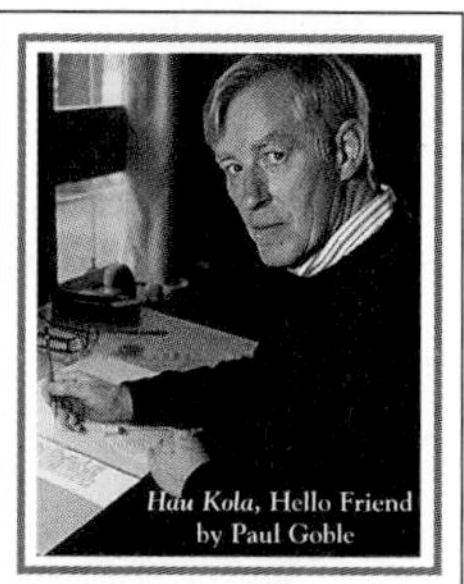

*Paul Goble wrote an **autobiography**, Hau Kola, Hello Friend, about his life.*

automatically
adverb

Automatically means something is done without effort or help.

*The door opens **automatically**. She doesn't have to push it.*

average
verb

When you **average** a set of numbers, you add the numbers together. Then you divide the sum by the number of items in the set.

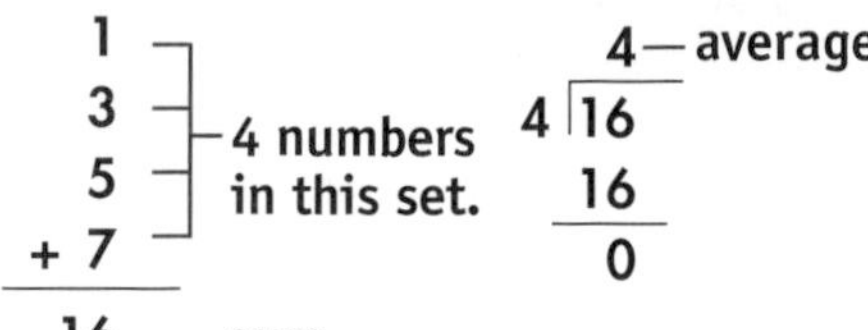

addition
1
3
5
+ 7
4 numbers in this set.
16 — sum
long division
4 — average
4 | 16
16
0

Bb

baby
noun

A **baby** is a very young child or animal.

kangaroo

joey

*The kangaroo carries her **baby** in a pouch.*

baker
noun

A **baker** makes cakes and breads to sell in a bakery.

balance
verb

You **balance** when you keep the same weight on both sides of something.

*This girl can **balance** on a beam.*

bandage
noun

You can use a **bandage** to keep a cut clean and dry.

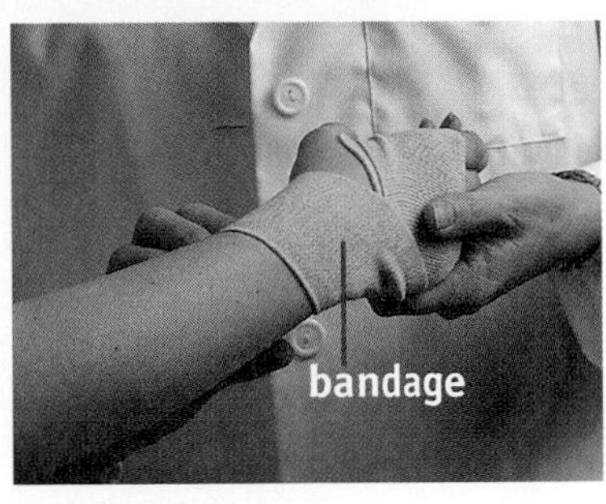

bar
noun

A **bar** has a shape that is longer than it is wide.

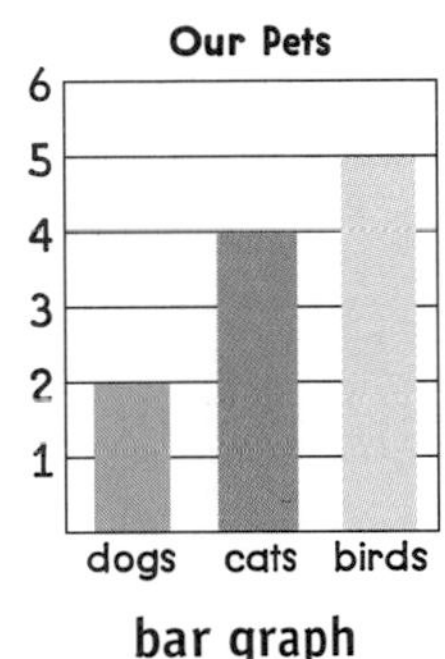

bar graph

candy bar

monkey bars

bargain
noun

Something is a **bargain** when it costs less than the usual price.

*This dress is a **bargain**.*

base
1 *noun*

A **base** is the bottom part of something. It holds up the top part.

statue

base

2 *noun*

A **base** is one of four corners in a baseball diamond.

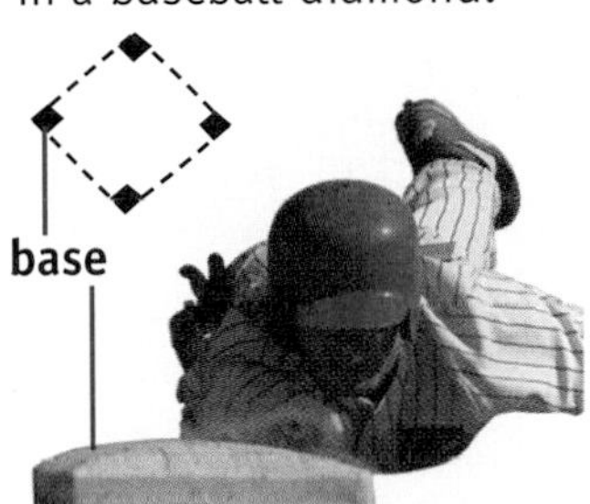

*The player slid into second **base**.*

bat
1 *noun*

A **bat** is a strong stick made of wood or metal. It is used to hit the ball in the game of baseball.

2 *noun*

A **bat** is a mammal that can fly.

*At night, **bats** hunt for insects to eat.*

A B C D E F G H I J K L M N O P Q R S T U V W X Y Z

battle

noun

A **battle** is a fight between two armies during a war. When both armies are from the same country, the war is called a civil war.

See also: ***freedom*****, page 40;**
slavery**, pages 100–101**

Battle of Gettysburg

In 1861, a civil war began in the United States. It was fought between the Northern States and the Southern States. One of the most terrible **battles** of the Civil War was the Battle of Gettysburg. It took place July 1–3, 1863, in Gettysburg, Pennsylvania. Over 38,000 soldiers died in this battle. The Civil War ended in 1865.

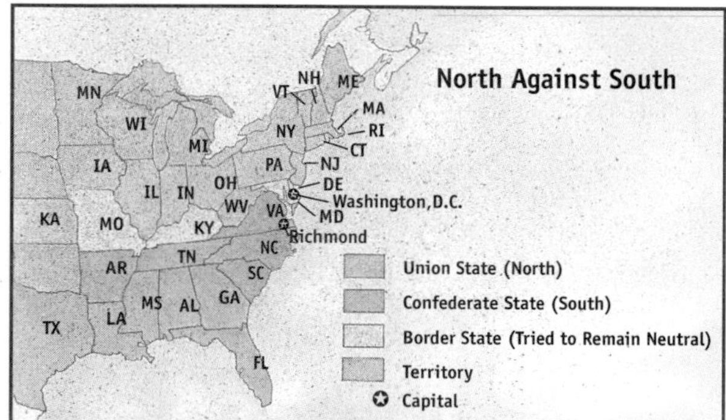

Gettysburg, Pennsylvania: Cemetery Ridge

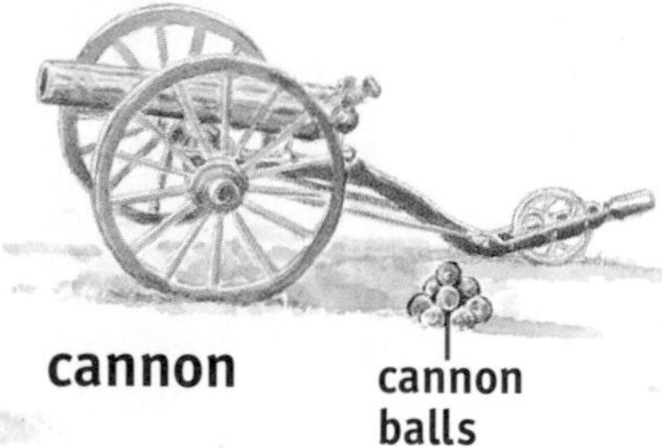

from a painting by Henry Phillippoteaux

field hospital

wagon

Why was there a war between the North and the South?

The states in the South used slaves to plant and harvest crops.

The states in the North passed laws to end slavery.

The states in the South decided they did not want to be part of the United States.

An Ordinance,

To dissolve the Union between the State of South Carolina and other States united with her under the compact entitled, "The Constitution of the United States of America."

We, the People of the State of South Carolina, in Convention assembled, do declare and ordain, and it is hereby declared and ordained,

That the Ordinance adopted by us in Convention, on the twenty-third day of May, in the year of our Lord one thousand seven hundred and eighty-eight, whereby the Constitution of the United States of America was ratified, and also, all Acts and parts of Acts of the General Assembly of this State, ratifying amendments of the said Constitution, are hereby repealed; and that the union now subsisting between South Carolina and other States, under the name of "The United States of America," is hereby dissolved.

President Abraham Lincoln wanted to keep the North and the South as one country.

For four long years the two sides battled. Finally, the North defeated the South. The Union stayed together.

beat

verb

You **beat** someone when you win and the other person loses.

*Marta **beats** Kane at tic-tac-toe.*

In the past:
She **beat** him.
She **has beaten** him.

Idiom:
Beat it!

When you say "**Beat it!**" you want someone or something to go away.

beautiful

adjective

Something that is very lovely is **beautiful**.

*Look at the **beautiful** garden!*

become

verb

Become means to change or grow into something different.

*A caterpillar may **become** a butterfly.*

In the past:
It **became** a butterfly.
It **has become** a butterfly.

bee

noun

A **bee** is an insect with four wings and a fuzzy body. A female bee has a stinger.

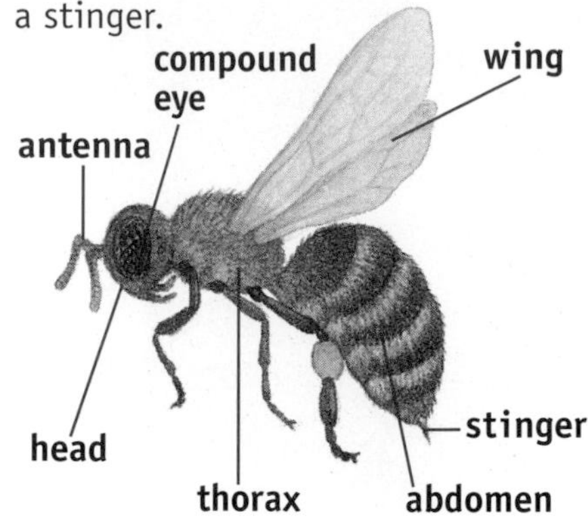

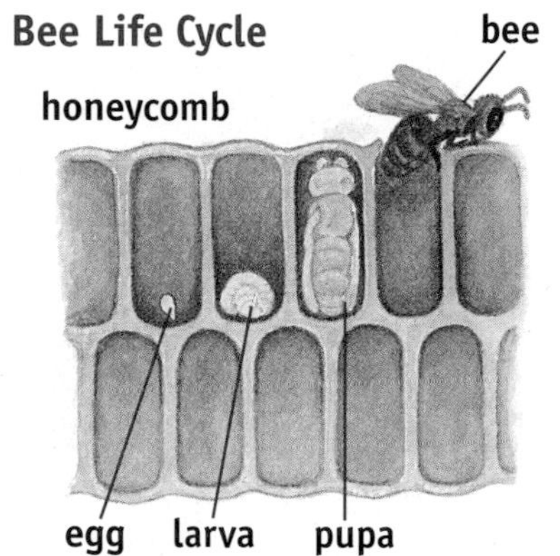

beehive

noun

A **beehive** is the home for a group, or colony, of bees.

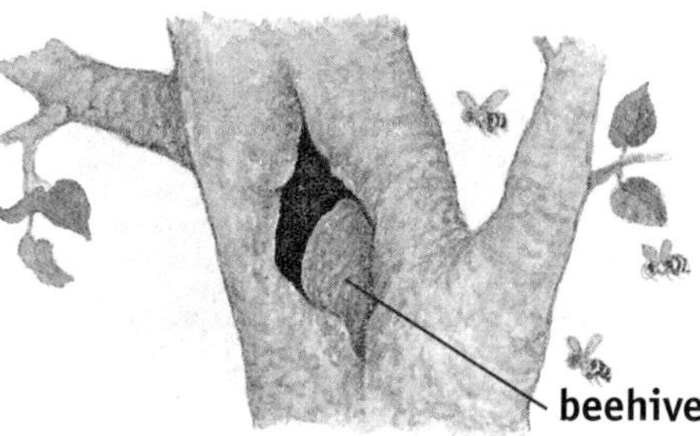

*Worker bees feed the queen and defend the **beehive**.*

begin

verb

You start something when you **begin**.

*Many fairy tales **begin** with the words, "Once upon a time."*

In the past:
You **began** to read.
You **have begun** to read.

behind

preposition

Behind means in back of something.

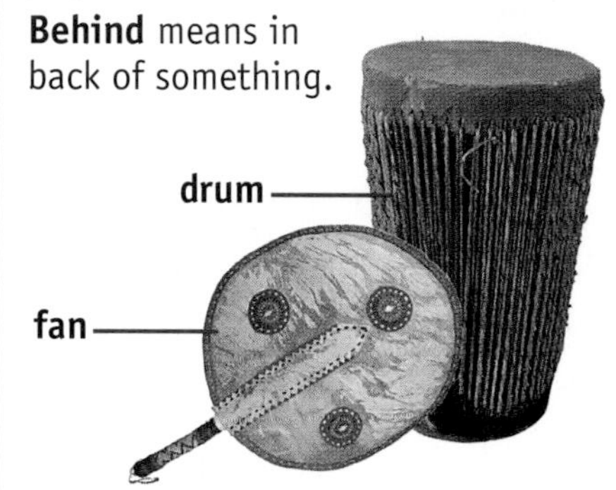

*The drum is **behind** the fan.*

believe

verb

When you **believe**, you feel certain that something is true.

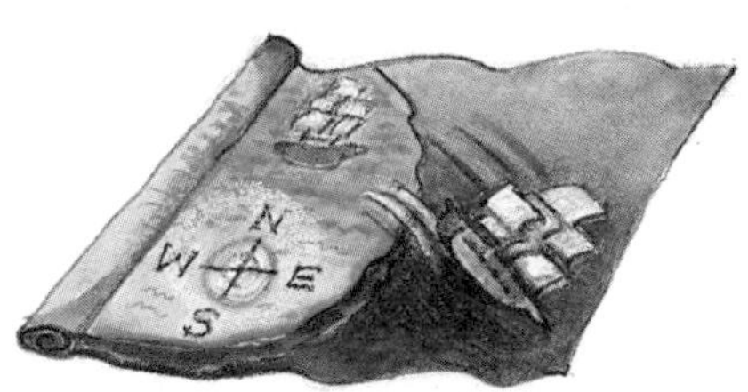

*Did early explorers really **believe** the world was flat?*

belong

verb

You **belong** when you are part of a group.

*These girls **belong** to a soccer team.*

between

preposition

Between means in the middle of two things.

*Elena does her homework **between** 4 and 6 o'clock.*

Idiom:
between a rock and a hard place

When you are **between a rock and a hard place**, you have to choose between two difficult things.

*Paul's choice of chores left him **between a rock and a hard place**.*

bill

❶ *noun*

A **bill** is a piece of paper money.

*This is a five-dollar **bill**.*

❷ *noun*

A **bill** is a list of items sold and their cost.

bill — VIDALIA'S TRUCK STOP

Check no	Tab	Ser	Time	Date
18083/1	1002	99	13:15	03/11/98

1 LG CAESAR SLD 9.20
2 BOWL OF FRIES 5.50

Food Sub Total 15.10

SUB TOTAL 15.10
5 % TAX .75

amount of money owed — TOTAL 15.95

Thank You for Dining at Vidalia's Truck Stop.

*When you eat in a restaurant, the **bill** shows how much you have to pay.*

biography

noun

A **biography** is the story of a person's life. It is written by another person.

*This is the **biography** of Mae Jemison by Gail Sakurai.*

bird

noun

A **bird** is an animal that has feathers and wings. Most birds use their wings to fly. There are many different kinds of birds.

See also: ***animal*****, pages 6–7**

Birds of Prey

Seabirds

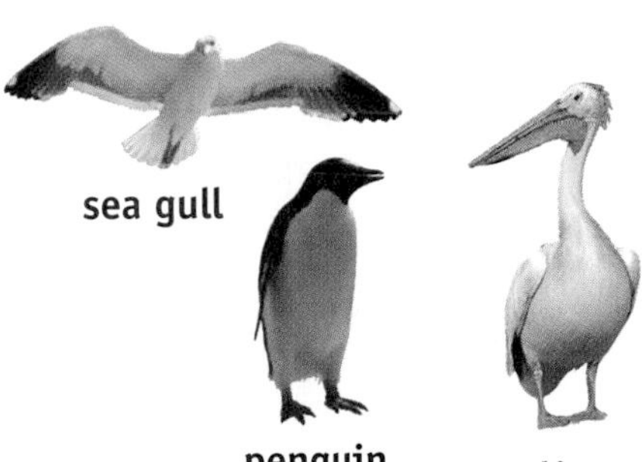

Tropical Birds

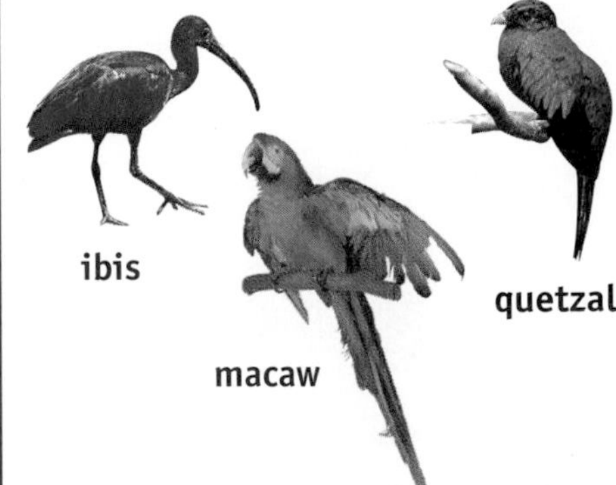

bite

verb

When you **bite** something, you cut into it with your teeth.

In the past:
She **bit** it.
She **has bitten** it.

blank

❶ *adjective*

Something is **blank** when it is not written on.

*This is a **blank** sheet of paper.*

❷ *noun*

A **blank** is an empty space to be filled in.

*She is writing her name in the **blank**.*

blizzard

noun

A **blizzard** is a heavy snowstorm with strong, cold winds.

blood

noun

Blood is the liquid that flows through your body. It flows—or circulates—through the circulatory system. Blood carries food and oxygen to all parts of the body. It also carries carbon dioxide and waste materials to organs that will get rid of them.

See also: ***bone*, page 15; *cell*, page 18; *digestion*, page 28**

The Circulatory System

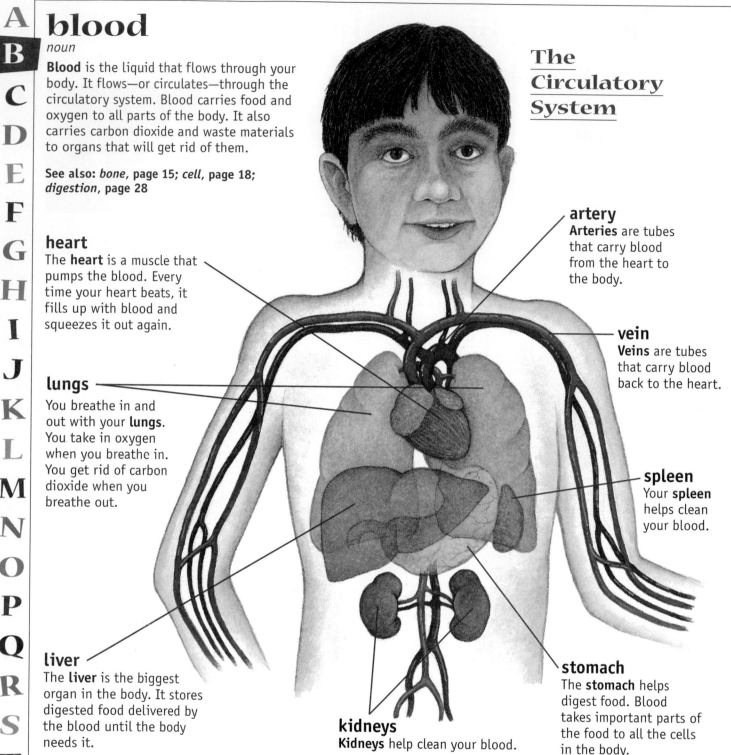

heart
The **heart** is a muscle that pumps the blood. Every time your heart beats, it fills up with blood and squeezes it out again.

lungs
You breathe in and out with your **lungs**. You take in oxygen when you breathe in. You get rid of carbon dioxide when you breathe out.

liver
The **liver** is the biggest organ in the body. It stores digested food delivered by the blood until the body needs it.

artery
Arteries are tubes that carry blood from the heart to the body.

vein
Veins are tubes that carry blood back to the heart.

spleen
Your **spleen** helps clean your blood.

stomach
The **stomach** helps digest food. Blood takes important parts of the food to all the cells in the body.

kidneys
Kidneys help clean your blood.

What do blood cells look like?

Red blood cells look like flattened doughnuts. Their job is to deliver oxygen and take away carbon dioxide.

White blood cells are much bigger than red blood cells. Their job is to fight infections.

Platelets are oval-shaped. Their job is to help you stop bleeding when you cut yourself.

red blood cells

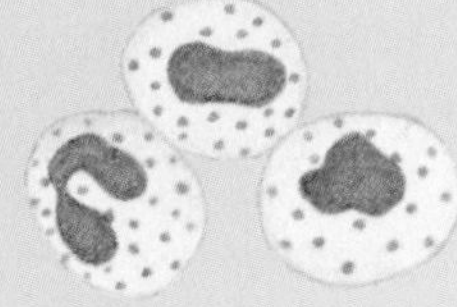

white blood cells

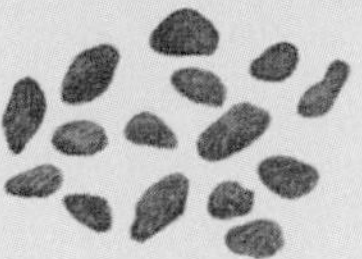

platelets

blossom
noun

A **blossom** is a flower.

*This **blossom** comes from a tree.*

boil
verb

When you **boil** water, you heat it until bubbles form and steam rises.

*Water **boils** at 212° Fahrenheit or 100° Celsius.*

bone
noun

A **bone** is one of the hard parts of the skeleton of a person or animal. Bones help give the body its shape.

See also: ***skeleton,*** **page 99**

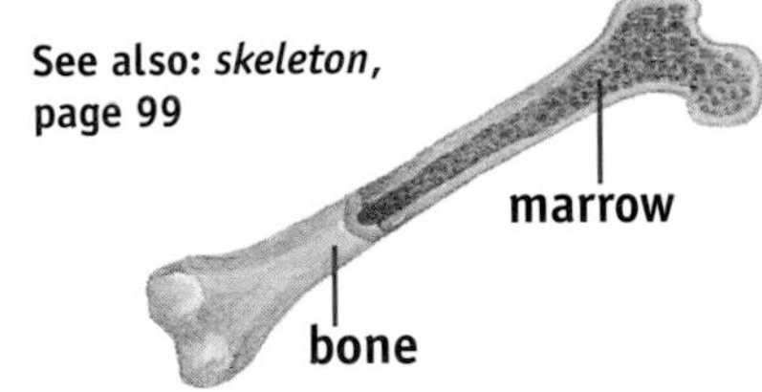

*New red blood cells are made in the marrow inside your **bones**.*

border
noun

A **border** is the line on a map that divides one country or state from another.

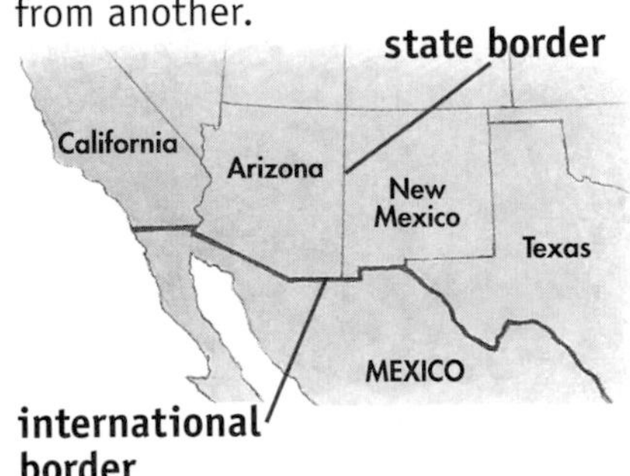

braid

1 *noun*

A **braid** is a length of hair in which three or more strands are woven together.

2 *verb*

When you **braid**, you weave three or more strands together.

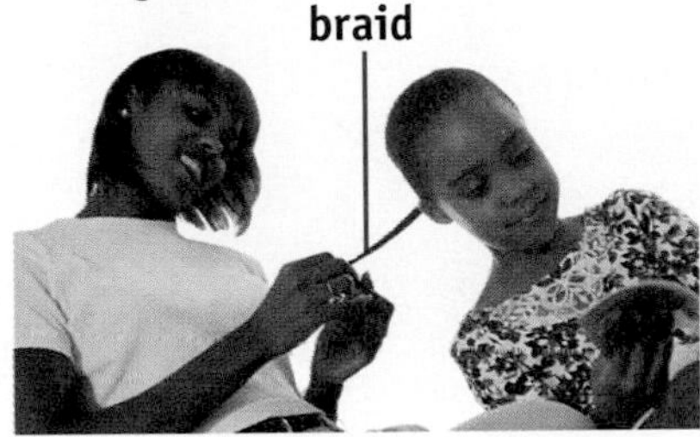

*The girl **braids** her sister's hair.*

brain
noun

Your **brain** is inside your skull. It helps you think, feel, learn, remember, and move.

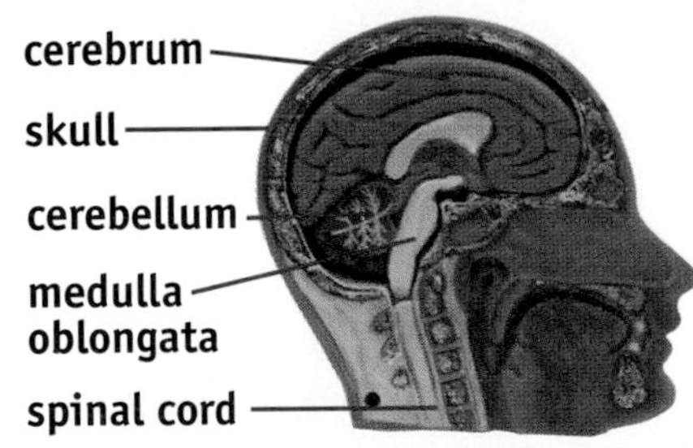

break
verb

When you **break** something, you crack it into pieces.

*He **breaks** an egg into the bowl.*

In the past:
He **broke** the egg.
He **has broken** the egg.

breath
noun

Your **breath** is the air that passes in and out of your lungs.

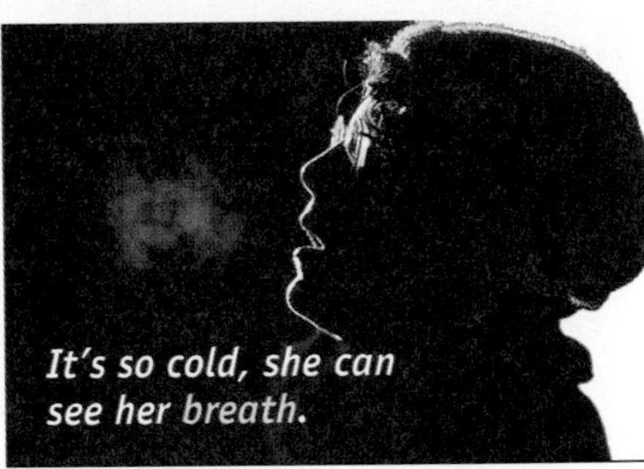

It's so cold, she can see her breath.

bride
noun

A **bride** is a woman who is just married or about to be married.

*This **bride** and bridegroom are dressed for their wedding.*

bridge
noun

A **bridge** is built over something that is hard to cross.

*This **bridge** goes over a river.*

bring
verb

You **bring** something when you carry or lead it somewhere.

*I **bring** my books home in a backpack.*

In the past:
We **brought** our books home.
We **have brought** our books home.

brush

❶ *noun*

A **brush** is a tool with bristles and a handle.

❷ *verb*

You **brush** when you use a brush to do something.

*He **brushes** his teeth every day.*

bubble

noun

A **bubble** is a round space filled with air or another gas.

*She's blowing a big **bubble** with bubble gum.*

buckle

noun

You use a **buckle** to fasten one end of a belt or strap to the other end.

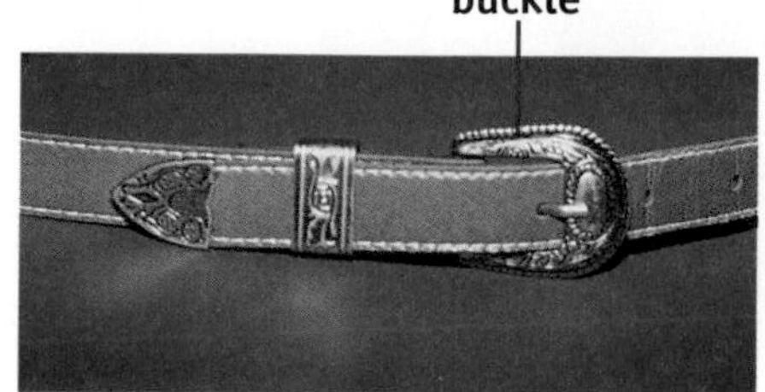

build

verb

You **build** something when you put materials or parts together to make it.

*They're working together to **build** an igloo.*

burn

verb

Something **burns** when it is set on fire.

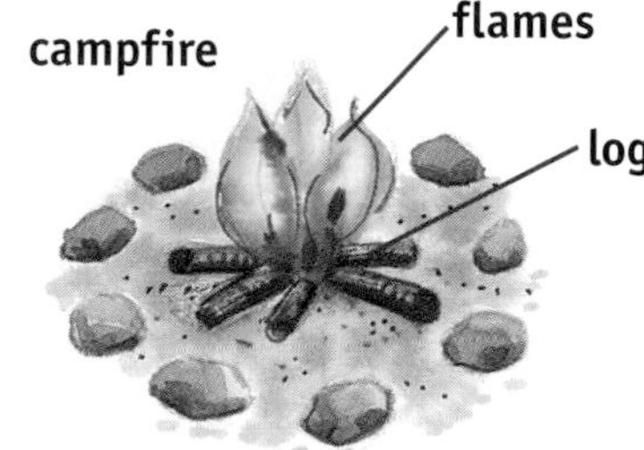

*The logs **burn** in the campfire.*

bury

verb

You **bury** something when you put it under the ground.

*Some turtles **bury** their eggs in the sand to keep them safe.*

bushel

noun

A **bushel** is a unit of measure equal to 32 quarts. It is used for fruit, vegetables, grain, and other dry products.

*The big basket holds a **bushel** of apples.*

business

noun

A **business** is a store, factory, or other company that buys and sells things.

busy

adjective

Busy means filled with work or activity.

*This street is a **busy** place.*

buy

verb

When you **buy** something, you pay money for it.

*He **buys** a newspaper every day.*

In the past:
He **bought** a newspaper.
He **has bought** a newspaper.

Cc

cabin

noun

A **cabin** is a small house made of wood or logs.

*Their **cabin** is in the country.*

cable

noun

A **cable** is made of electrical wires inside a plastic cover.

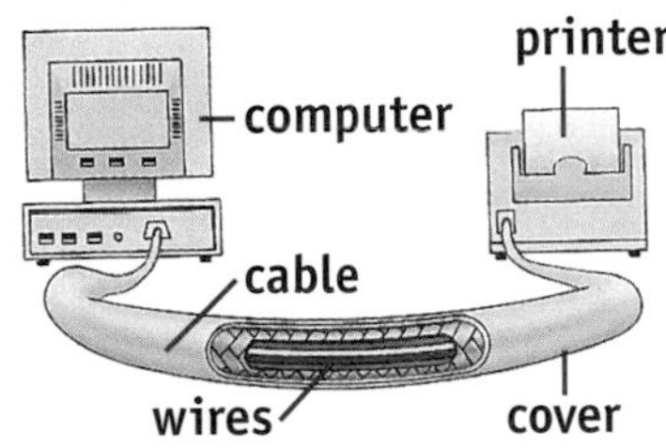

*A **cable** connects the computer to the printer.*

calcium

noun

Calcium is a white mineral found in rocks and plants.

*The **calcium** in milk helps keep your teeth and bones strong.*

call

1 *verb*

You can **call** someone to speak with them.

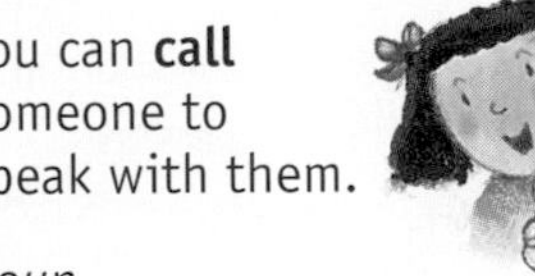

2 *noun*

When you make a **call**, you contact someone by telephone.

*On Sunday, I **call** my grandmother. We enjoy our weekly **call**.*

Idiom:

call it a day

You **call it a day** when you decide to stop doing something.

*The workers **call it a day** at 5:00.*

camouflage

noun

Some animals use camouflage to hide from their enemies.

Frogs use their color for camouflage.

canal

noun

A **canal** is a narrow street made of water.

capital

noun

The government of a nation or state is located in its **capital**.

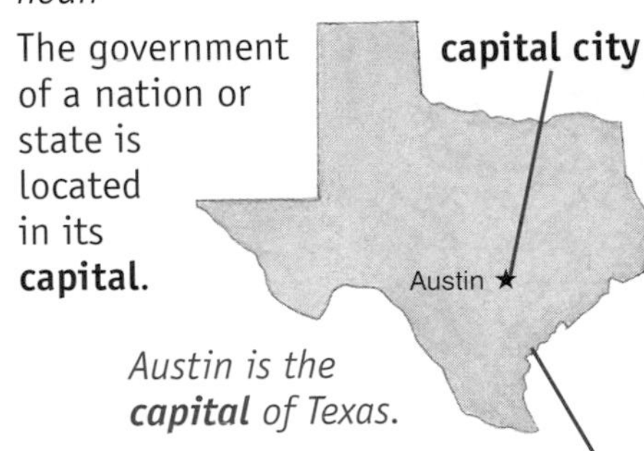

*Austin is the **capital** of Texas.*

See also: *state*, page 105

caption

noun

A **caption** is a word or sentence that explains a picture.

caption

photograph

In addition to vegetable farms, there are many other types of farms that produce food. Let's visit some.

*This **caption** gives you information about the field.*

capture

verb

You **capture** something when you catch it and keep it.

butterfly

net

I used a net to capture the butterfly.

cause

noun

The **cause** is the reason that something happens.

*The snowstorm was the **cause** of the traffic accident.*

celebrate

verb

You **celebrate** when you do something special on a holiday.

Hanukkah Celebration

Kwanzaa Celebration

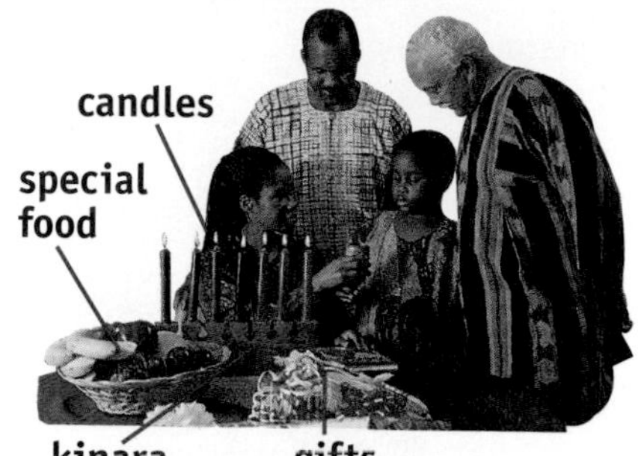

*People light candles when they **celebrate** Kwanzaa and Hanukkah.*

cell

noun

A **cell** is a very small, basic part of all plants and animals.

Plant Cell

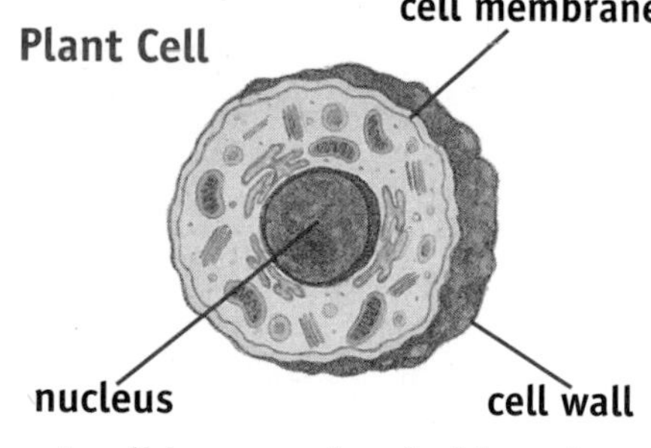

*A **cell** has a nucleus inside and a cell wall around it.*

How Cells Divide

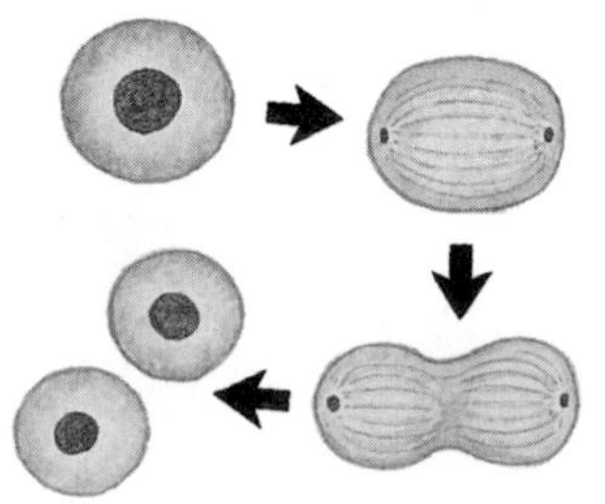

*A **cell** can divide to make new cells.*

See also: ***blood*, page 14**

center

❶ *noun*

The **center** of something is its middle.

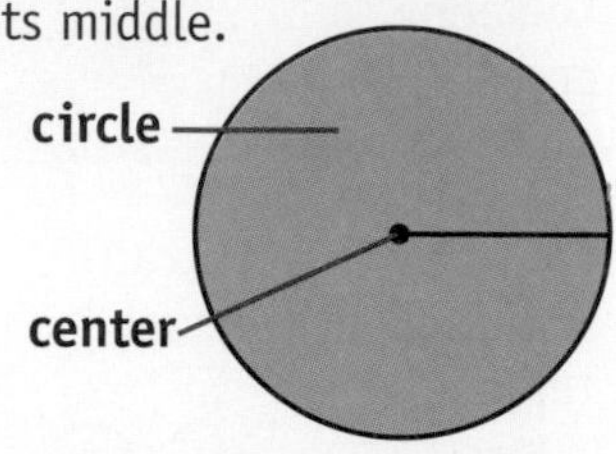

*You can measure the distance between the **center** and the edge of a circle.*

❷ *noun*

A **center** is a place where people meet.

*You can go to a youth **center** to meet friends.*

central

adjective

When something is **central**, it is near the middle.

Time Zones

*Chicago is in the **Central** Time Zone.*

century

noun

A **century** equals 100 years of time.

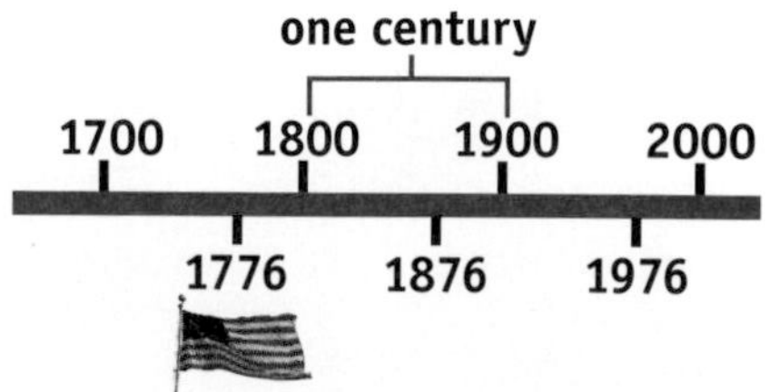

*The United States of America has been an independent nation for more than two **centuries**.*

cereal

noun

A **cereal** is a kind of grass. It has seeds that we can eat.

*Wheat is a **cereal** often used in breakfast foods.*

certain

adjective

When something is **certain**, there is no question about it.

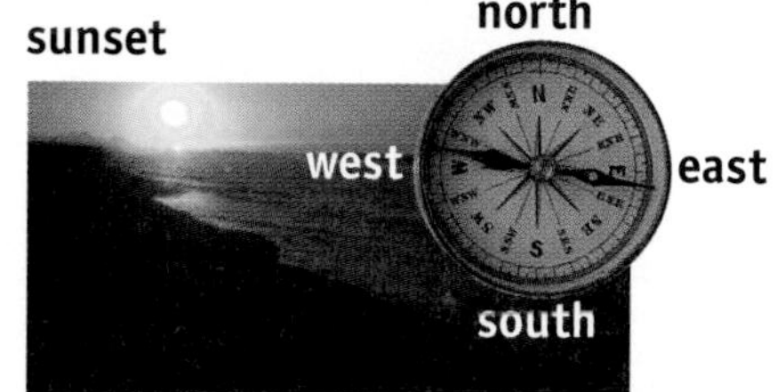

*You can be **certain** the sun will set in the west.*

certificate

noun

A **certificate** is a paper with important information.

name
date of birth
place of birth
Cook County
Vital Statistics
Chicago, Illinois
name Peter Sean Brown
date May 23, 1984
hospital Chicago Lying In

*Your birth **certificate** tells when and where you were born.*

change

verb

When something **changes**, it becomes different.

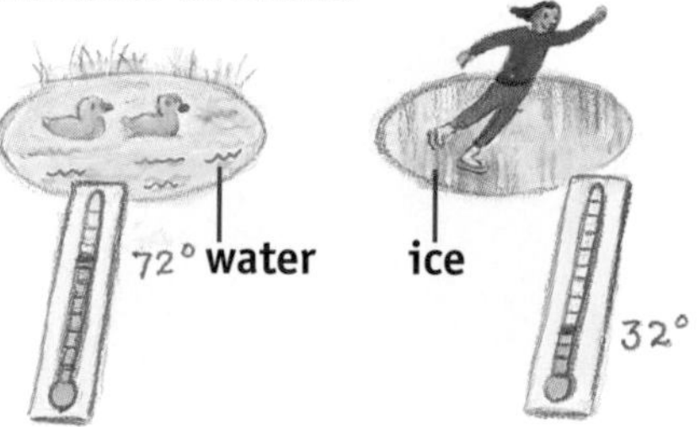

*Water will **change** to ice at 32 degrees Fahrenheit.*

chapter
noun

Some books are divided into several parts, or **chapters**.

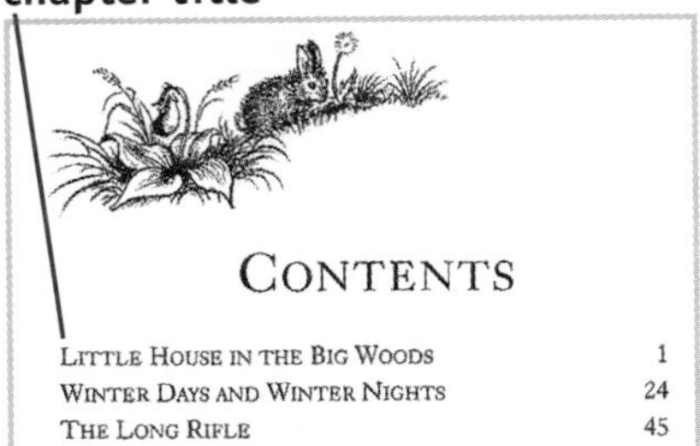

CONTENTS

character
noun

A **character** is a person in a story, a book, a movie, or a play.

*Laura is the main **character** in Little House in the Big Woods.*

characteristic
noun

A **characteristic** is a feature or quality that helps make each person different from others.

*Helpfulness is one of Laura's **characteristics**.*

chart
noun

A **chart** is a clear way to show facts.

chart — title of book

Little House in the Big Woods	
Characters	Characteristics
Pa	brave caring playful
Laura	cheerful helpful kind

*This **chart** describes two characters in the book.*

cheerful
adjective

A **cheerful** person smiles and enjoys life.

*Laura was a **cheerful** person.*

chemical reaction
noun

A **chemical reaction**, or change, can happen when two liquids combine.

*Always wear safety goggles when you are near a **chemical reaction**.*

child
noun

A **child** is a young boy or girl.

*This **child** is learning to cut paper.*

More than one:
Two **children** can cut paper.

chill
verb

You **chill** something when you make it cold.

*You need to **chill** milk to keep it fresh.*

Idiom:
chill out

You ask children to **chill out** when you want them to calm down.

choice
noun

A **choice** is a decision you make when you choose between different things.

*It can be hard to make a **choice**.*

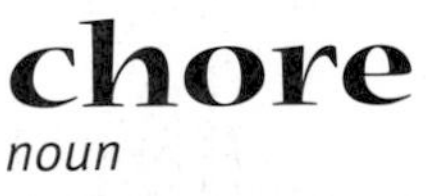

chore
noun

A **chore** is a small job that has to be done.

*Vacuuming the living room is my brother's weekly **chore**.*

A B C D E F G H I J K L M N O P Q R S T U V W X Y Z

circuit

noun

A **circuit** is the complete path of an electric current.

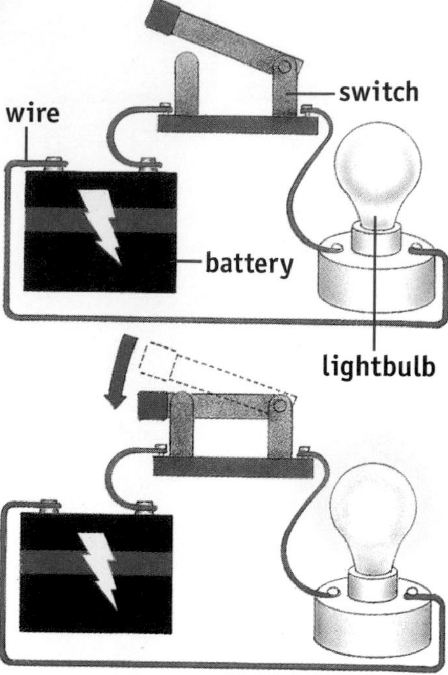

*When you close the switch, electric current flows through the **circuit**. This makes the bulb light up.*

See also: *electricity*, **page 31**

circumference

noun

The **circumference** is the distance around a circle.

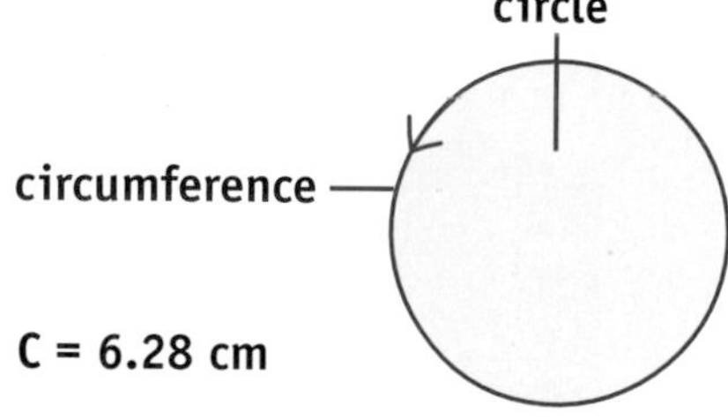

*The **circumference** of this circle is 6.28 centimeters.*

citizen

noun

A **citizen** is a person who is born in or becomes a member of a nation.

*They have just become **citizens** of the United States.*

civilization

noun

A **civilization** is the way of life of a group of people or a nation. It includes their government, their arts, and their system of beliefs.

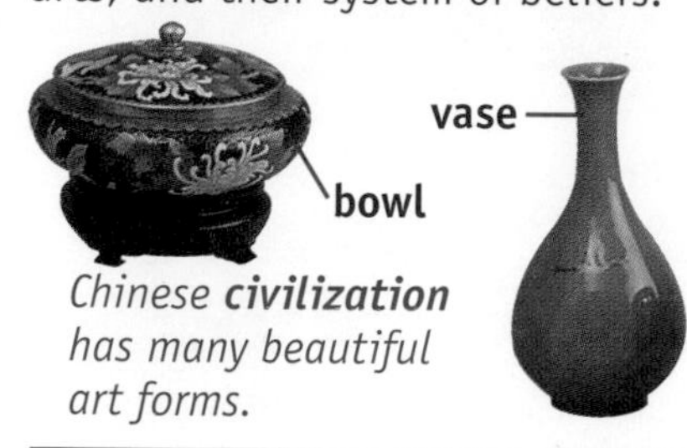

*Chinese **civilization** has many beautiful art forms.*

clan

noun

A **clan** is a group of families with a common ancestor.

*These families belong to the same **clan**.*

See also: *ancestor*, **page 6**

classify

verb

You **classify** things when you put them in groups that are alike in some way.

*You can **classify** leaves by their shape.*

climate

noun

Climate is the kind of weather a region usually has. The earth is divided into three climate zones.

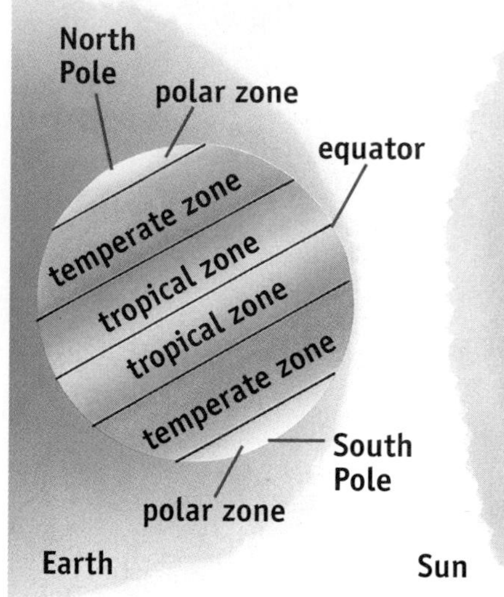

*Tropical **climates** are hot. Temperate climates change with the season. Polar climates are cold. With Earth at this angle, it is summer in the Southern Hemisphere.*

cloud

noun

A cloud is a mass of tiny drops of water floating in the air.

clue

noun

A **clue** is a hint that helps you solve a problem.

*What does throw mean? The teacher is giving a **clue**.*

cluster

noun

A **cluster** is a group of similar items.

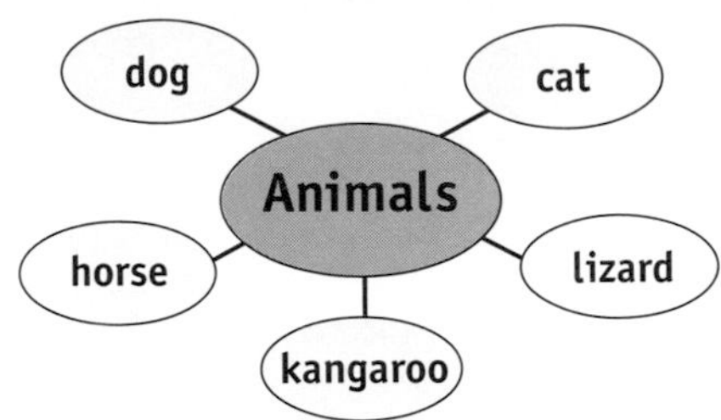
dog
cat
Animals
horse
lizard
kangaroo

*This **cluster** shows several kinds of animals.*

code

noun

A **code** is a set of symbols. You can use a code to write a message.

Some Morse Code Symbols

E •	O ••
H ••••	S •••
L —	V •••—
N —•	W •——

*Use the **code** to read this message:*

•••• • — — ••

collect

verb

When you **collect** things, you gather them together.

*We **collect** newspapers to recycle.*

college

noun

A **college** is a school to go to after high school. You can study for a career or profession in college.

*This is William and Mary **College**.*

See also: *university*, page 114

colony

noun

A **colony** is a place that belongs to another country.

See also: *community*, page 23; *pilgrim*, pages 80-81; *revolution*, page 91; *United States*, page 113

England

England's Colonies in America

More than two centuries ago, there were 13 **colonies** in America. They belonged to England. The colonists fought England to win their freedom. The free colonies became the first 13 states of the United States of America.

The Thirteen Colonies

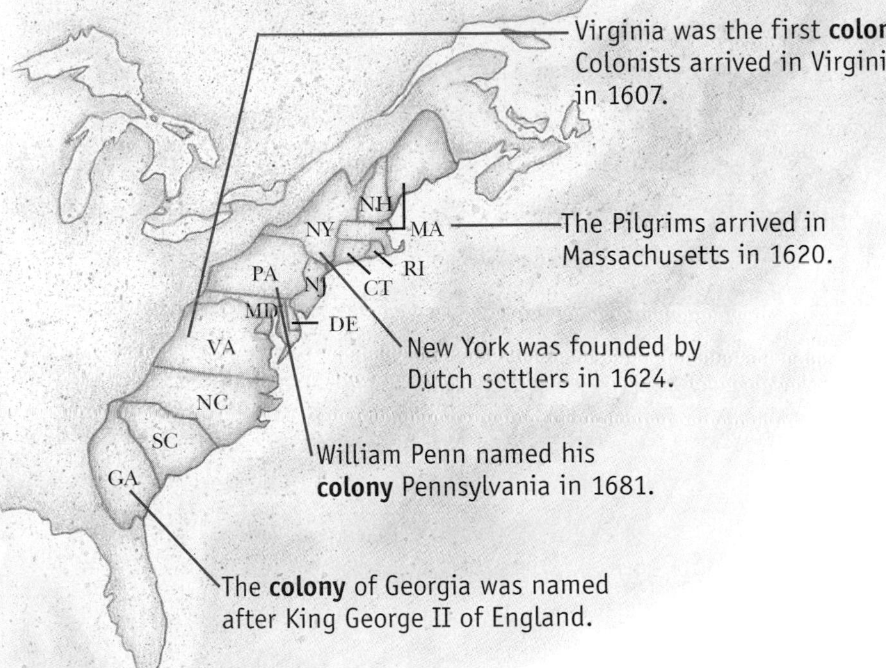
NH
NY
MA
RI
CT
PA
NJ
MD
DE
VA
NC
SC
GA
Virginia was the first **colony**. Colonists arrived in Virginia in 1607.
The Pilgrims arrived in Massachusetts in 1620.
New York was founded by Dutch settlers in 1624.
William Penn named his **colony** Pennsylvania in 1681.
The **colony** of Georgia was named after King George II of England.

Colonial Life

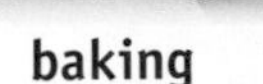

baking

spinning

marching in a band

A B C D E F G H I J K L M N O P Q R S T U V W X Y Z

column

❶ *noun*

A **column** is used to support part of a building.

❷ *noun*

A **column** is a vertical section. It fills a space from top to bottom.

*This page has three **columns**.*

comma

noun

A **comma** is a punctuation mark that separates words or phrases in a sentence.

commas

I like math, social studies, and English.

*Use **commas** to separate items in a series.*

committee

noun

A **committee** is a group of people. They work together on a project.

*This **committee** signed the Declaration of Independence.*

communication

noun

Communication happens when people send and receive messages.

See also: ***satellite*****, page 93**

Letter carriers deliver mail to people.

Communication Throughout History

Throughout history, people have used many kinds of **communication**.

490 B.C.E.

The Greeks used runners to bring news from town to town.

117 A.D.

Roman soldiers used torches to send signals.

1750 A.D.

Native Americans sent messages with smoke signals.

1860 A.D.

Pony Express riders took mail from Missouri to California.

1861 A.D.

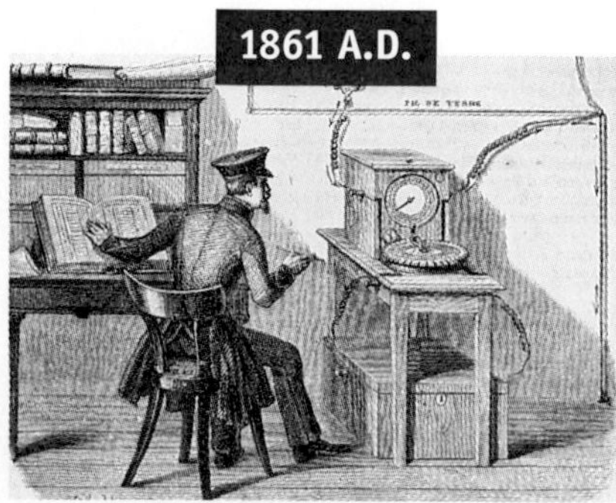

The telegraph uses a code to send messages.

TODAY

People can fax, e-mail, and talk using telephones and computers.

community

noun

A **community** is a group of people who live in the same place. They have the same laws and government. A community can change and grow.

The Community of Philadelphia, Pennsylvania

PHILADELPHIA, 1682

The **community** of Philadelphia began in 1682 in the colony of Pennsylvania. It had 500 people. Most of them came from England. The name of their community means "City of Brotherly Love."

PHILADELPHIA, 1720

Artist Peter Cooper painted this scene of his home town, Philadelphia, in 1720. It shows ships on the Delaware River and many buildings. By 1760, 20,000 people lived in Philadelphia. It was the largest **community** in the English colonies of America.

PHILADELPHIA, 1856

In 1856, the docks along the Delaware River were busier than ever. People came to ice skate there in winter. By 1880, the **community** of Philadelphia was very large. About 500,000 people lived there.

PHILADELPHIA, TODAY

Now more than 1 million people live in Philadelphia. Many tourists come every year to visit the historic city, home of the Liberty Bell.

Liberty Bell

A B C D E F G H I J K L M N O P Q R S T U V W X Y Z

compare

verb

When you **compare** two things, you see how they are the same and how they are different.

***Compare** these two beetles.*

complete

verb

When you **complete** something, you finish it.

Homework

1. 8 ÷ 2 = 4
2. 4 x 6 = 24
3. 27 ÷ 9 = 3
4. 5 x 2 = 10
5. 24 ÷ 8 =

*This student needs to **complete** the homework. One problem has no answer.*

computer

noun

A **computer** is a machine. You can use it to write, do math, store information, or play games.

a computer

*This boy uses the **computer** to do his homework.*

See also: ***disk*, page 29; *keyboard*, page 55; *modem* and *mouse*, page 67; *network*, page 71; *scroll*, page 93; *software*, page 102; *surf*, page 105**

conclusion

noun

The **conclusion** is the end of something.

introduction — title

The California Missions

There are 21 missions in California. They were founded by the Franciscan father Junípero Serra.

body — The first mission, San Diego de Alcalá, was founded in 1769 in present-day San Diego. The last one, Mission San Francisco Solano, was founded in 1823 in Sonoma.

Today, the California missions are treasures that remind us of Spain's rule in early California. — conclusion

*This report has a strong **conclusion**.*

cone

noun

A **cone** is a shape. It is round at one end and has a point at the other end.

round end

cone

point

conjunction

noun

A **conjunction** is a word that connects two words, phrases, or sentences.

conjunctions

I like peanut butter **and** jelly, **but** I don't like mustard.

*There are two **conjunctions** in this sentence.*

connect

verb

When you **connect** two things, you join them together.

*A plug **connects** this cable to the electrical outlet.*

constellation

noun

A constellation is a group of stars that form a shape.

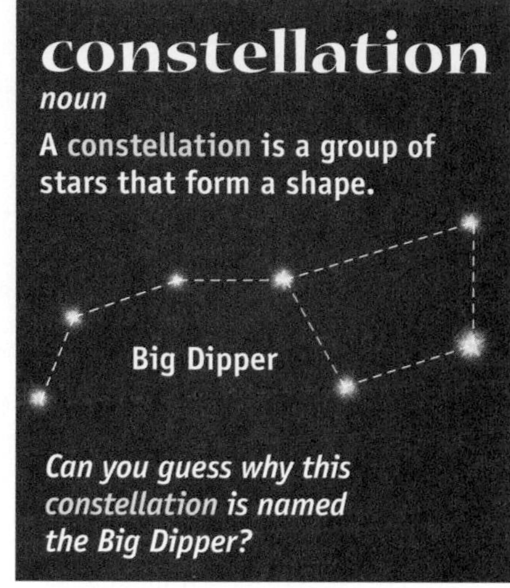

Can you guess why this constellation is named the Big Dipper?

constitution

noun

A **constitution** is a set of rules followed by the government and citizens of a country.

See also: ***government*, pages 44-45**

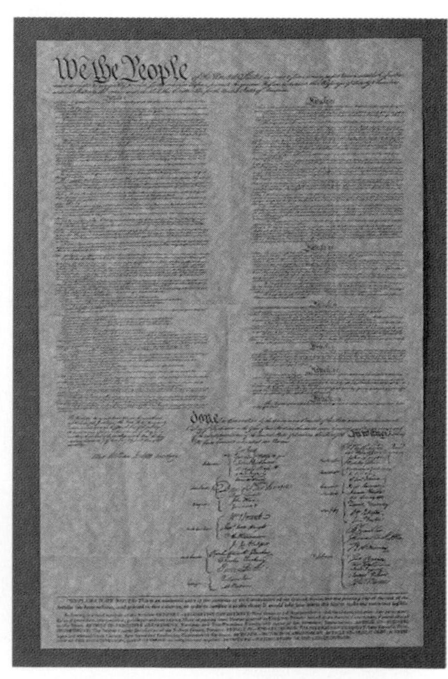

*The **Constitution** of the United States was written in 1787.*

continent
noun

A **continent** is a large body of land.

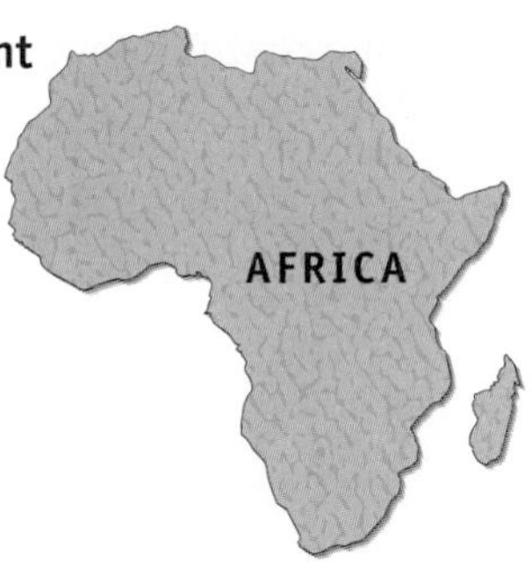

*Africa is one of the seven **continents** on Earth.*

contraction
noun

A **contraction** is a word made by putting two words together and leaving out one or more letters.

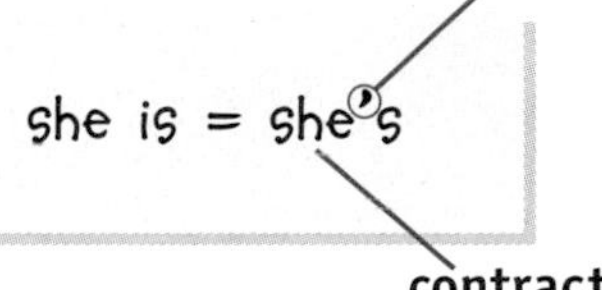

*In this **contraction**, the apostrophe takes the place of the i in is.*

conversation
noun

When two or more people talk together, they have a **conversation**.

*The teachers are having a **conversation**.*

cooperate
verb

When you **cooperate**, you work well with other people.

*Kim and her mother **cooperate** when they make cupcakes.*

correct
adjective

Something is **correct** when it has no mistakes.

Test
1. 8 ÷ 2 = 4
2. 4 x 6 = 24
3. 27 ÷ 9 = 3
4. 5 x 2 = 10
5. 24 ÷ 8 = 3

*All the answers on this test are **correct**.*

cost
noun

The **cost** is the amount of money you must pay for something.

*The **cost** of this clock is $9.95.*

country
noun

A **country** is a nation with its land and people.

*Mali is a **country** in Africa.*

create
verb

You **create** something when you make it yourself.

*Did you ever **create** a Mother's Day card?*

curious
adjective

When you are **curious**, you really want to know about something.

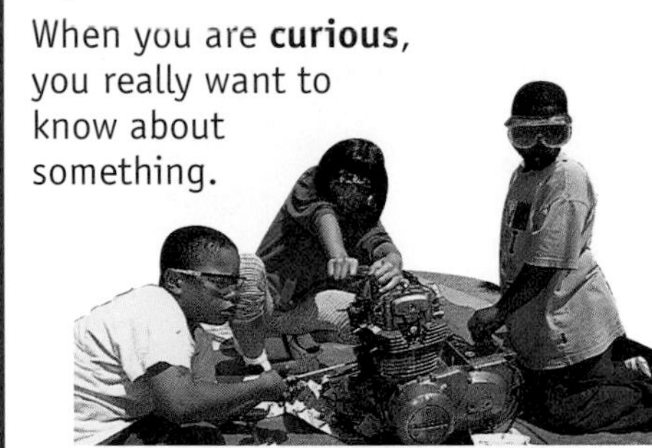

*These kids are **curious** about how this engine works.*

current

❶ *adjective*

Something that is **current** is happening now.

*Today's news is about the hurricane. It is a **current** event.*

❷ *noun*

A **current** is water or air that is moving.

*It's very difficult to paddle against the **current**.*

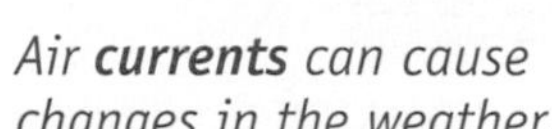

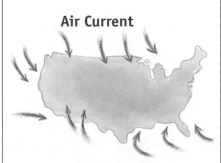

*Air **currents** can cause changes in the weather.*

A B C D E F G H I J K L M N O P Q R S T U V W X Y Z

custom

noun

When something is a **custom**, people have done it that way for a long time.

mask

costume

It is a ***custom*** *to wear costumes for Halloween.*

See also: *tradition*, page 108

cut

verb

When you **cut** something, you use a tool to divide it.

She will ***cut*** *it with a knife.*

In the past:
She **cut**.
She **has cut**.

Idiom:
cut it out

You ask someone to **cut it out** when you want them to stop what they are doing.

His dad asked him to ***cut it out.***

cycle

noun

A **cycle** is a series of changes that happen over again in the same order.

spring

summer

fall

winter

It takes one year for the seasons to complete one ***cycle.***

Dd

dam

noun

A **dam** is a wall built across a river.

People build ***dams*** *to collect water.*

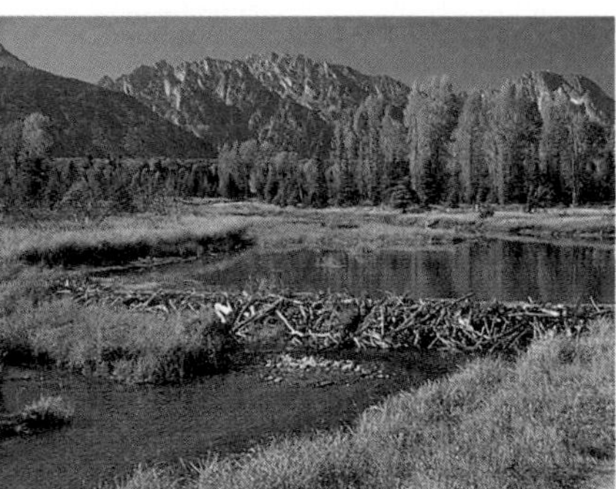

Beavers use mud and sticks to build a ***dam*** *to live in.*

dance

verb

When you **dance**, you move your body in time to music.

These dancers ***dance*** *to Mexican music.*

dangerous

adjective

Something that is **dangerous** can hurt you.

Crossing this street can be very ***dangerous.***

data

noun

Data are facts and information.

The library has ***data*** *in books and on compact discs, called CD-ROMs.*

daughter

noun

A **daughter** is a female child in a family.

dawn

noun

Dawn is the first light that shows at the beginning of the day.

dead

adjective

When something is **dead**, it is no longer alive.

*One plant is **dead** because no one watered it.*

deaf

adjective

A person who is **deaf** cannot hear.

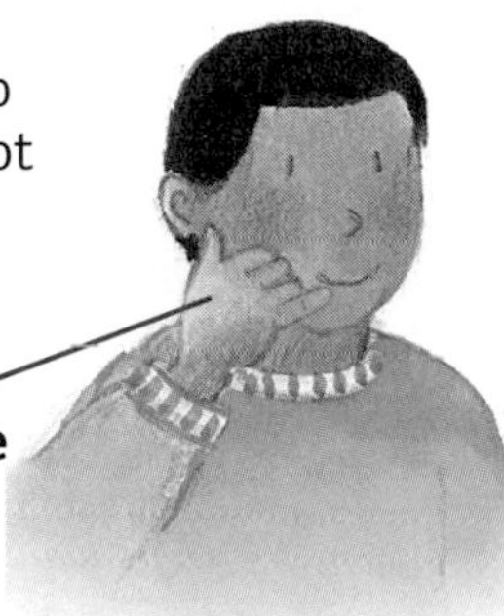

*Many **deaf** people use sign language to communicate.*

debate

verb

When people **debate**, they give arguments for or against something.

*Rosa and Jacob **debate** the issue of school uniforms.*

decimal

noun

A **decimal** is a fraction that is expressed in multiples of 10.

decimal point

$$4.5 = 4\frac{5}{10}$$

*You read the **decimal** 4.5 as "four and five tenths" or "four point five."*

decompose

verb

Decompose means to break down into small parts.

*Logs and leaves **decompose** and rot into the forest soil.*

delicious

adjective

Food that is **delicious** smells and tastes good.

*This spaghetti is **delicious**!*

depend

verb

You **depend** on someone or something when you need them to help you.

*This woman **depends** on her seeing-eye dog.*

design

noun

A **design** is a drawing showing how something is made.

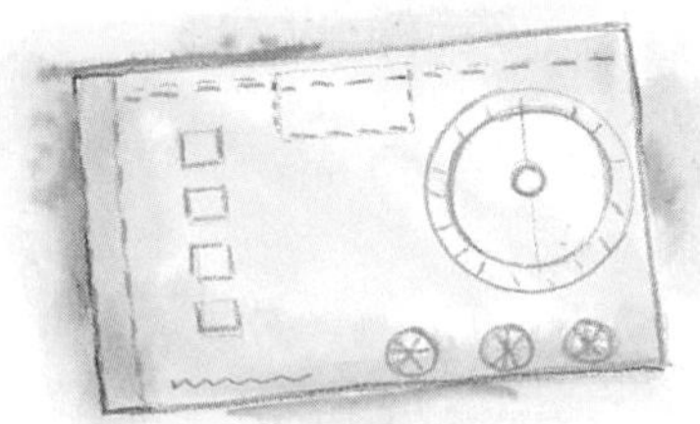

*This is the **design** for the new playground.*

develop

verb

When something **develops**, it grows and changes over time.

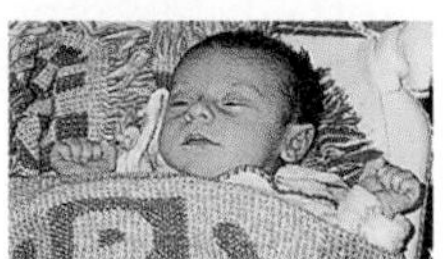

infant

toddler

child

teenager

middle-aged adult

elder

*A human being begins life as an infant and **develops** into an adult.*

diameter

noun

The **diameter** is the distance of a straight line drawn through the center of a circle.

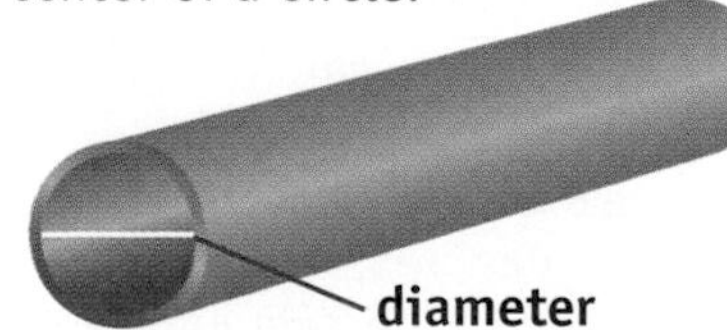

*The straight line shows the **diameter** of this pipe.*

See also: ***circumference*****, page 20**

digestion

noun

Digestion is the process your body uses to break down the food you eat into smaller pieces so it can be absorbed. The process of digestion takes place in your digestive system.

See also: ***blood*****, page 14**

The Digestive System

mouth

Digestion starts in your **mouth**. The **teeth** cut the food into small pieces when you chew. Your **tongue** mixes the food with saliva. Saliva is a juice that makes food easy to swallow. It is made in the **salivary glands**.

esophagus

When you swallow, the food goes into your **esophagus**. The sides of the esophagus move in and out. The movement pushes the food all the way down the esophagus and into your **stomach**.

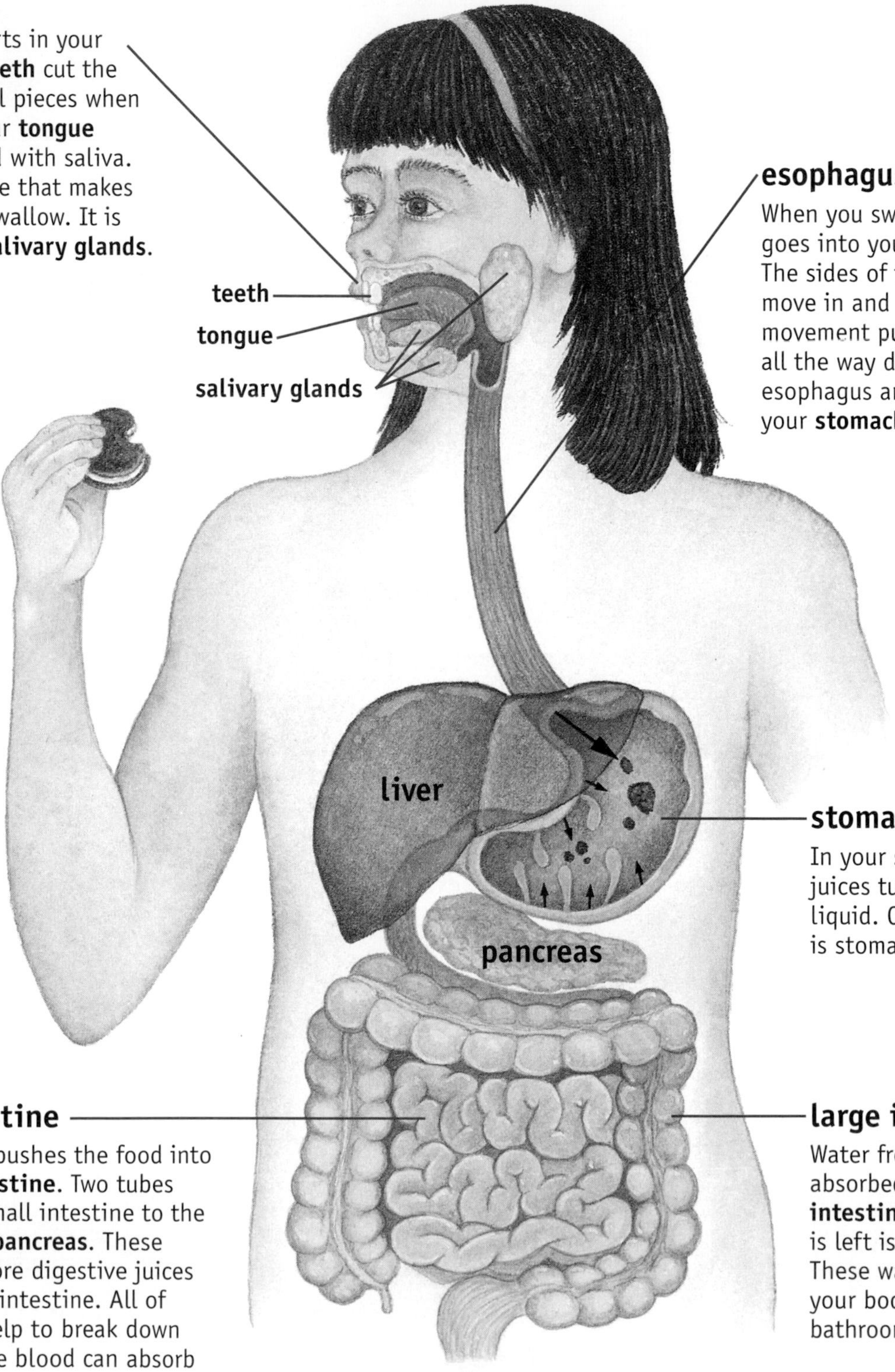

stomach

In your **stomach**, digestive juices turn the food into a liquid. One of these juices is stomach acid.

small intestine

Your stomach pushes the food into the **small intestine.** Two tubes connect the small intestine to the **liver** and the **pancreas.** These tubes carry more digestive juices into the small intestine. All of these juices help to break down the food so the blood can absorb nutrients from the food.

large intestine

Water from the food is absorbed in the **large intestine.** The material that is left is called solid waste. These waste products leave your body when you use the bathroom.

dinosaur

noun

Dinosaurs were large reptiles that lived millions of years ago. Hardened bits of animal and plant life from those times, called *fossils,* provide clues about the lives of dinosaurs.

*You can study the fossil remains of a **dinosaur** in the field.*

See also: *extinct*, page 36; *fossil*, page 39

directions

noun

Directions tell you how to do something.

*This recipe has **directions** for making a snack.*

discover

verb

You **discover** something when you find it for the first time.

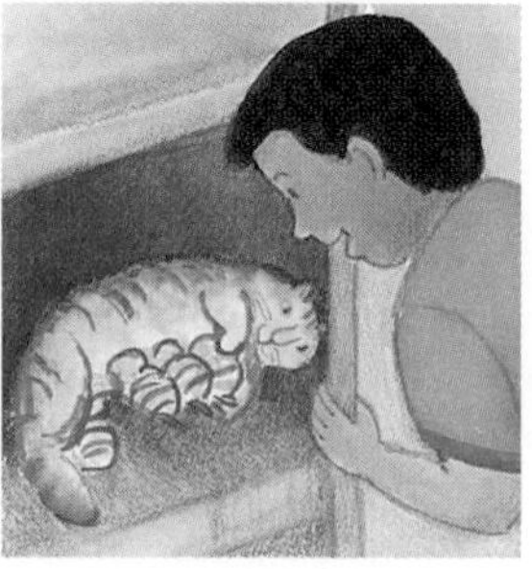

*Ned **discovers** the mother cat with her kittens.*

discuss

verb

When you **discuss** something, you talk it over with other people.

*We **discuss** our class project every day.*

disk

noun

A **disk** is a flat object that stores information for use in a computer.

*You place a floppy **disk** or a CD-ROM into a slot called a drive on the computer.*

See also: *computer*, page 24

dissolve

verb

When something **dissolves**, it breaks down into tiny pieces and is absorbed by a liquid.

*The sugar will **dissolve** into the water.*

distance

noun

Distance is the amount of space between two things.

*The **distance** from San Francisco to Los Angeles is about 400 miles.*

Idiom:

keep your distance

You **keep your distance** when you stay away from something.

*He will **keep his distance** from the donkey.*

divide

verb

You **divide** to see how many times one number is contained in another.

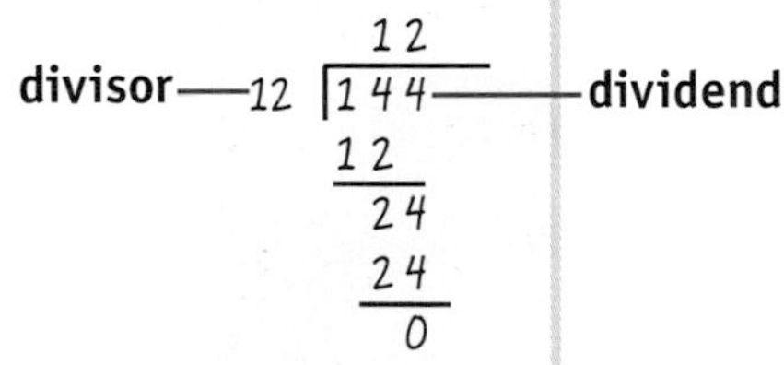

*When you **divide** 144 by 12, you get 12.*

drought

noun

A **drought** is a long period of time when there is no rain.

*The long **drought** caused the crops to dry up and die.*

Ee

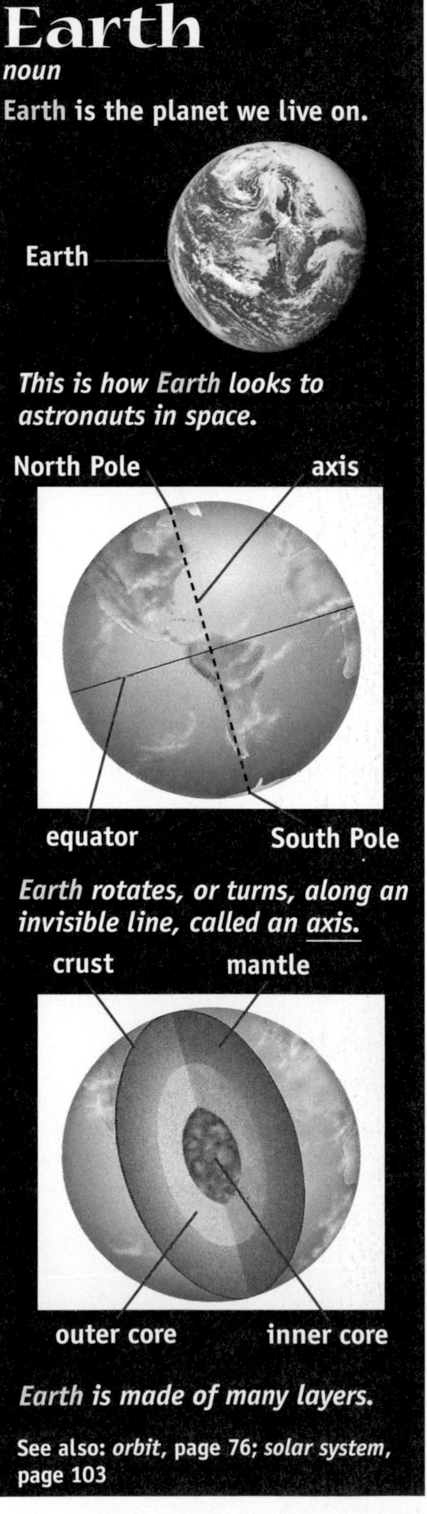

Earth

noun

Earth is the planet we live on.

This is how Earth looks to astronauts in space.

Earth rotates, or turns, along an invisible line, called an axis.

Earth is made of many layers.

See also: *orbit*, page 76; *solar system*, page 103

earthquake

noun

An **earthquake** is a sudden shaking of the ground.

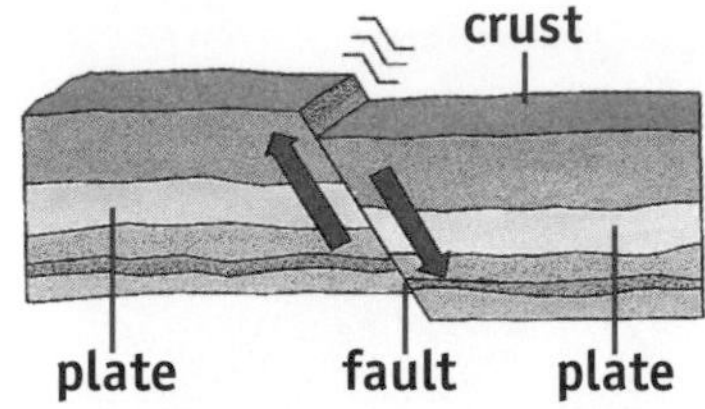

When two of Earth's plates move against each other, ***earthquakes*** *happen.*

easy

adjective

Something is **easy** when it is not hard to do.

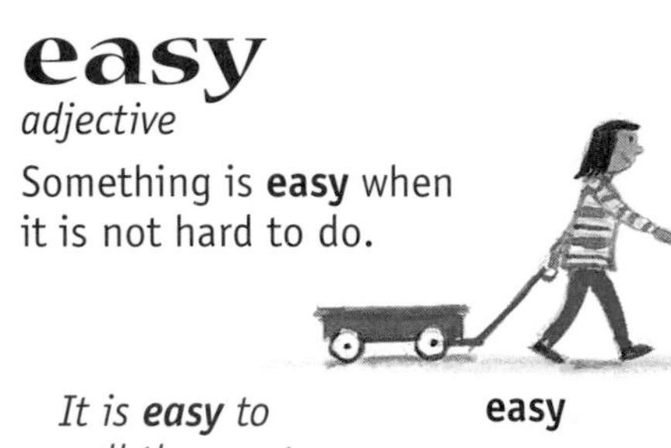

It is ***easy*** *to pull the empty wagon.*

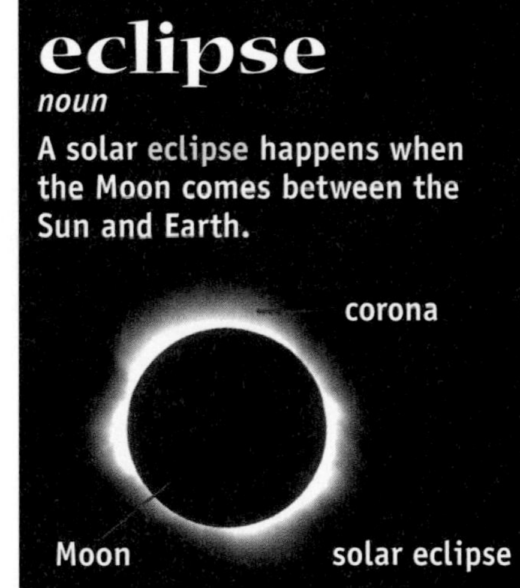

eclipse

noun

A solar eclipse happens when the Moon comes between the Sun and Earth.

edge

noun

An **edge** is the place where two faces of a solid object meet.

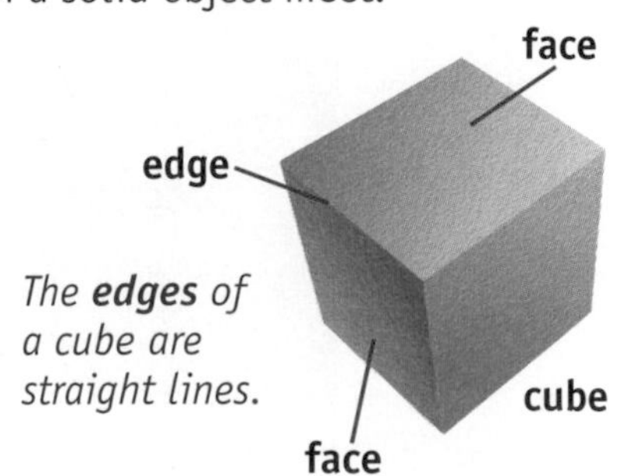

The ***edges*** *of a cube are straight lines.*

editorial

noun

An **editorial** is a newspaper article that gives the writer's opinion about an issue. An editorial writer wants others to share the same opinion.

Bigelow Bee

January 12, 2002

Why We Need More Computers

by Joe Jackson

We must have more computers at school! Every classroom should have at least one computer. We also need a computer in the library so we can look things up on the Internet. A 21st century school needs 21st century tools!

egg

noun

An **egg** is a round or oval object covered with a shell. Most birds, fish, and reptiles develop inside eggs.

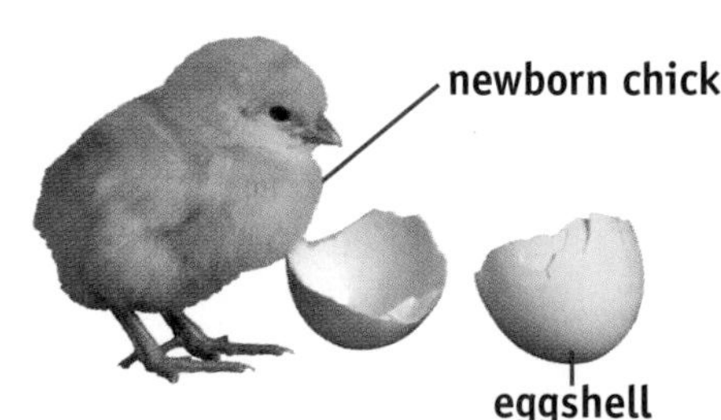

Idiom:

egg on your face

You have **egg on your face** when you do something embarrassing.

She had ***egg on her face*** *when she dropped all her papers.*

See also: *embarrassed*, page 31

elect
verb

Elect means to choose.

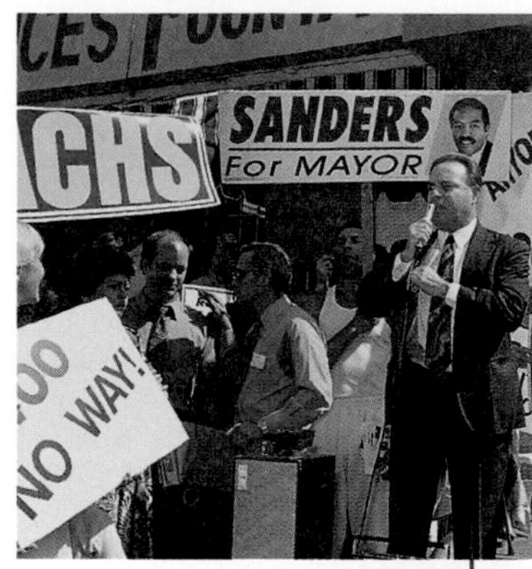

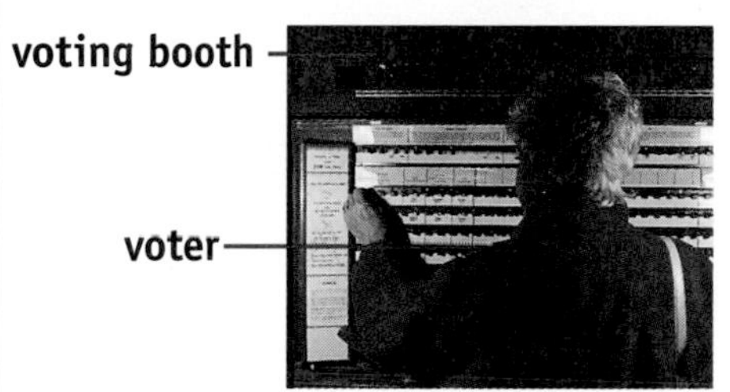

*People vote for the candidate they want to **elect**.*

See also: *government*, page 44-45

electricity
noun

Electricity is a form of energy that can produce light, heat, and power.

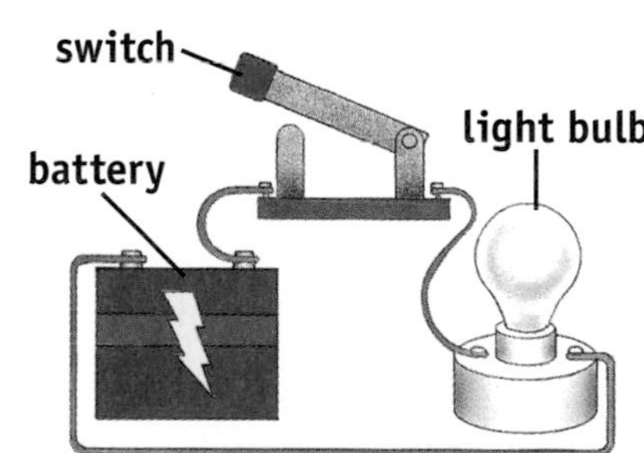

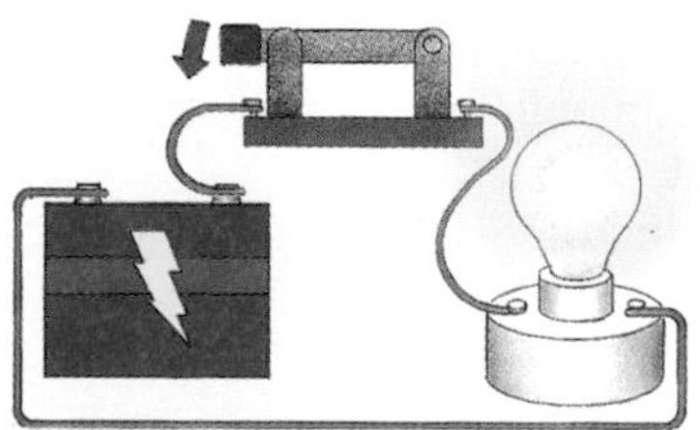

***Electricity** is produced when an electric charge moves through wire in a closed circuit.*

See also: *circuit*, page 20

embarrassed
adjective

When you are **embarrassed**, you feel uncomfortable about something.

*If you make a mess, you may feel **embarrassed**.*

emergency
noun

An emergency is a problem that needs fast action.

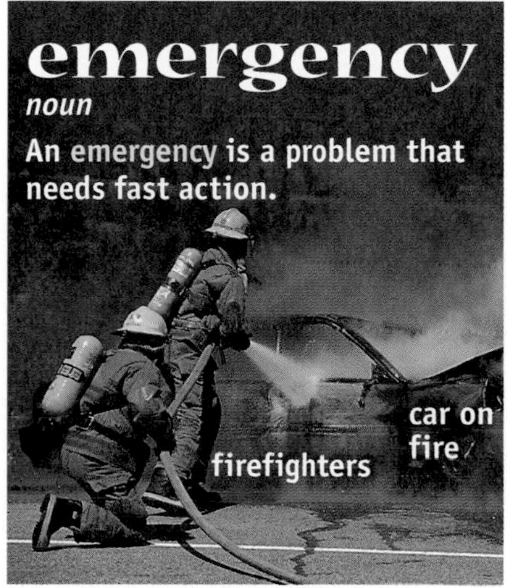

encyclopedia
noun

An **encyclopedia** is a set of books with information on many topics.

*This volume of the **encyclopedia** is full of facts on whales.*

endangered
adjective

An animal is **endangered** when very few like it are still alive.

*Only 200 Siberian tigers remain in the wild. They are **endangered** animals.*

energy
noun

Energy is the power to do work.

Some Sources of Energy

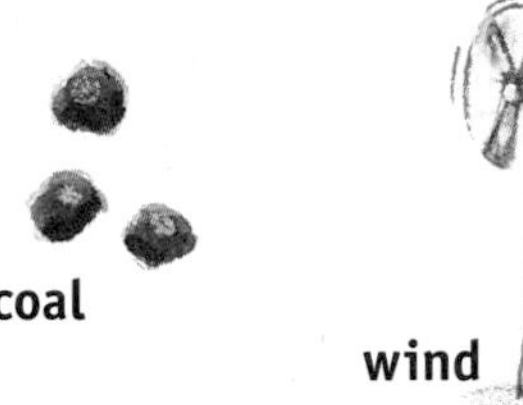

Energy from Food

*Food gives your body the **energy** to work and play.*

See also: *natural resource*, page 70

enjoy
verb

You **enjoy** something when it makes you happy.

*This father and daughter **enjoy** cooking.*

enter
verb

When you **enter** a place, you go in.

*Children **enter** the school in the morning.*

A B C D E F G H I J K L M N O P Q R S T U V W X Y Z

environment

noun

The **environment** is all the things around us. It includes the air, land, and water. The environment affects the lives of people, animals, and plants.

See also: *landfill*, page 57; *natural resource*, page 70; *pollution*, page 84; *recycle*, page 87

*The mountains are a beautiful natural **environment**.*

Ways to Protect the Environment

End pollution.

Pick up litter.

Recycle.

Help clean the air. Plant a tree.

equipment

noun

Equipment is a collection of things needed for a special purpose.

*This **equipment** is used to play baseball.*

equivalent

adjective

Things are **equivalent** if they are equal.

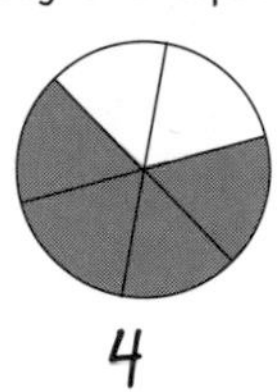

*These fractions are **equivalent**. They both equal the same amount.*

escape

verb

Escape means to break loose or get free.

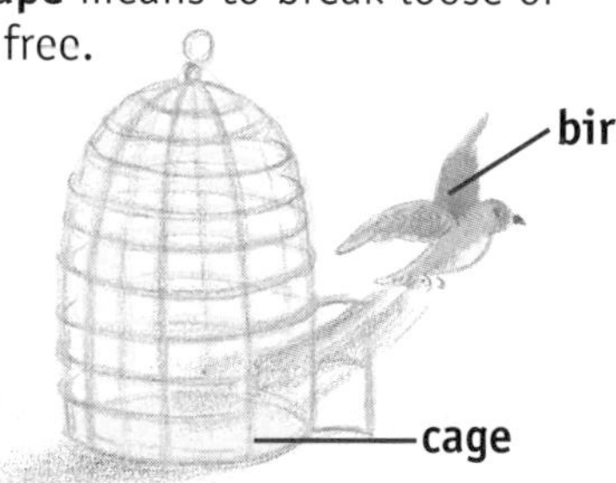

*The bird can **escape** from the cage if the door is open.*

estimate

verb

When you guess about size, number, or cost, you **estimate**.

*She **estimates** that there are 200 books in the bookcase.*

event
noun

An **event** is an activity that happens.

*The Bake Sale was a big **event** at school.*

exactly
adverb

When you do something exactly, you don't make any mistakes.

To do the experiment, he must measure exactly.

example
noun

An **example** is one of many similar items.

*An orchid is an **example** of a flower.*

excellent
adjective

Something is **excellent** when it is very, very good.

Report Card		
name	subject	grade
Tai	Spelling:	A
	Reading:	A
	Math:	A
	Science:	A

*Tai brought home an **excellent** report card!*

exchange
verb

You **exchange** something when you trade it for something else.

*These friends **exchange** snacks.*

exercise
verb

When you **exercise**, you move your body to keep it strong and healthy.

*We **exercise** in gym class.*

expand
verb

Something **expands** when it becomes larger.

*You can blow into a balloon to **expand** it.*

expensive
adjective

Something is **expensive** when it costs a lot of money.

*An automobile is very **expensive**.*

experiment
noun

You can do an **experiment** to discover something.

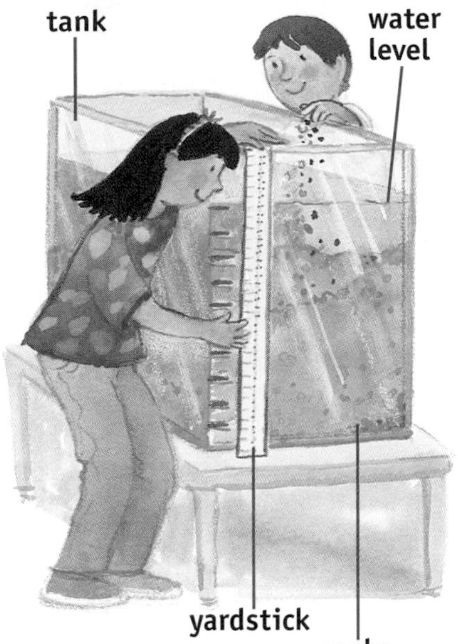

*Our **experiment** showed how adding rocks can raise the water level in a tank.*

See also: ***laboratory*, page 57**

expert
noun

An **expert** is a person who knows a lot about a topic.

*Professor Gregg is an **expert**. He knows all about sea stars.*

explode
verb

When something **explodes**, it blows up.

*Balloons can **explode** when they get too full of air.*

explore

verb

When you **explore**, you travel to discover things or places. A person who explores is an explorer.

Early Explorers

Marco Polo

Marco Polo began to **explore** the world in 1271. He traveled from Italy to China by sea and by land. When he came back to Italy, he wrote a book about his trip.

Hudson Bay
ENGLAND
EUROPE
PORTUGAL
SPAIN
ITALY
NORTH AMERICA
ATLANTIC OCEAN
AFRICA
PACIFIC OCEAN
SOUTH AMERICA
ATLANTIC OCEAN
Cape of Good Hope
Strait of Magellan

Christopher Columbus

Christopher Columbus read a book by explorer Marco Polo. In 1492, Columbus sailed across the Atlantic Ocean, hoping to find India and China. But Columbus landed in the Americas instead.

Bartolomeu Dias

Bartolomeu Dias was an explorer from Portugal. In 1487, he was the first European to discover the tip of Africa. Dias called it the Cape of Storms, but later the King of Portugal renamed it the Cape of Good Hope.

What new foods did explorers bring to Europe?

John Cabot brought codfish from North America to England. Other English explorers and traders sold tea from India and China to the English people.

When returning from India in 1499, Vasco da Gama filled his ships with pepper and cinnamon. He delivered these exotic spices to his home port of Lisbon. They soon became very popular.

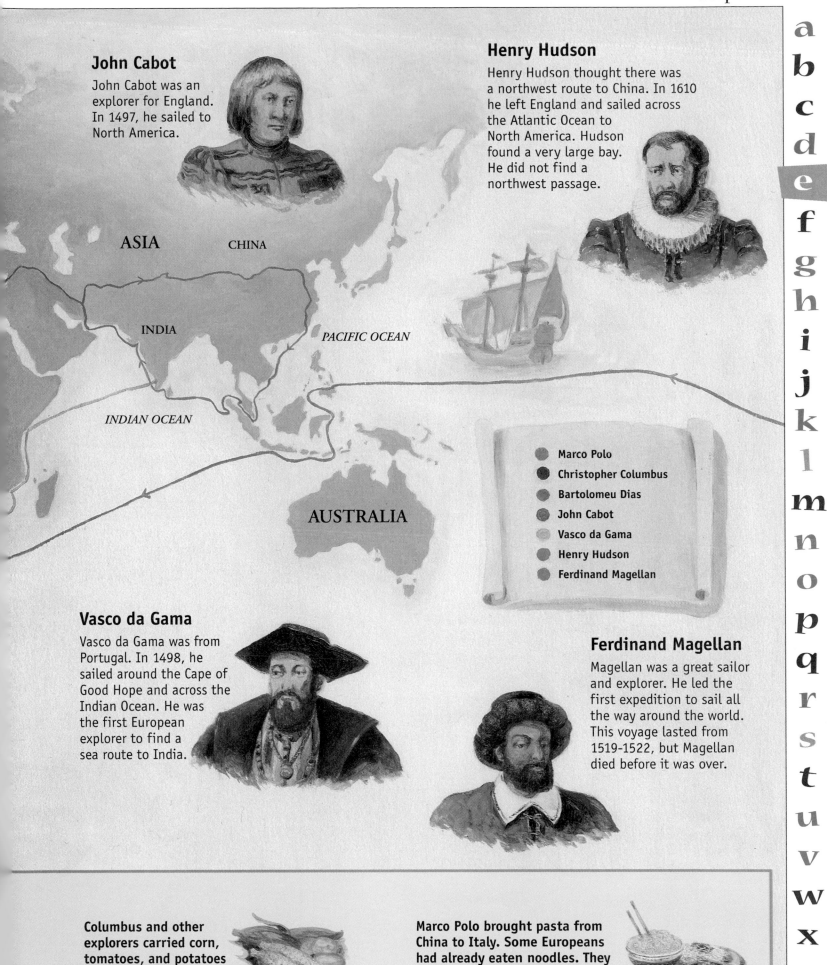

John Cabot

John Cabot was an explorer for England. In 1497, he sailed to North America.

Henry Hudson

Henry Hudson thought there was a northwest route to China. In 1610 he left England and sailed across the Atlantic Ocean to North America. Hudson found a very large bay. He did not find a northwest passage.

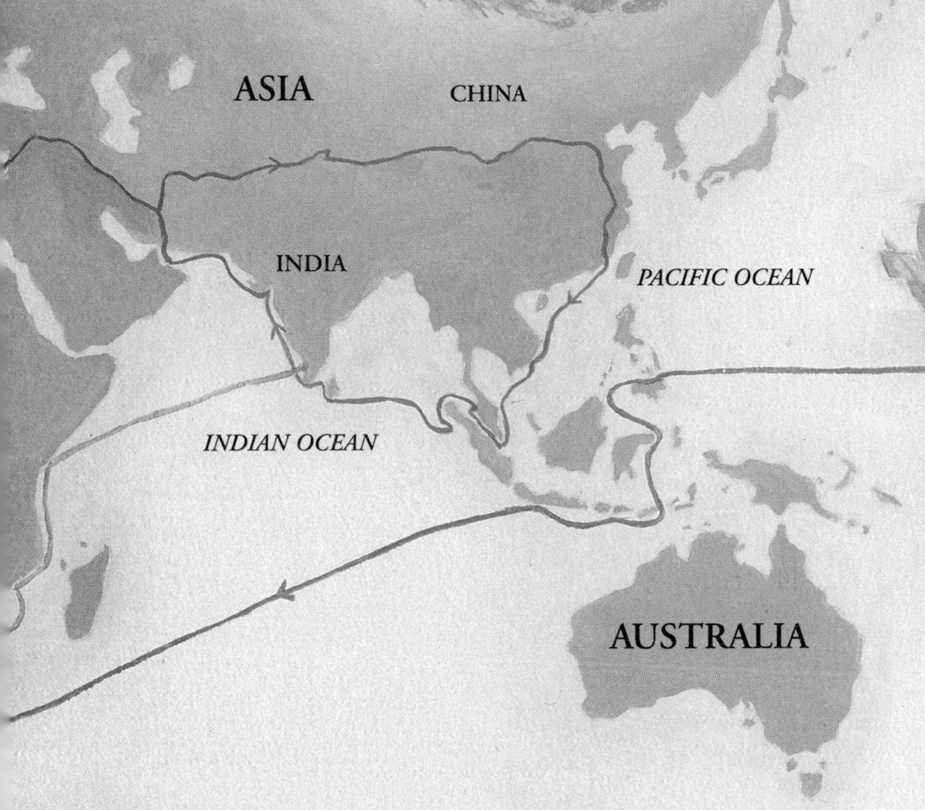

ASIA

CHINA

INDIA

PACIFIC OCEAN

INDIAN OCEAN

AUSTRALIA

- Marco Polo
- Christopher Columbus
- Bartolomeu Dias
- John Cabot
- Vasco da Gama
- Henry Hudson
- Ferdinand Magellan

Vasco da Gama

Vasco da Gama was from Portugal. In 1498, he sailed around the Cape of Good Hope and across the Indian Ocean. He was the first European explorer to find a sea route to India.

Ferdinand Magellan

Magellan was a great sailor and explorer. He led the first expedition to sail all the way around the world. This voyage lasted from 1519-1522, but Magellan died before it was over.

Columbus and other explorers carried corn, tomatoes, and potatoes from the Americas to Europe.

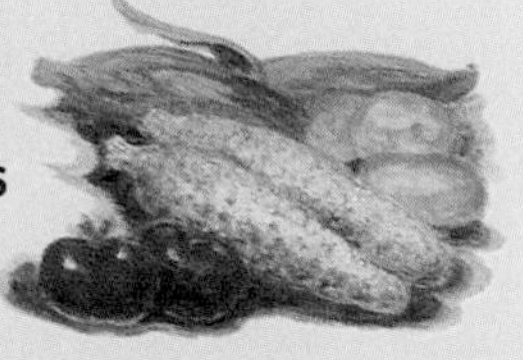

Marco Polo brought pasta from China to Italy. Some Europeans had already eaten noodles. They had been brought from China through the Middle East to Spain.

extinct
adjective
When a plant or animal is **extinct**, it does not exist anymore.

*These animals are **extinct**. There are no more left on Earth.*

See also: ***dinosaur,*** **page 29**

extra
adjective
Something is **extra** when it is more than you need.

*Matt gives Dora his **extra** pencil.*

eye
noun
An **eye** is the part of the body you see with.

Idiom:
keep an eye on
You **keep an eye on** something when you watch it carefully.

*It's good to **keep an eye on** children at the beach.*

Ff

fable
noun
A **fable** is a story that teaches a lesson.

*"The Tortoise and the Hare" is an old **fable**.*

face
❶ *noun*
Your **face** is part of your head.

Idiom:
make a face

When you **make a face**, you change the way your face looks for a moment.

❷ *noun*
A **face** is any one side of a solid shape.

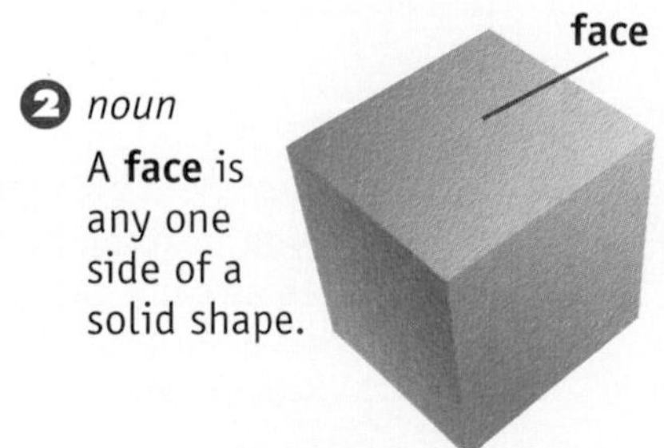

fact
noun
A **fact** is information that is true.

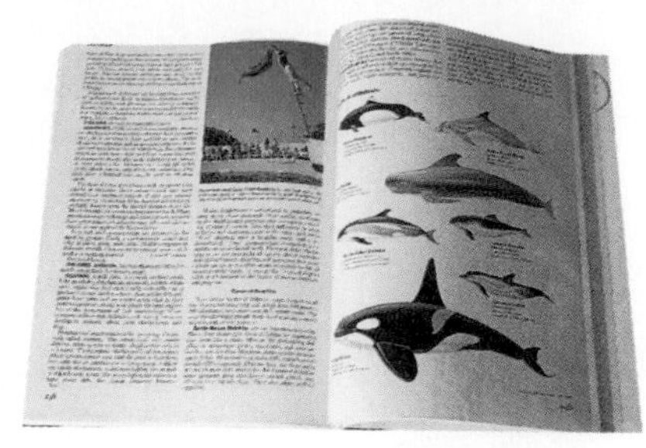

*An encyclopedia is full of **facts**.*

factory
noun
People work with machines in a **factory**. They make products.

See also: ***manufacture,*** **page 63**

fade
verb
When something **fades**, it gets lighter.

*Jeans **fade** when they are washed many times.*

fairy tale
noun
A **fairy tale** is a story about make-believe people, animals, and spirits.

*"Little Red Riding Hood" is a **fairy tale** about a girl and a wolf.*

famous
adjective

Something is **famous** when many people know about it.

*The Statue of Liberty is one of the most **famous** statues in the world.*

fantasy
noun

A **fantasy** is a story about something that could never happen.

*This book is a **fantasy** about traveling to another planet on a flying dinosaur.*

fasten
verb

You make two things stay together when you **fasten** them.

*Always **fasten** your seatbelt.*

favorite
adjective

Your **favorite** food is the one you like best.

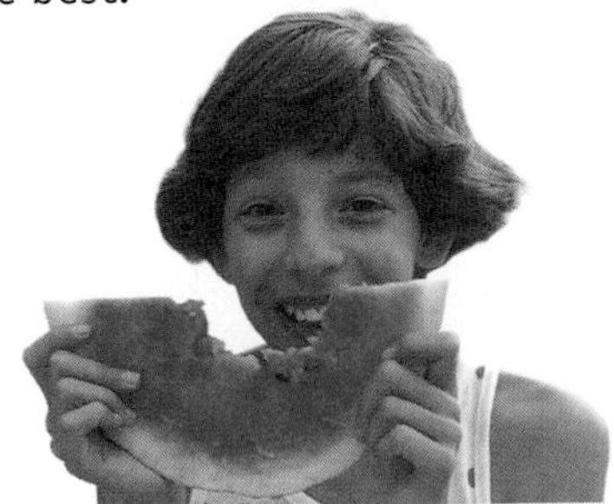

*Watermelon is her **favorite** fruit.*

In the past:
You **fed** the dog.
You **have fed** the dog.

Idiom:
fed up

When you are **fed up** with something, you have had enough of it.

*She is **fed up** with the cartoons.*

fertile
adjective

When soil is **fertile**, crops and plants grow well in it.

*Iowa has **fertile** land for farming.*

N O P Q R S T U V W X Y Z

fight

verb

When you **fight**, you struggle against someone or something.

*The firefighters must **fight** the raging blaze.*

In the past:
They **fought**.
They **have fought**.

fill

verb

When you **fill** something, you put as much as you can into it.

*He will **fill** all the glasses with milk.*

float

verb

Something floats when it rests on the surface of water without sinking.

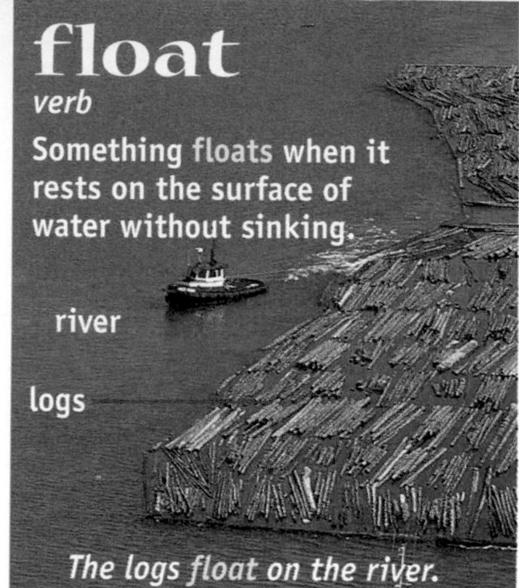

The logs float on the river.

flood

noun

A **flood** happens when water flows over land that is normally dry.

*Too much rain can cause a **flood**.*

❷ *verb*

To **fly**, an animal uses wings to travel through the air.

*Birds use their wings to **fly** through the air.*

In the past:
They **flew**.
They **have flown**.

Idiom:
fly off the handle

When you **fly off the handle**, you get very mad.

food chain

noun

A **food chain** is made up of a group of plants and animals. They each feed on one member of the chain and are themselves food for another.

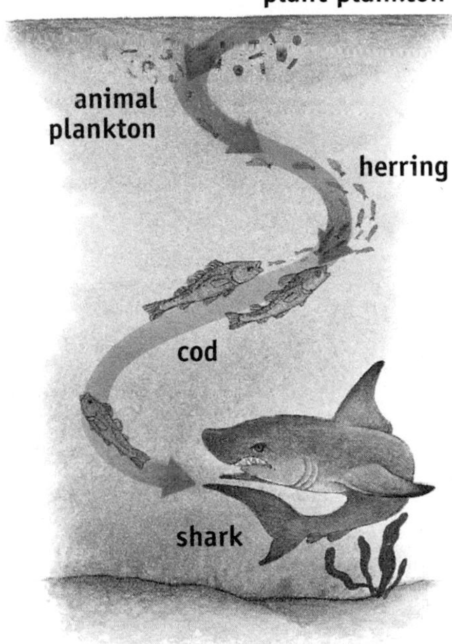

foolish

adjective

Something **foolish** is silly or has no sense.

*The boy planted money to make it grow. What a **foolish** thing to do!*

force

noun

A **force** is anything that causes, changes, or stops motion.

*Pushing and pulling are both **forces** that will make this boat move faster.*

foreign

adjective

Something is **foreign** when it comes from outside your country.

*You can't spend **foreign** money in the United States.*

forest

noun

A **forest** is a large area where many trees grow. Animals and birds of many kinds live in a forest.

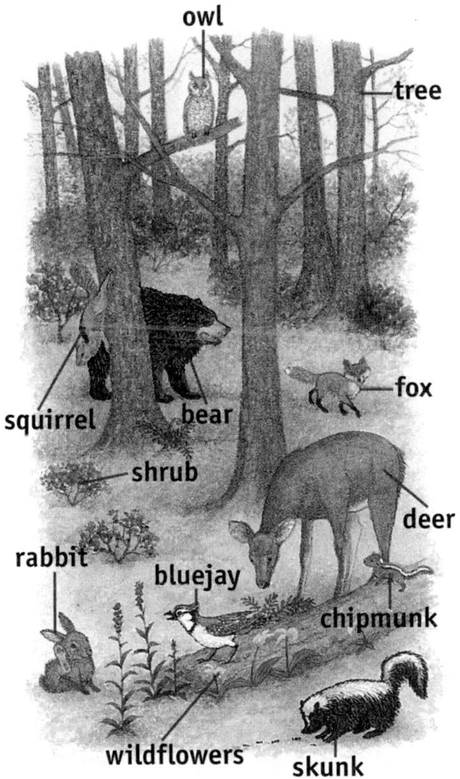

forever

adverb

Forever means that something will never end.

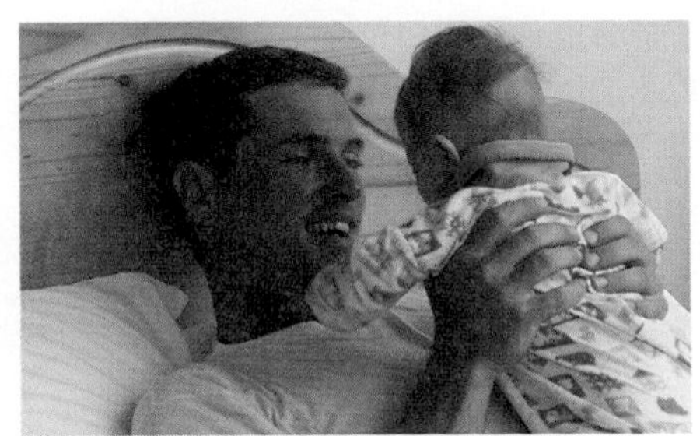

*Bob will love his son **forever**.*

forget

verb

You **forget** something when you are unable to remember it.

*Marcel often **forgets** his lunch.*

In the past:
He **forgot**.
He **has forgotten**.

fossil

noun

A **fossil** is the hardened remains or impression of something that lived long ago.

dinosaur footprint fossil

See also: *dinosaur*, page 29; *extinct*, page 36

fraction

noun

A **fraction** is one or more of the equal parts of a whole.

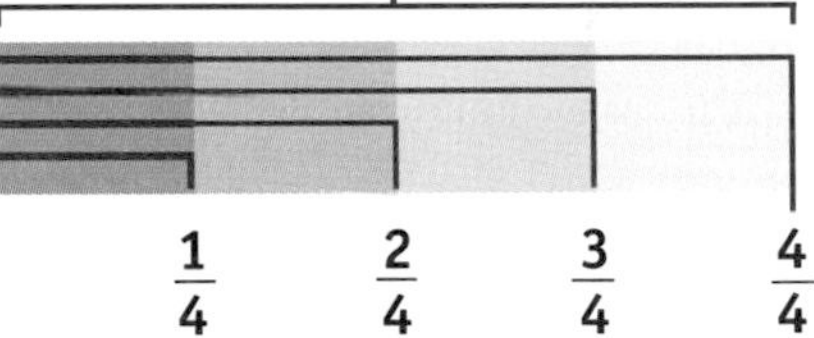

$\frac{1}{4}$ $\frac{2}{4}$ $\frac{3}{4}$ $\frac{4}{4}$

*The bottom number in each **fraction** tells how many parts there are in the whole bar.*

free

adjective

Something is **free** when it can choose to move around anywhere it wants.

*Buffalo are **free** to roam on the plains.*

buffalo

freedom

noun

Freedom is the condition of being free—not under the control of other people.

See also: ***slavery*, pages 100–101**

The Underground Railroad—Route to Freedom

For over 200 years, most African Americans in the United States were not free. They worked as slaves on Southern plantations, or large farms. To gain their **freedom**, thousands of slaves ran away. Many found their way to states in the North and to Canada. To get there, they used something called the Underground Railroad. This was not a railroad. It was a secret network, or system, of people who helped slaves escape to freedom in the North.

1. "Conductors" met slaves who wanted to escape. At night, they led the slaves away from the plantation. The "Drinking Gourd"—a group of stars we call the Big Dipper—pointed the way north.

2. Families who were against slavery hid runaway slaves in their homes. These stops on the Underground Railroad were called "stations." Runaways moved from station to station.

3. Conductors carried runaways across the Ohio River in boats. Across the river was the North—and **freedom.**

4. In the North, runaways were no longer slaves. They could live as free people.

fresh
adjective

Something is **fresh** when it is newly made or gathered.

*She buys **fresh** vegetables at the store.*

frontier
noun

A **frontier** is the newest area to be settled. In America, the frontier moved slowly to the west as settlers crossed the land.

See also: *settler*, pages 96–97

furniture
noun

Beds, tables, chairs, and couches are all **furniture**.

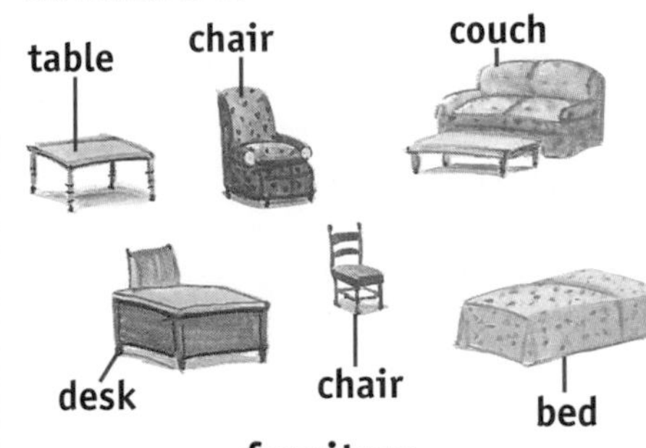

Gg

gain
verb

When you **gain** something, you get it or win it.

*She is about to **gain** control of the ball.*

game
noun

A **game** is an activity you play for fun. Each game has its own rules.

*I enjoy board **games** and outdoor games.*

gas
1 *noun*

A **gas** is a substance that is not a solid or a liquid.

*You can buy a balloon filled with helium **gas**.*

2 *noun*

Gas, or gasoline, is a fuel used to run the motors in cars, planes, and other machines.

*A car runs on **gas**.*

See also: *liquid*, page 62; *solid*, page 104

gather
verb

You **gather** things when you collect them in one place.

*Let's **gather** up all the trash and put it in the trash barrels.*

gaze
verb

When you **gaze** at something, you stare at it for a long time.

*I love to sit and **gaze** at the sea.*

gear

1 *noun*

Gears are special wheels that turn together to make a machine work.

2 *noun*

Gear is equipment you need for a special purpose.

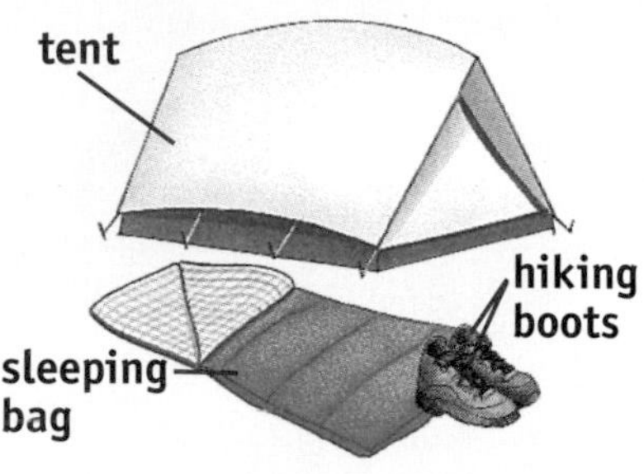

*You need to take a lot of **gear** on a camping trip.*

generation

noun

A **generation** is all the people born around the same period of time.

*There are three **generations** of people here.*

gentle

adjective

A **gentle** person is kind, careful, and quiet.

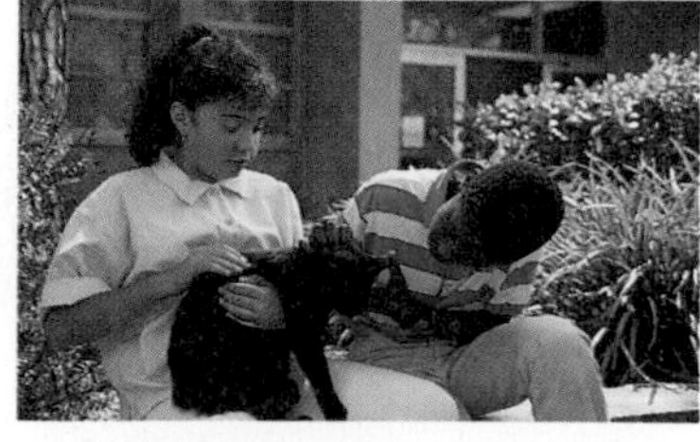

*Use a **gentle** touch when you pet a cat.*

geography

noun

Geography is the study of Earth's surface.

*You learn about many countries when you study **geography**.*

geologist

noun

A **geologist** is someone who studies the earth and what it is made of.

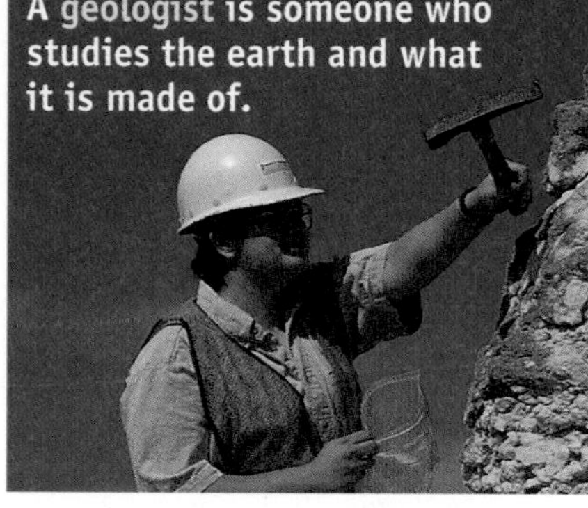

giant

1 *noun*

A **giant** is a huge make-believe character in a fairy tale.

*This **giant** tried to catch Jack in "Jack and the Beanstalk."*

2 *adjective*

Something is **giant** when it is very large.

*You can look at the stars through a **giant** telescope.*

gingerbread

noun

Gingerbread is a dark cookie or cake made with ginger. Ginger comes from the root of the ginger plant.

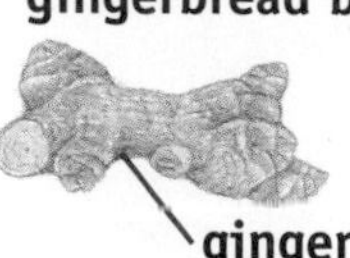

*Many people love the spicy taste of **gingerbread**.*

give

verb

When you **give** something, you offer it to another person.

*Molly will **give** Tara a gift.*

In the past:
She **gave** a gift.
She **has given** a gift.

glacier

noun

A **glacier** is a huge mass of ice that is moved downhill by gravity.

*Long ago, **glaciers** covered much of the earth.*

See also: ***landforms*****, pages 58–59**

glad

adjective

When you are **glad**, you are pleased and happy.

*I'm so **glad** my uncle is here for a visit!*

glass

noun

Glass is made of sand and other materials that are melted together.

*This artist has turned liquid **glass** into a vase.*

gleam

verb

Something **gleams** when it shines or glows.

*The clean glass window **gleams** in the sunlight.*

globe

noun

A **globe** is a sphere with the map of the world on it.

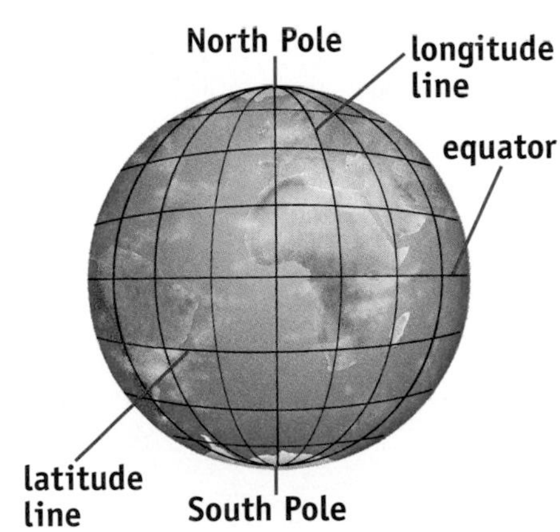

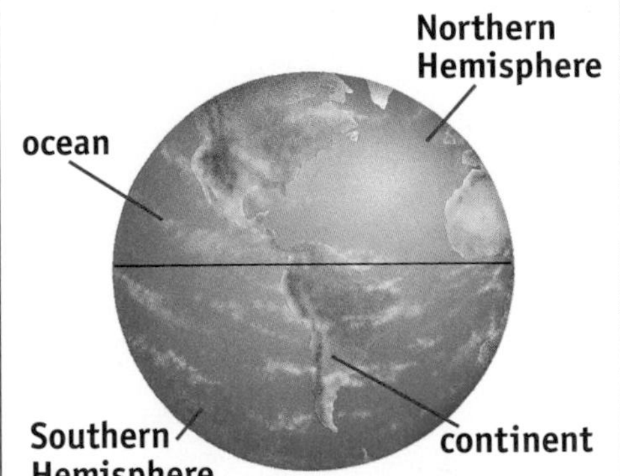

glossary

noun

A **glossary** is a list of special words and their meanings.

GLOSSARY
L
landform a shape on the surface of the Earth, such as a mountain or valley
language a system of words that people use to communicate with each other
legend a story that has been told over and over again

*You can look up new words in the **glossary** at the back of a book.*

gnaw

verb

When you **gnaw** something, you chew it again and again.

*This dog loves to **gnaw** his favorite bone.*

go

verb

When you **go**, you move from one place to another.

*He will **go** home.*

In the past:
He **went** home.
He **has gone** home.

Idiom:
go for it

You **go for it** when you try hard to do something.

*All the runners will **go for it** in the race.*

goal

❶ *noun*

When you have a **goal**, you have a purpose or an aim.

*Jody-Anne's **goal** was to win the Spelling Bee.*

❷ *noun*

In sports, your team scores a **goal** when the ball crosses a special line.

*He kicked the soccer ball into the net and scored a **goal**!*

good

adjective

Something **good** is of high quality, useful, or pleasant.

*The first, second, and third place winners are all **good** runners.*

goods

noun

Goods are things that can be bought, sold, or traded.

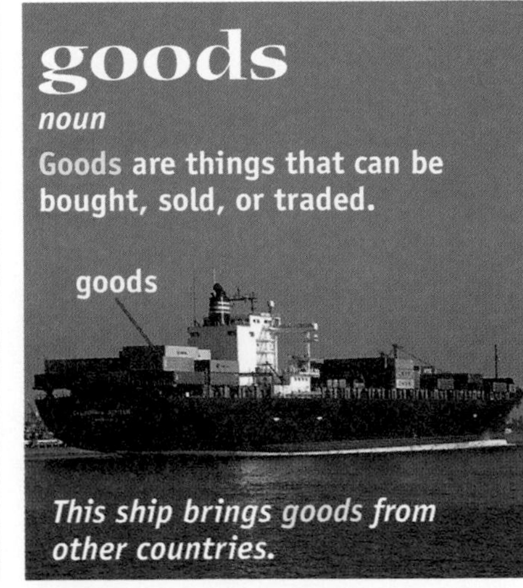

This ship brings goods from other countries.

government

noun

The **government** is the group of people who make laws for a country, a state, or a city.

See also: ***constitution*****, page 24**

Federal Government

In the United States, the **federal government** has three parts, or branches. The federal government makes laws for the whole country. The overall plan for these laws is called the *Constitution*.

Legislative Branch

Capitol Building

The **legislative branch** has two parts: the Senate and the House of Representatives. Both senators and representatives can suggest ideas for new laws, called *bills*.

The legislators all vote to decide if a bill should become a law of the United States. If more than half vote for the bill, it goes to the president for signature.

Executive Branch

White House

The president, the vice-president, and the cabinet belong to the **executive branch**. The vice-president and members of the cabinet give the president help and advice.

The president can agree or disagree with the legislative branch about which bills should be laws. If the president signs a bill it becomes law.

Judicial Branch

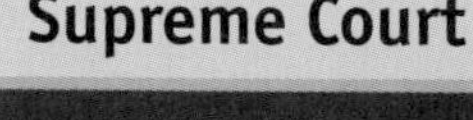

Supreme Court

The **judicial branch** is headed by the Supreme Court.

The Supreme Court is made up of nine judges, or justices. They decide if laws follow the United States Constitution.

Bills

Laws

State Government

Each state has a government. It makes laws for that state. The head of the state government is called a *governor*.

New Jersey Governor Christie Todd Whitman

Texas state capitol

California State Senator Liz Figueroa

Local Government

Each city, town, or county has a **local government**. Citizens work together to make decisions about their community.

City Council, Laguna Niguel, CA

School field trip to study government in action

How do we elect a class president?

A class can elect a president at school. First, students are nominated, or invited to be candidates for president.

Candidates try to convince the voters to choose them on election day.

Students vote to choose the candidate they want. They mark the name on a *ballot*.

The candidate with the most votes is the winner.

grain

noun

Grain is the seed of wheat, corn, and other plants we eat.

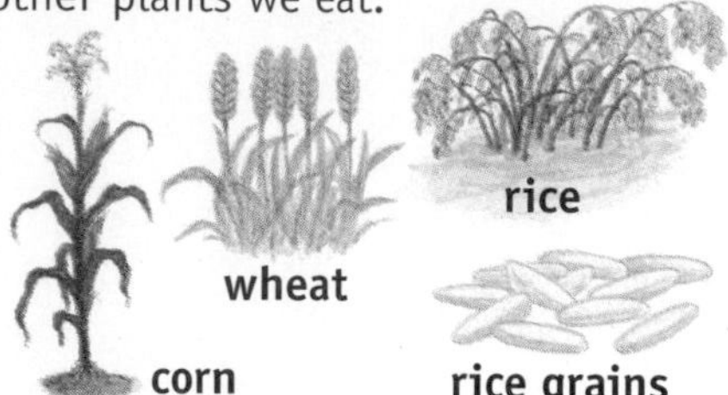

*The **grains** of rice look like this before you cook them.*

graph

noun

A **graph** is a drawing showing how certain facts are related.

Immigration to the U.S. from Asia, Europe, and South America

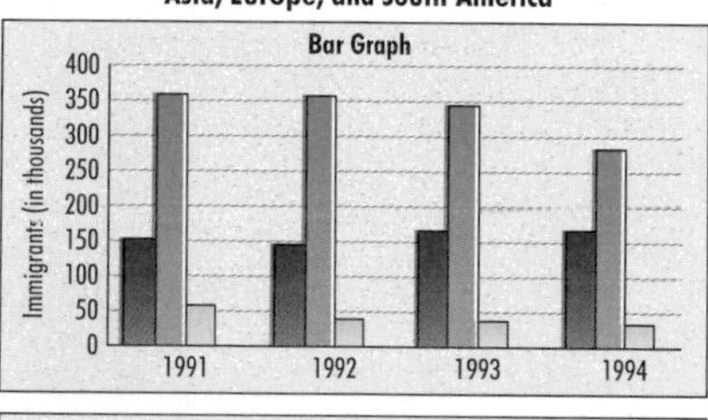

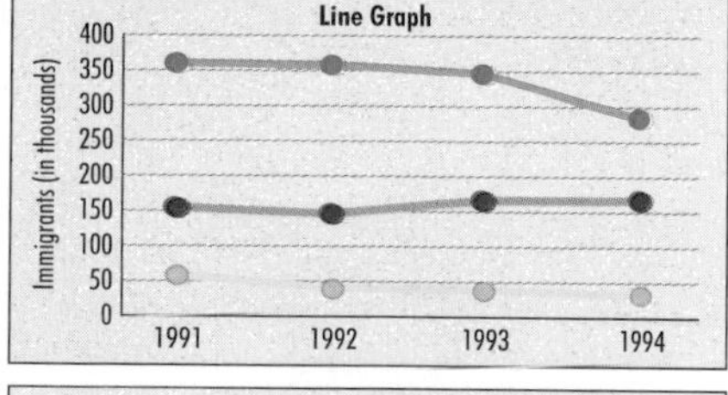

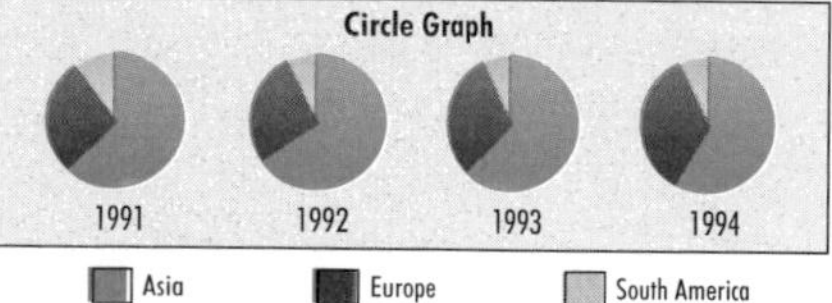

*These **graphs** show facts about immigration to the United States.*

gravity

noun

Gravity is a force that pulls things down toward Earth's center.

*When you drop a ball, **gravity** pulls it down.*

great

❶ *adjective*

Something is **great** when it is of very high quality or wonderful.

*Charlotte's Web is a **great** book.*

❷ *adjective*

Something is **great** when it is very large.

*The **Great** Wall of China is 4,000 miles long.*

grind

verb

You **grind** something when you crush it into tiny pieces or powder.

*You can **grind** corn on a special stone.*

In the past:
You **ground** corn.
You **have ground** corn.

group

noun

A **group** is a number of persons or things gathered together.

*This **group** of children is working on a project.*

growth

noun

Growth is the way something becomes larger and changes as it gets older.

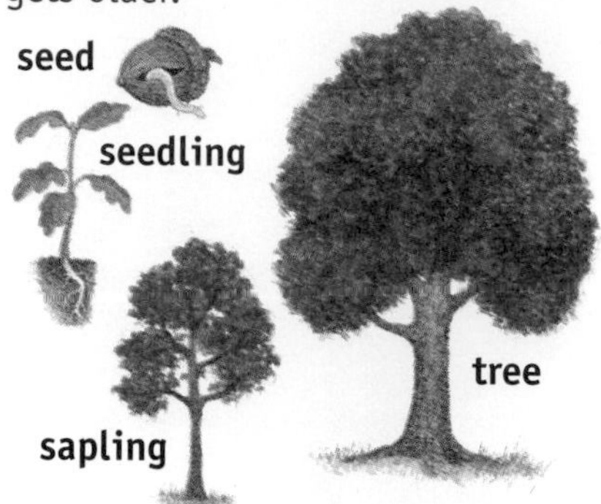

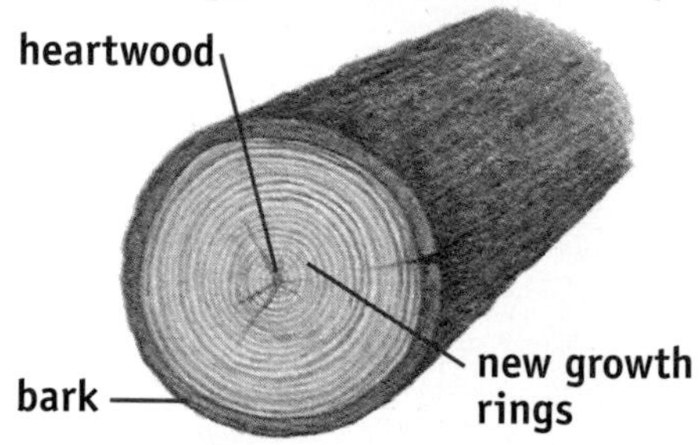

*The **growth** of a tree takes place over many years. The number of rings in a tree trunk shows how old the tree is.*

guess

verb

When you **guess**, you use clues to figure out an answer.

*You can use clues in the picture to **guess** the meaning of the word exit.*

guitar

noun

A **guitar** is a stringed instrument. To play it, you pluck the strings with fingers or a pick.

*An electric **guitar** is often used to play rock and roll music.*

Hh

habitat

noun

A **habitat** is a place where an animal or plant can live and do well.

rain forest

A tropical rain forest is a warm, wet **habitat**. It has many kinds of plants and animals. A rain forest may get 150 inches of rain each year.

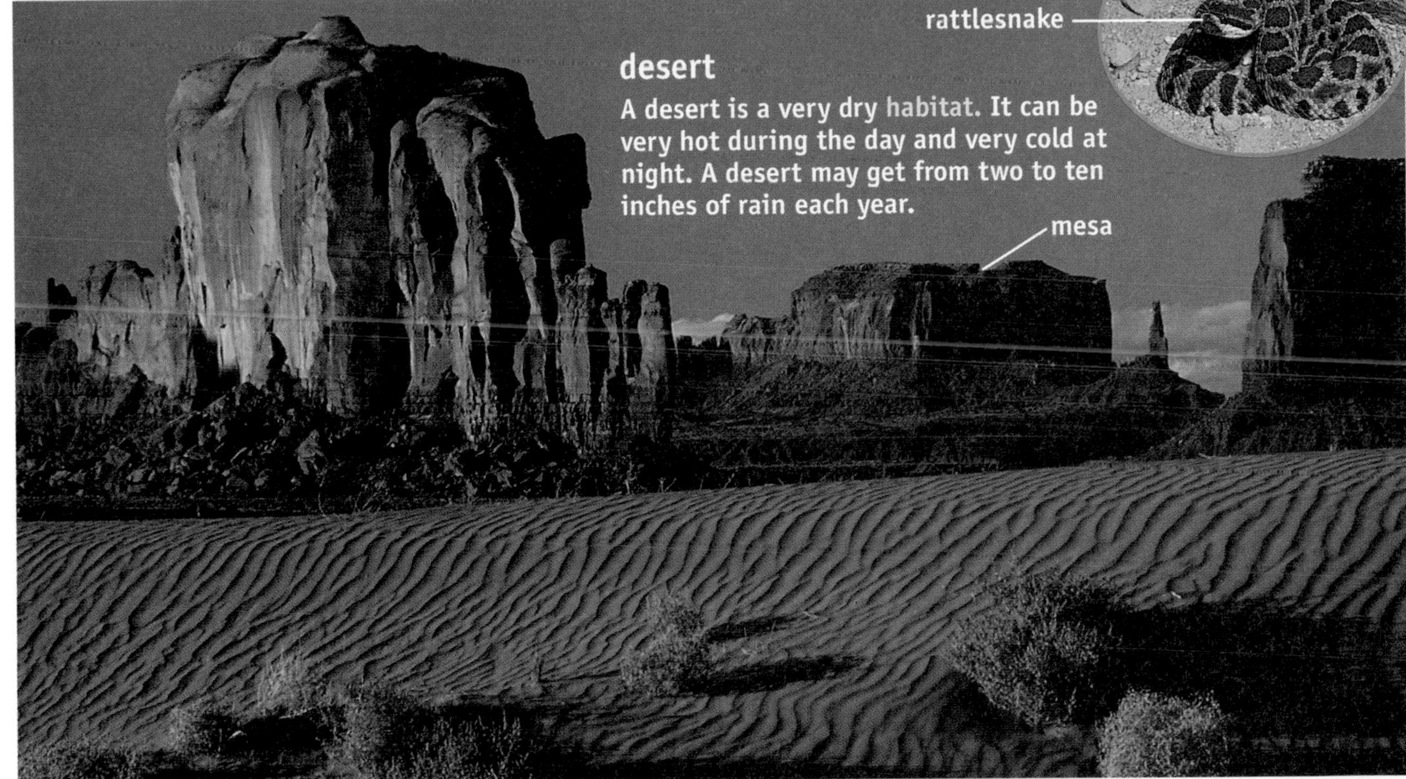

desert

A desert is a very dry habitat. It can be very hot during the day and very cold at night. A desert may get from two to ten inches of rain each year.

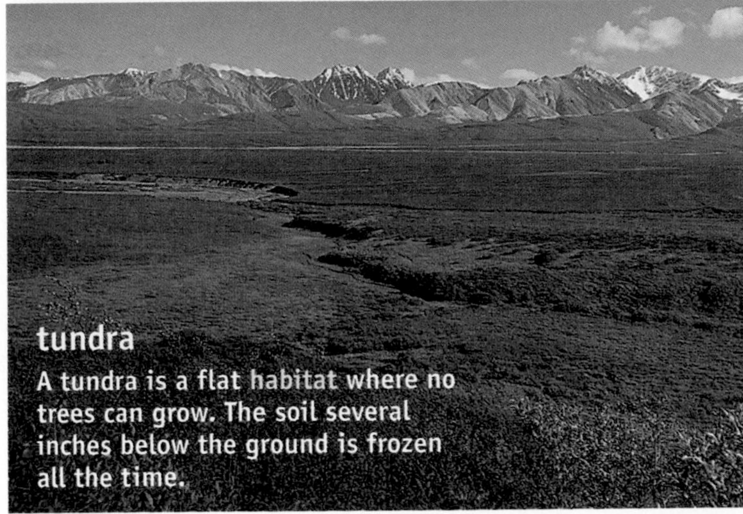

tundra

A tundra is a flat habitat where no trees can grow. The soil several inches below the ground is frozen all the time.

grassland

A grassland is a **habitat** with no hills and lots of grass. Another name for a grassland is *prairie*.

A B C D E F G H I J K L M N O P Q R S T U V W X Y Z

half

noun

A **half** is one of two equal parts.

More than one: Two **halves** make a whole.

*We each get one **half** of the sandwich.*

handle

❶ *noun*

A **handle** is the part of something that is made especially to carry or hold with your hand.

❷ *verb*

When you **handle** something, you touch, feel, or use it.

*He will **handle** the model with care.*

handsome

adjective

Handsome means good-looking.

*This white horse is very **handsome**.*

hardware

❶ *noun*

Tools and utensils made from metal are **hardware.**

❷ *noun*

The machines that make a computer work are called **hardware.**

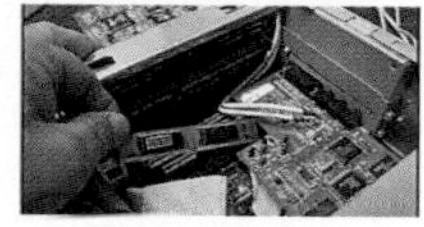

*The monitor, keyboard, and disk drive unit are computer **hardware**.*

healthy

adjective

Something is **healthy** when it is strong and well.

*These children are **healthy**.*

height

noun

Height is the measurement of how tall someone or something is.

*The **height** of this child is 4 feet, or 1.2 meters.*

heritage

noun

Your **heritage** includes the traditions, ideas, and language that come from your ancestors.

See also: *ancestor,* **page 6**

*Playing a traditional instrument is part of this boy's Hmong **heritage**.*

hero

noun

A **hero** is a person admired by others for being brave.

*The firefighter who saved the child is a **hero**.*

hibernate

verb

When an animal **hibernates**, it spends the winter resting.

*Chipmunks **hibernate** underground for most of the winter.*

history

noun

History is the study of events and people from the past. When you read about history, you are reading true stories.

See also: ***battle*****, pages 10–11;** ***freedom*****, page 40;** ***frontier*****, page 41;** ***railroad*****, page 87;** ***revolution*****, page 91;** ***settler*****, pages 96–97**

History of the California Gold Rush

The Discovery of Gold (1848)

John Sutter owned a farm in California. He had a sawmill to cut up trees. James Marshall worked at the sawmill. On January 24, 1848, Marshall discovered gold in the river near the sawmill.

John Sutter's sawmill

The Gold Rush Begins

News about the gold traveled across the United States. Thousands of people went to California to look for gold. They were called *49ers* because they arrived in 1849.

49ers with mules, picks, and shovels

Prospecting for gold with a pan *(middle)* and a cradle *(left)*

Those Amazing 49ers

People from all over the world came to California. They did not all find gold. But many stayed and helped to build the state of California.

hit

1 *noun*

Something is a **hit** if it is a great success.

*This movie is a **hit**. Everyone wants to see it.*

2 *verb*

When you **hit** something, you bump it or strike it.

*In table tennis, you **hit** the ball with a paddle.*

hold

verb

When you **hold** something, you take it and keep it in your hands.

*Two children **hold** the ropes while one jumps.*

In the past:
They **held** it.
They **have held** it.

Idiom:
Hold it!

When someone says, **"Hold it!"** you should stop.

holiday

noun

A **holiday** is a special day when many people do not work.

*People enjoy a parade on this **holiday**, the Fourth of July.*

horizontal

adjective

When something is **horizontal**, it lies along a flat line in front of you.

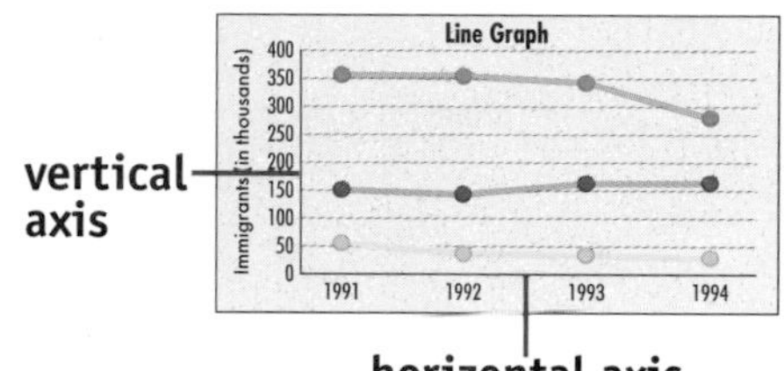

*On this graph, the **horizontal** axis, or line, has information about time.*

house

noun

A **house** is a building for people to live in.

*A **house** shelters people from the weather.*

human

noun

A **human** is a person.

*We are all **humans**.*

humorous

adjective

Something is **humorous** when it is funny.

*Cartoons are usually **humorous**.*

hurry

verb

When you **hurry**, you move or act quickly.

***Hurry!** You'll be late for the school bus!*

husband

noun

When a man and a woman marry, the man is called the **husband**.

Ii

iceberg

noun

An **iceberg** is a large mass of ice floating in the sea.

*Only a small part of an **iceberg** is above the water.*

Idiom:
just the tip of the iceberg

Something is **just the tip of the iceburg** if it is much more complicated than you thought.

laugh
calf

rough
bough

*Learning to speak in English is **just the tip of the iceberg**. You also have to learn to write some hard words.*

idea

noun

An **idea** is something you think, believe, or imagine.

*He had a good **idea** for blowing out his birthday candles.*

identical

adjective

Things are **identical** if they are exactly alike.

*Twins often wear **identical** clothes.*

imitate

verb

When you **imitate** something, you try to copy it.

*All the children **imitate** the leader in this game.*

immediately

adverb

When something happens **immediately**, it happens right away.

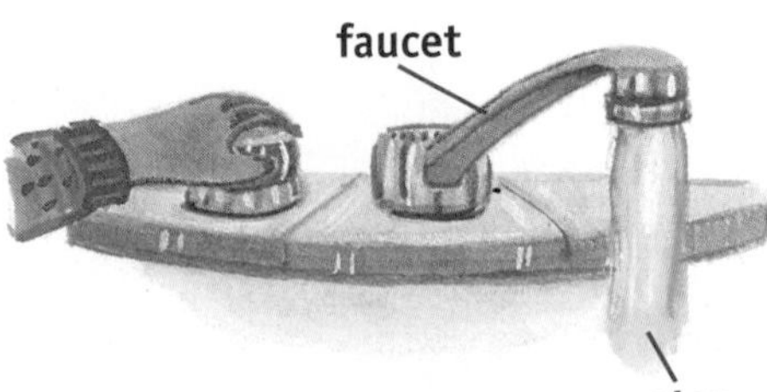

*When you turn on a faucet, water flows **immediately**.*

immigration

noun

Immigration is the act of coming into a foreign country to live.

Russian Immigrants, 1905

Between 1901 and 1920, more than 2,500,000 Russians came to the United States to escape poverty, hunger, and religious persecution.

Vietnamese Immigrants, 1978

Between 1971 and 1980, more than 170,000 Vietnamese came to the United States to escape war in their homeland.

Salvadoran Immigrants, 1981

Between 1981 and 1993, 315,000 Salvadorans came to the United States. They were escaping a civil war in El Salvador.

A B C D E F G H I J K L M N O P Q R S T U V W X Y Z

important

adjective

Something is **important** when it has great meaning or value.

*The U.S. Capitol is an **important** government building.*

improve

verb

You **improve** something when you make it better.

*These neighbors have worked to **improve** an empty lot.*

increase

verb

Something **increases** when it grows in size or numbers.

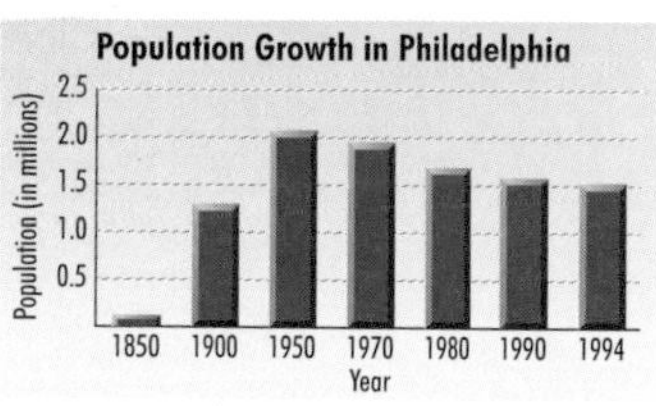

*This graph shows how population can **increase** and then decrease over time.*

index

noun

An **index** is a list that tells how to find different topics in a book.

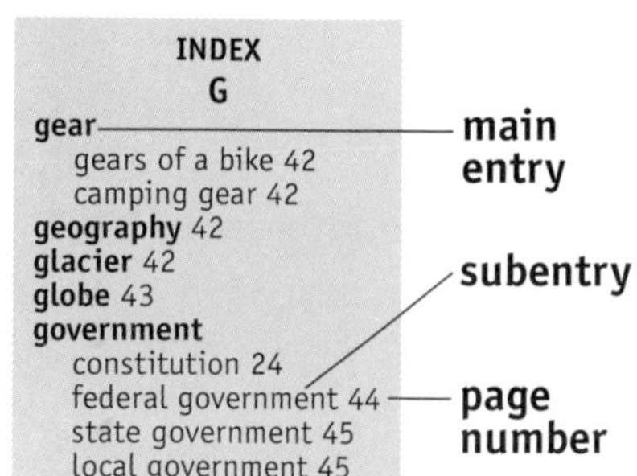

INDEX
G
gear
gears of a bike 42
camping gear 42
geography 42
glacier 42
globe 43
government
constitution 24
federal government 44
state government 45
local government 45

industry

noun

An **industry** is any branch of business or manufacturing.

*The textile **industry** makes many kinds of cloth.*

information

noun

Information is facts about a subject or subjects.

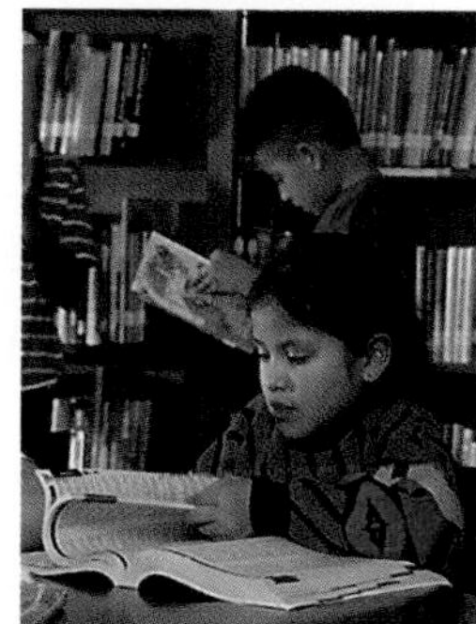

*You can get **information** from books, newspapers, or a computer.*

insect

noun

An **insect** is a small animal with no backbone. It has six legs, two antennae, and its body is divided into three parts.

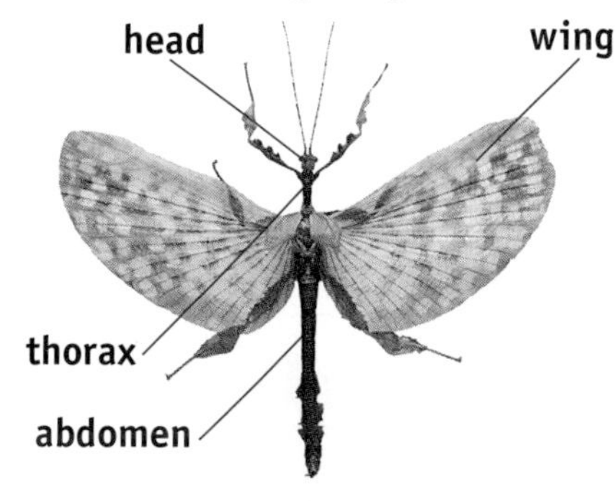

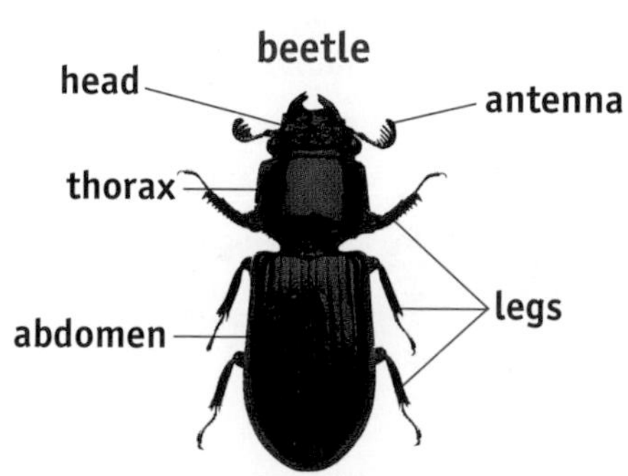

See also: *bee*, page 12; *fly*, page 38

interjection

noun

An **interjection** is a word that shows strong feeling.

*"Ouch!" is an **interjection** you use when you feel pain.*

Internet

noun

The **Internet** is a group of computer networks linked together.

See also: *modem*, page 67; *surf*, page 105; *web*, page 118

*You can find lots of information on the **Internet**.*

interview

1 *verb*

When you **interview** people, you ask them questions.

*Emilio will **interview** Dr. Brown about her work.*

2 *noun*

An **interview** is a written report of a meeting where people ask and answer questions.

*You can read Emilio's **interview** with Dr. Brown in the school newspaper.*

invention

noun

An **invention** is something new or a new way of doing something.

Young Inventors

All **inventions** start as an idea. Some ideas are brand new. Others improve older inventions. Sometimes the best inventions are from kids!

Hands-on Basketball *Christopher Haas, age 11*

Christopher invented Hands-on Basketball—a basketball with hands drawn on it. The hands show where to place your own hands when shooting a basketball, so you can't miss!

Shake Awake *Laura Keiter, age 13*

Laura invented the Shake Awake pillow to do two things. It vibrates to wake you up. It can also alert a hearing-impaired person in case of a fire. What a life-saving **invention**!

Inventions that Help Us Learn

computer

You can use computers to look for information and to write about what you learn.

video camera

You can do your own research and use a video camera to record what you learn on video.

microscope

You can study science using a microscope.

invertebrate

noun

An **invertebrate** is an animal that does not have a backbone.

See also: *vertebrate*, page 114

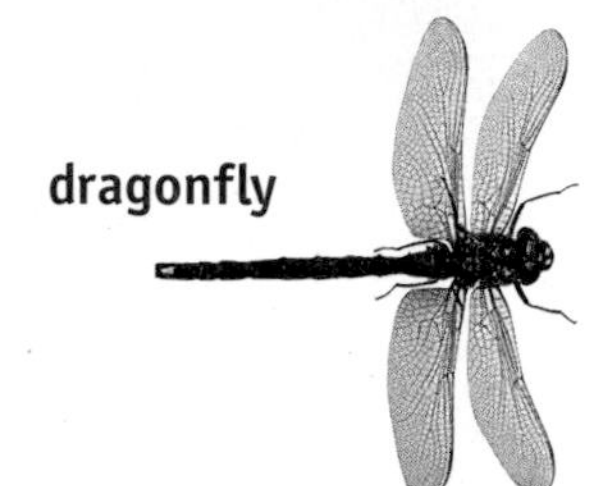

*Most animals are **invertebrates**.*

iron

❶ *noun*

Iron is a metal we find in the Earth's crust.

*All these items contain **iron**.*

❷ *verb*

When you **iron** clothes, you press out all the wrinkles.

Idiom:

iron out

When you **iron out** a problem, you solve it.

*These boys need to **iron out** their problem.*

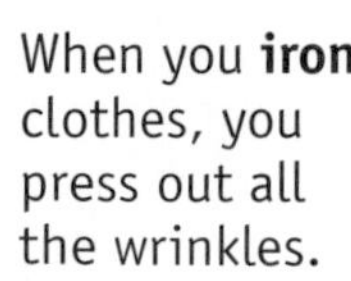

Jj

jealous

adjective

People are **jealous** when they want something that somebody else has.

*Jan is **jealous** of Michael because he got a new puppy.*

jewelry

noun

Jewelry is decoration for the body made of beautiful stones and metals.

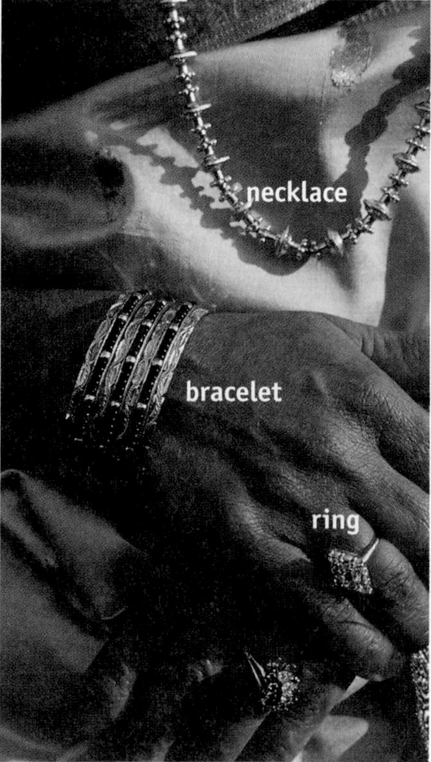

*Rings are a kind of **jewelry**.*

jiggle

verb

When something **jiggles**, it shakes a little.

*The children think it is funny to **jiggle** their dessert.*

jog

verb

When you **jog**, you run slowly.

*They **jog** in the park every morning.*

join

verb

When you **join** a group, you become a member.

*This girl will **join** a jazz band.*

joke

noun

A **joke** is a short, funny story that makes people laugh.

*My grandparents always laugh at my **jokes**.*

journal

noun

In a **journal**, you can write about what you do and what you are thinking.

journal from Lewis and Clark expedition

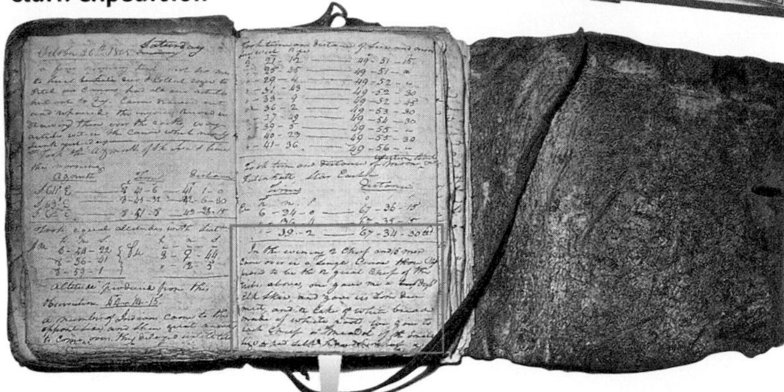

excerpt from journal

In the evening 2 Chief and 15 men Come over in a Single Canoe those Chf proved to be the 2 great Chief of the Tribe above, one gave me a Elk Skin, and gave us some Deer meet, and 2 Cakes of White bread

*The explorer William Clark kept a **journal** to remember what he saw during his travels.*

journey

noun

A **journey** is a trip.

See also: ***immigration*****, page 51**

immigrants arriving at Ellis Island

*Many families have made the long **journey** from their homelands to the United States.*

justice

noun

Justice is the fair and correct treatment of people.

courtroom

*In a court, the judge and jury decide how **justice** should be carried out.*

Kk

kayak

noun

A **kayak** is a small canoe with a narrow opening for the seat.

*This man and his son enjoy using their **kayak**.*

keyboard

❶ *noun*

A **keyboard** is a row of keys that you press to make music.

*A musical **keyboard** has black and white keys.*

❷ *noun*

A **keyboard** is a set of keys that you use for typing.

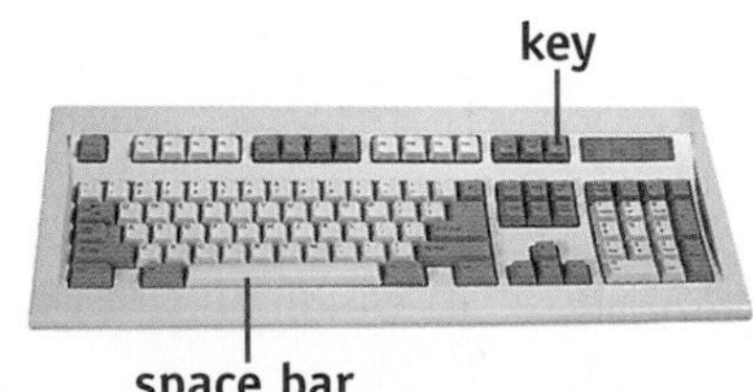

*A computer **keyboard** has letters, numbers, and punctuation marks.*

kind

❶ *noun*

When things belong to the same category, they are the same **kind** of thing.

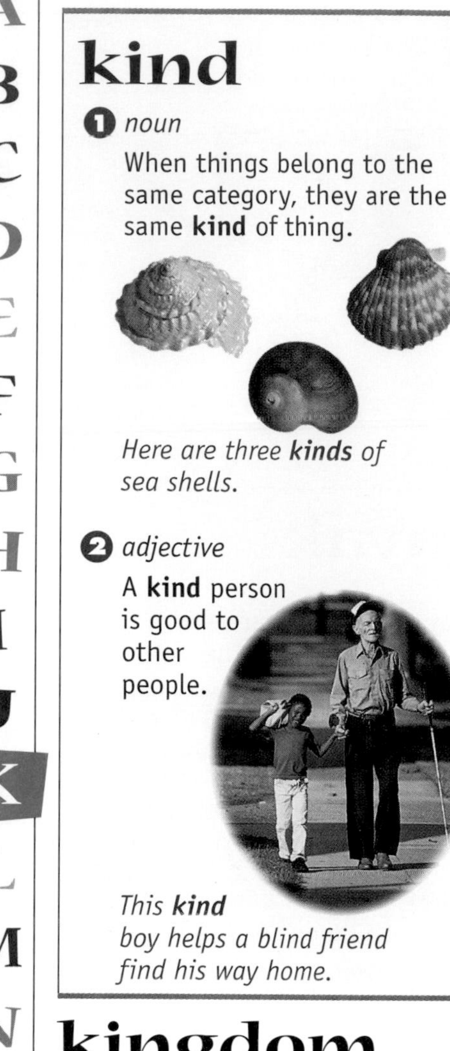

*Here are three **kinds** of sea shells.*

❷ *adjective*

A **kind** person is good to other people.

*This **kind** boy helps a blind friend find his way home.*

kingdom

noun

A **kingdom** is a country ruled by a king or queen.

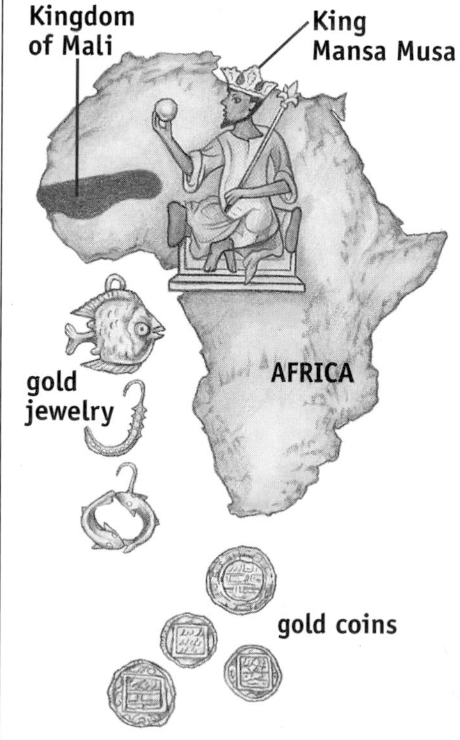

*In ancient Mali, the king owned all the gold in the **kingdom**.*

kite

noun

A **kite** is a toy that can fly in the wind.

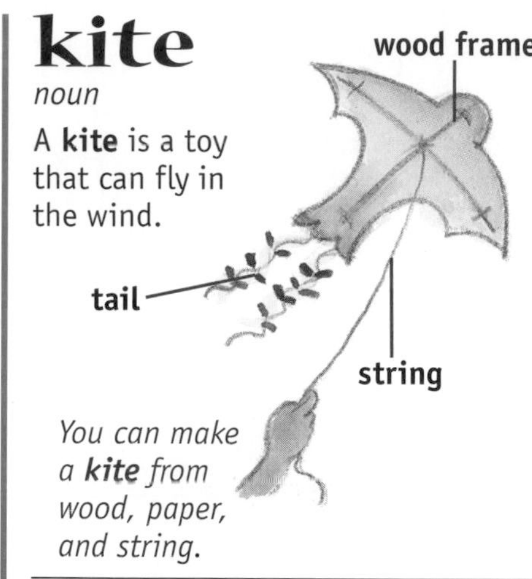

*You can make a **kite** from wood, paper, and string.*

kneel

verb

When you **kneel**, you rest one or both knees on the ground.

*A knight would **kneel** in front of his king to show loyalty.*

In the past:
He **knelt.**
He **has knelt.**

knight

noun

In ancient times, a **knight** was a soldier who fought for a king.

*A **knight** wore armor to protect himself in battle.*

knit

verb

You use yarn and special needles to **knit** something.

*Can you **knit** a warm scarf for yourself?*

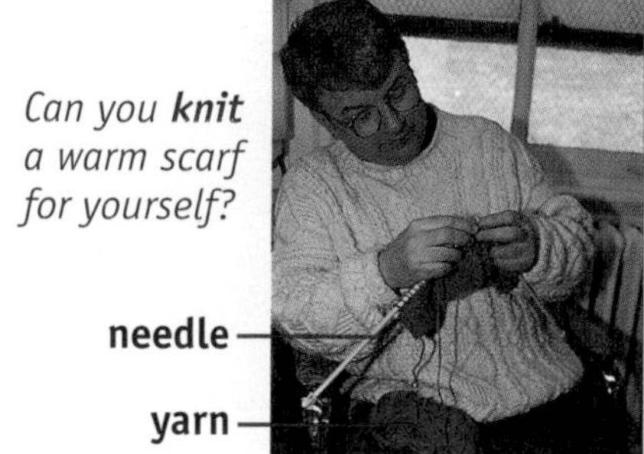

knob

noun

A **knob** is a round handle.

*You can pull on a **knob** to open something.*

knot

noun

You make a **knot** when you loop and tie string or rope.

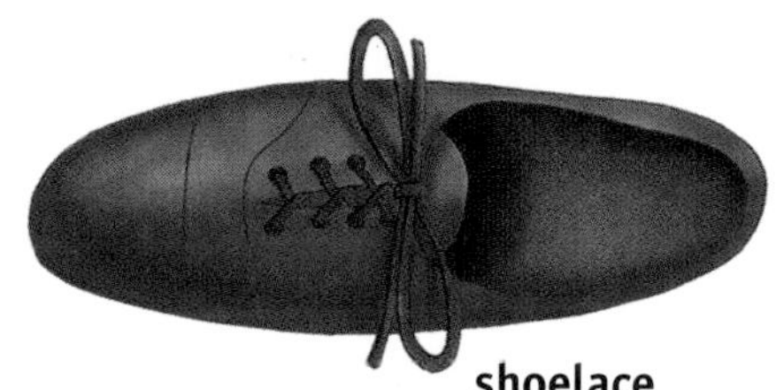

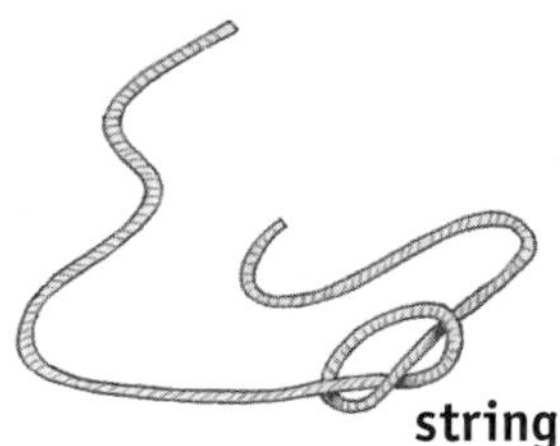

knowledge

noun

Knowledge is what you or others have learned.

*Teachers share their **knowledge** with students in class.*

life cycle

noun

A **life cycle** is a series of stages in plant or animal growth. A stage is a major change. Each kind of plant or animal passes through its stages in the same order.

See also: ***develop*, page 27; *growth*, page 46**

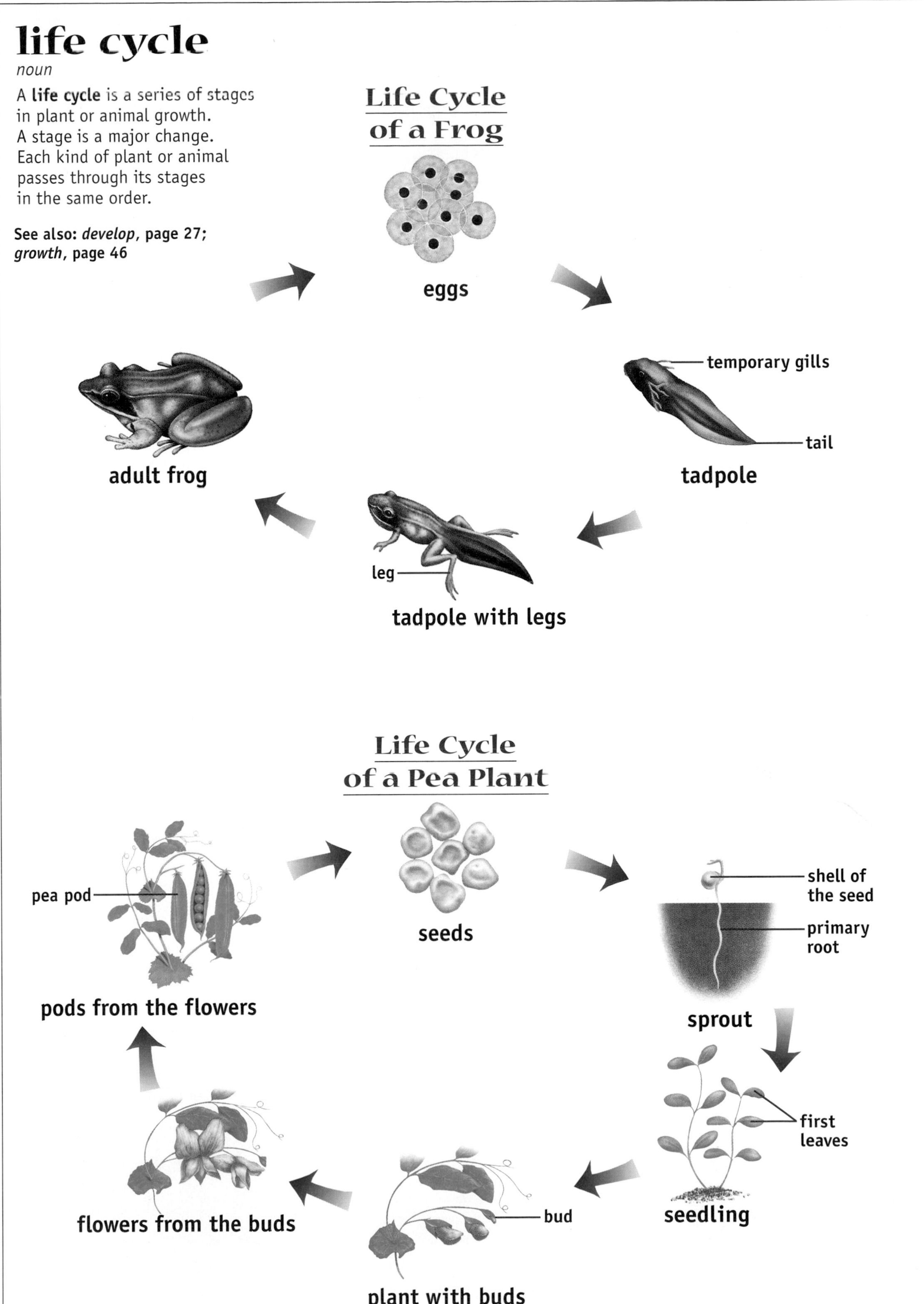

light

1 *noun*

Light is a form of energy that we can see.

__Light__ from the sun is called sunlight.

2 *noun*

A light is something that shines in the dark and helps us see.

Here are two __lights__ we can use to see at night.

line

noun

A **line** is a thin mark.

You can use a ruler to draw a straight __line__.

Idiom:

line up

You **line up** when you form a line with other people.

The children __line up__ at the bus stop.

liquid

noun

A **liquid** is something wet that you can pour. Liquid changes shape to fit its container.

Milk is a __liquid__ that we drink.

See also: ***gas*, page 41; *solid*, page 104**

lizard

noun

A **lizard** is a reptile. There are about 3,000 kinds of lizards.

A row of scaly spines goes down the back of this __lizard__.

load

noun

A **load** is something being carried.

This llama is carrying a __load__ of straw.

locate

verb

When you **locate** something, you find it.

I'm lost. Can you help me __locate__ Crest Road?

lock

1 *noun*

A **lock** is something you can open and close with a key.

You can use a __lock__ to keep your bike safe.

2 *verb*

When you **lock** something, you use a key to keep it closed.

Be sure to __lock__ the door when you leave the house.

lonely

adjective

When you are **lonely**, you feel sad because you are alone.

Chad is __lonely__ because everyone has gone home.

lovely

adjective

Something is **lovely** when it is beautiful or enjoyable.

The garden looks __lovely__ with so many bright flowers.

Mm

magician

noun

A **magician** is a person who can do magic tricks.

*This **magician** waved his wand, and a bird appeared.*

make

verb

When you **make** something, you build it or create it yourself.

*You can **make** a bowl out of clay.*

In the past:
You **made** something.
You **have made** something.

Idiom:
make do

You **make do** when you use what you have instead of what you want.

*Eric would like a new bike, but he will **make do** with his old one.*

machine

noun

A **machine** has many parts that work together to do a job.

sewing machine

***Machines** can make work easier for people.*

magnet

noun

A **magnet** is a piece of metal with a force that attracts iron.

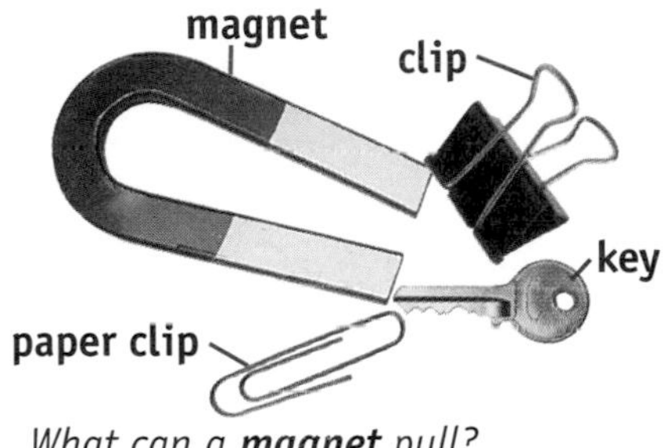

*What can a **magnet** pull?*

magnify

verb

When you **magnify** something, you make it look bigger than it really is.

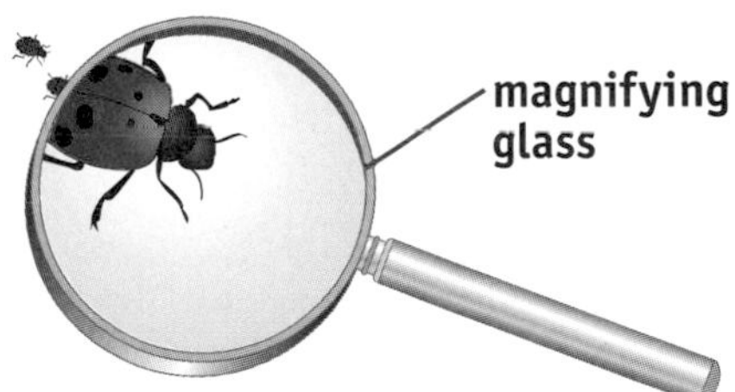

*When you **magnify** a bug, its body looks big.*

mammal

noun

A **mammal** is a warm-blooded vertebrate with hair or fur.

*A baby **mammal** drinks milk from its mother.*

See also: ***animal***, **pages 6–7;** ***vertebrate***, **page 114**

magazine

noun

A **magazine** is a printed collection of news articles or stories.

*This **magazine** comes in the mail once a month.*

main

adjective

The **main** character is the most important character in a story or play.

*A coyote is the **main** character in many Native American tales.*

manufacture

verb

You **manufacture** something when you use a machine to turn raw materials into another product.

*Workers use wood to **manufacture** chairs at this factory.*

map

noun

A **map** is a drawing of the Earth's surface or a part of it. Some maps show continents, countries, and landforms. Others may show cities, roads, climate, or products.

See also: ***globe*****, page 43**

Map of the World

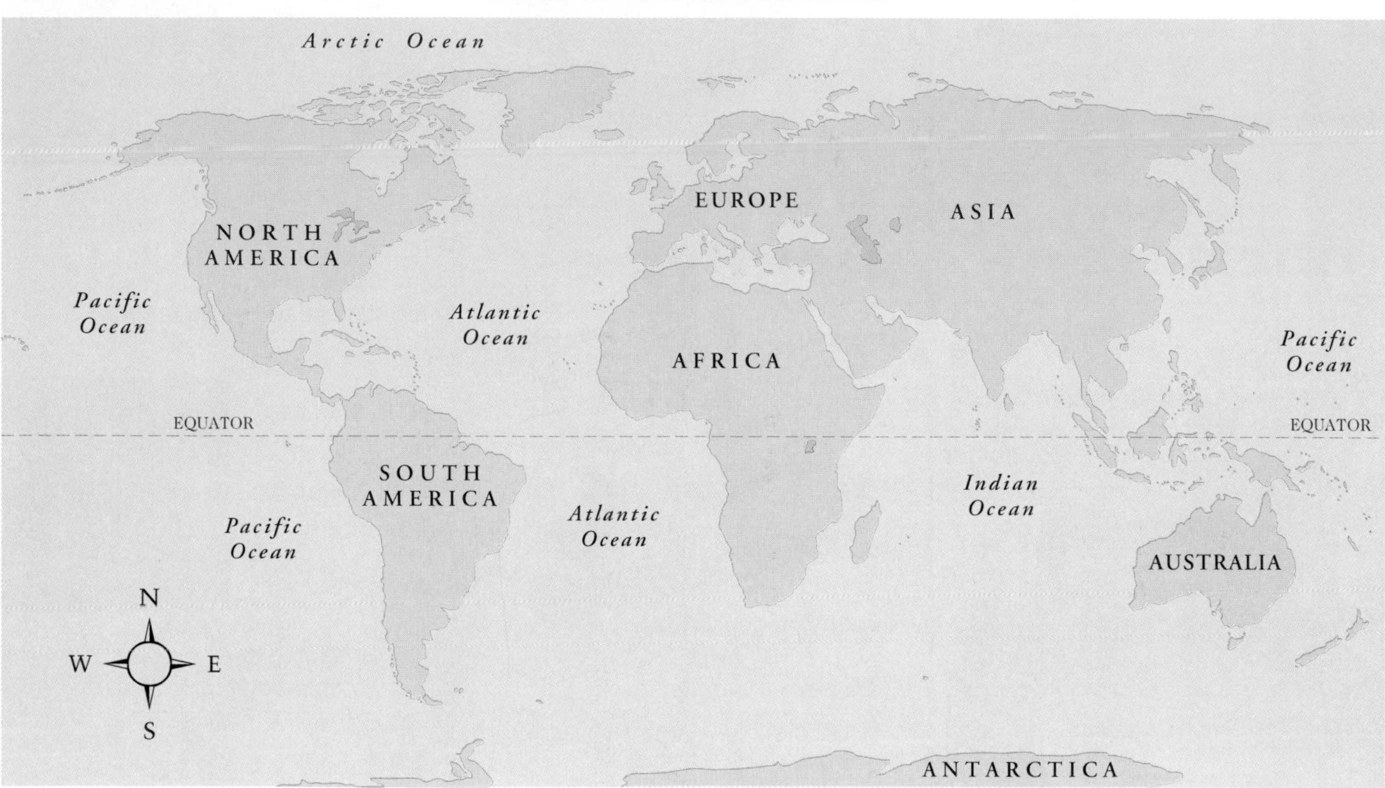

Product Map of the United States

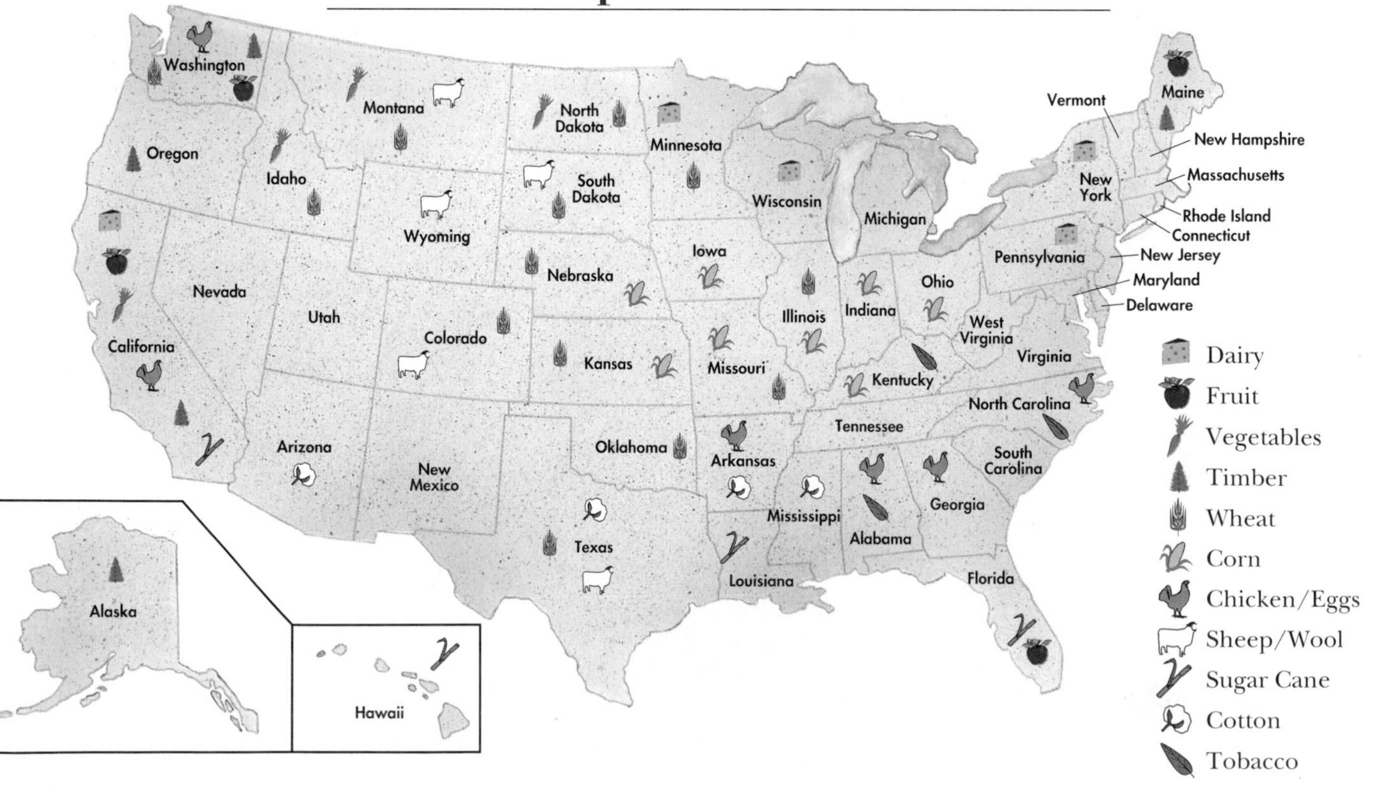

modem

noun

A **modem** connects computers to each other using telephone lines.

You need a ***modem*** *to use the Internet.*

See also: *Internet*, page 52

moisture

noun

Moisture is small drops of liquid in the air or on things.

Steam turns into ***moisture*** *when it hits the cold window.*

money

noun

Money is the coins and paper bills that people use to buy things.

Each country has its own type of ***money****.*

moon

noun

A **moon** is a natural satellite that travels around a planet.

mountain

lunar craft

surface of the Moon

Astronauts first walked on Earth's ***moon*** *in July of 1969.*

See also: *phase*, page 79; *satellite*, page 93

mouse

❶ *noun*

A **mouse** is a small, furry animal in the rodent family.

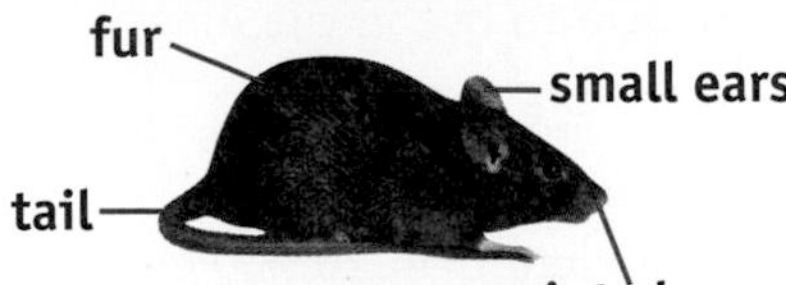

More than one:
Mice can live in a grassy habitat and eat plant seeds.

❷ *noun*

A **mouse** is a piece of computer equipment. You touch the mouse to move the cursor.

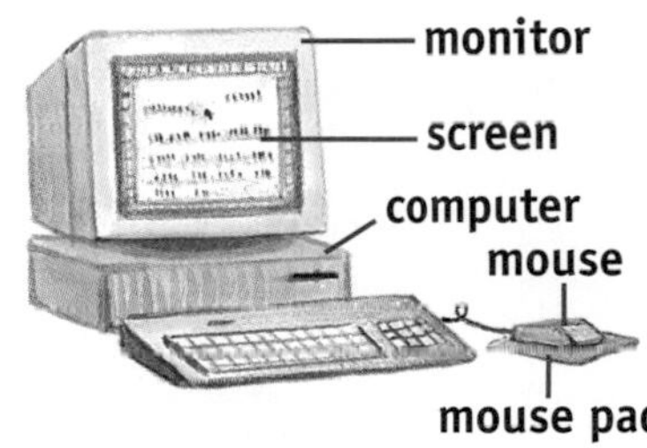

mouth

noun

Your **mouth** is the opening in your face that you use to eat and speak.

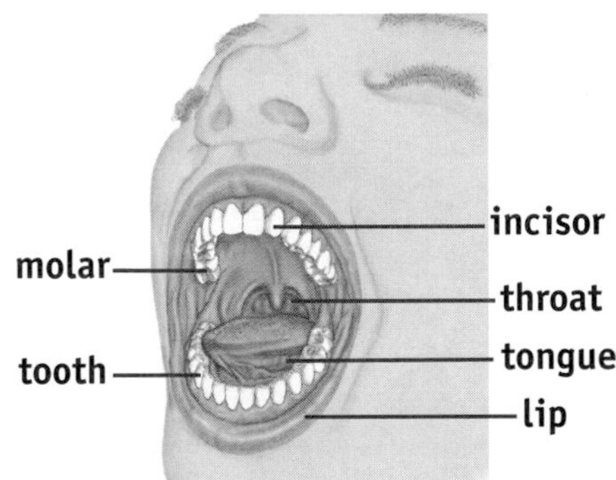

Idiom:
big mouth

If you have a **big mouth**, you tell things that should be secret.

multiply

verb

To **multiply** a number, you add it to itself several times.

$$\begin{array}{r} 9 \\ +9 \\ +9 \\ +9 \\ +9 \\ \hline 45 \end{array}$$

In math class you learn how to ***multiply*** *numbers.*

multiplicand

multiplier

$$\begin{array}{r} 9 \\ \times 5 \\ \hline 45 \end{array}$$

product

muscle

noun

A **muscle** is the part of the body beneath your skin and attached to your bones that helps your body move.

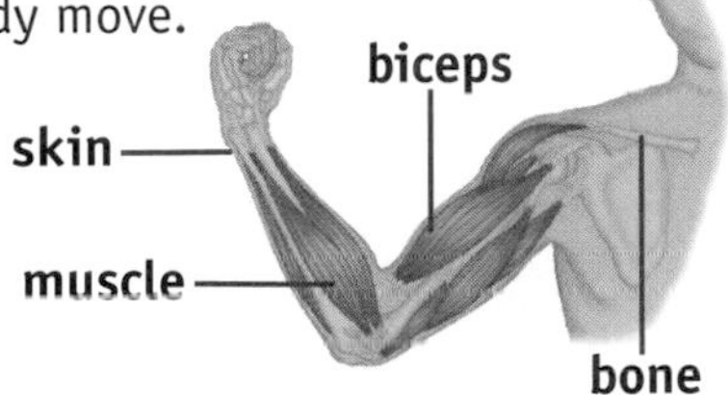

When you exercise, you build strong ***muscles****.*

museum

noun

A **museum** is a building where objects related to science, history, or art are displayed.

There are models of animals at the natural history ***museum****.*

musician

noun

A **musician** is a person who plays or composes music.

This young ***musician*** *enjoys playing the violin.*

Nn

nation

1 *noun*

The people who live together in a country under one government form a **nation**.

Poland is a ***nation*** *in Eastern Europe.*

2 *noun*

A **nation** is a group of people who share the same heritage and traditions.

The people of the Inuit ***nation*** *live in the Arctic region.*

native

adjective

Something is native to the place it originally comes from.

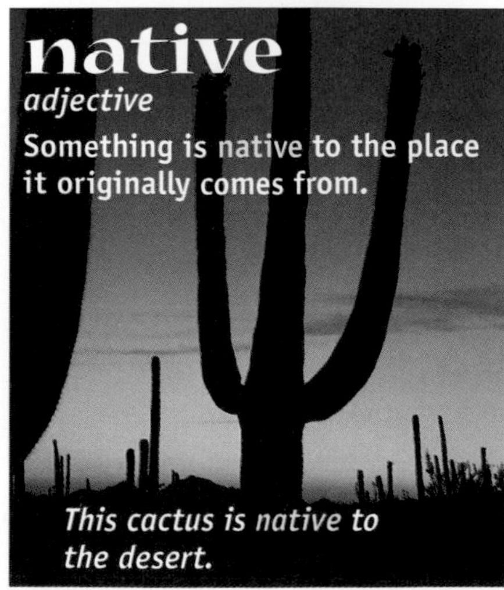

This cactus is native to the desert.

Native Americans

noun

Native Americans were the first people to live in the Americas.

Many scientists believe that the first **Native Americans** came from Asia more than 20,000 years ago. They walked across an ice bridge into what is now Alaska.

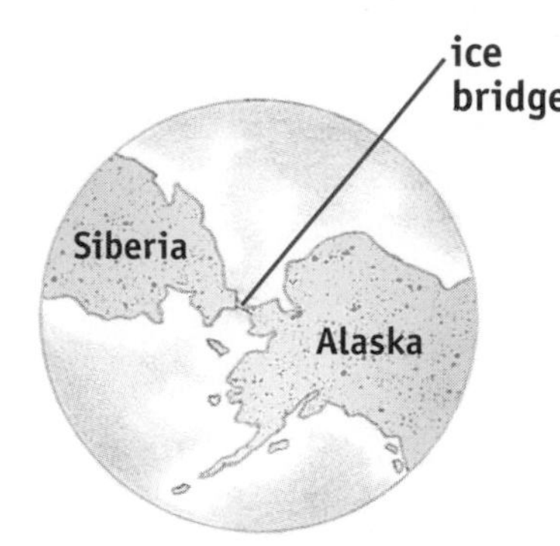

Native American Cultures

Native Americans across the continent developed very different cultures. Each native nation has its own types of clothing, housing, and daily customs.

See also: *powwow*, **page 85**

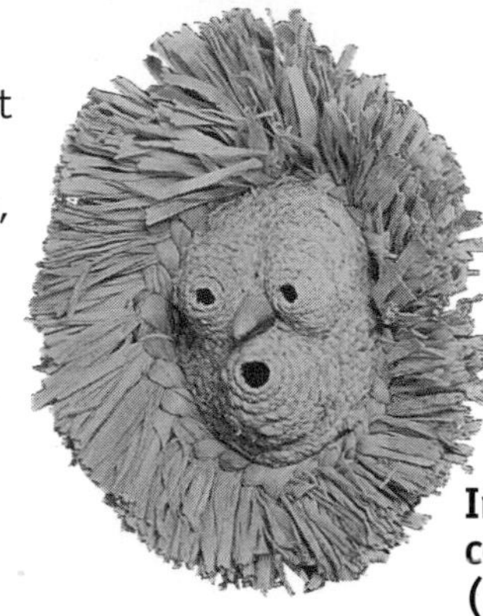

Iroquois corn husk mask (Northeast)

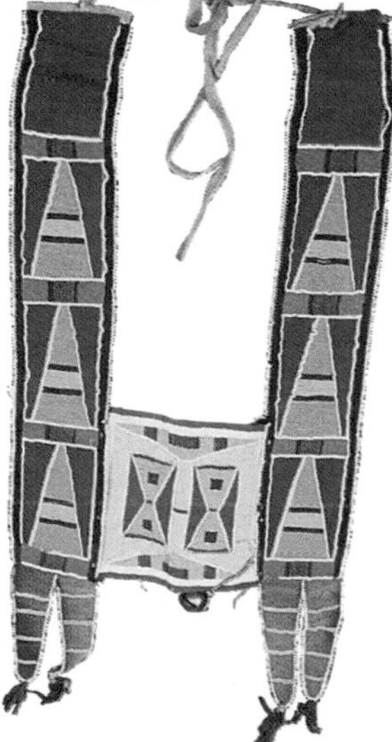

Crow beaded horse decoration (Plains)

Navajo woven blanket (Southwest)

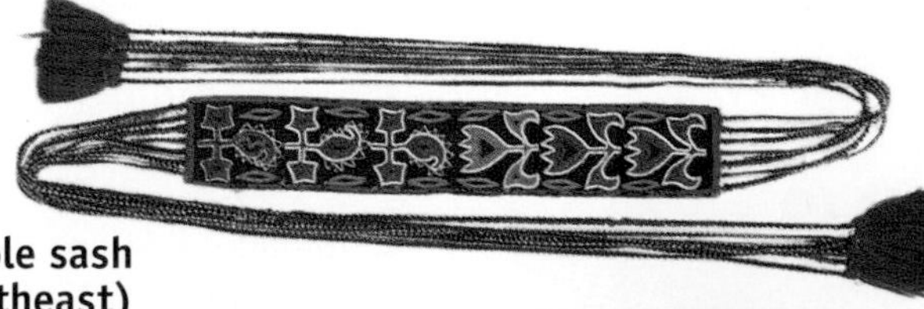

Seminole sash (Southeast)

Tlingit feast bowl (Northwest)

Pomo gift basket (West Coast)

Native Americans Before European Contact

In the 1500s, when the first European explorers arrived on the continent, there were at least 600 **Native American** tribes living in North America. There may have been as many as 18 million Native Americans at that time.

See also: *tribe*, page 111

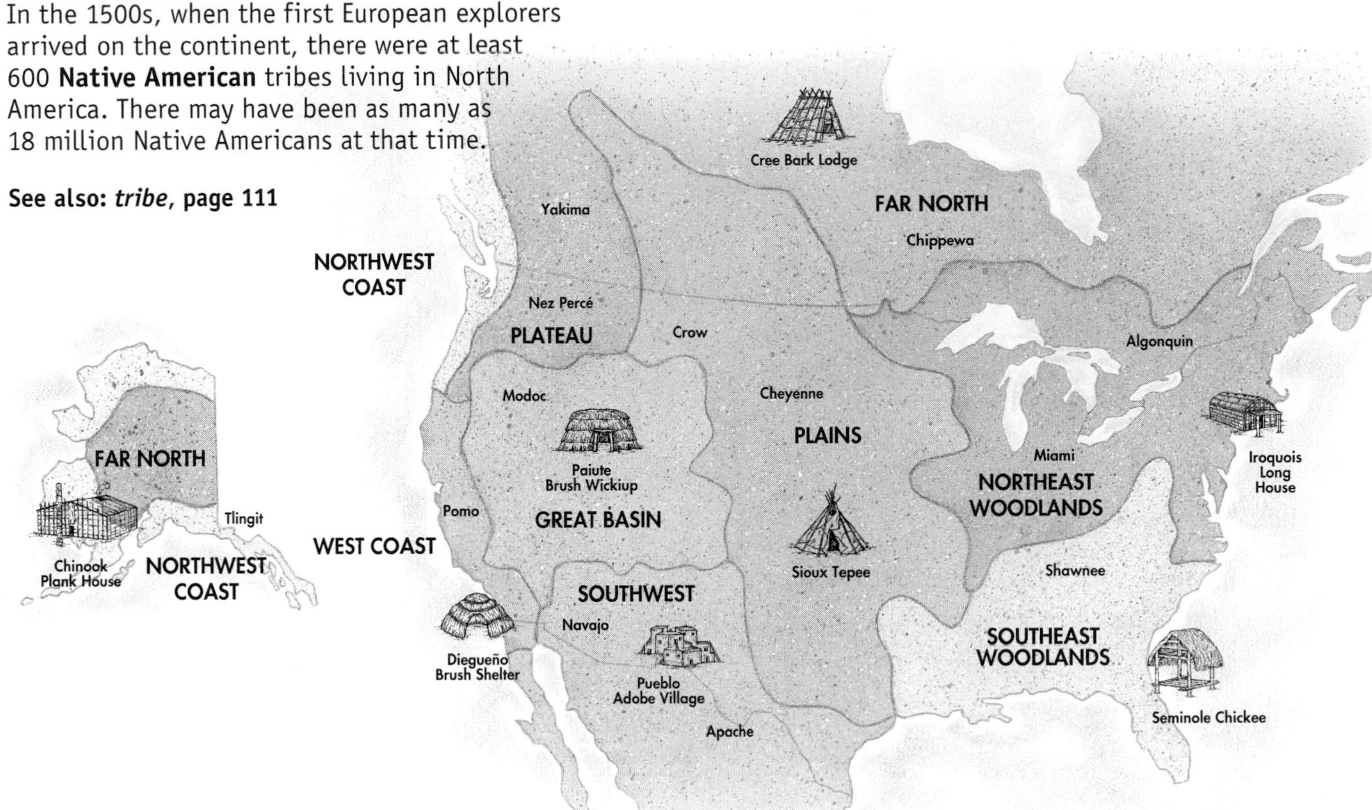

Native Americans Today

Today, there are over two million **Native Americans** living in the United States. Some live on special Native American lands called *reservations*. Others live in cities and towns across America. Many U.S. place names come from Native American tribal names and words.

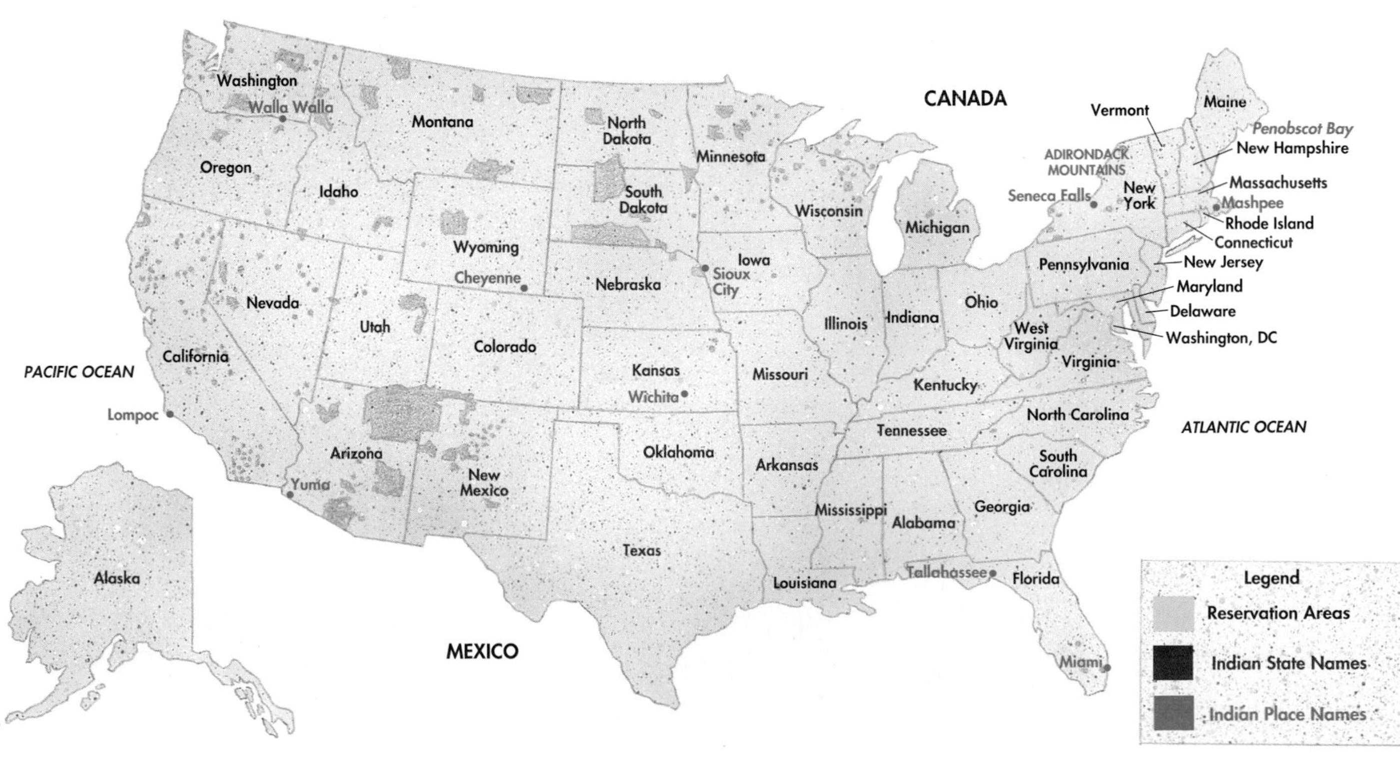

natural resource

noun

Natural resources are valuable plants, animals or minerals that are found in nature.

*Many **natural resources** are made into products that we use every day.*

Natural Resources	How Do We Take the Resources?	How Do We Prepare Resources for Use?	Everyday Products
petroleum	Oil wells pump out petroleum.	Petroleum is processed at the oil refinery.	gasoline
tree	Lumberjacks cut down trees.	Tree trunks are cut up at the saw mill.	lumber paper
fish	Fishing boats catch fish.	A cannery puts the fish in cans.	food

nature

noun

Nature includes everything in the physical world that is not made by humans. It includes all living things.

*Many people visit national parks to enjoy the beauty of **nature**.*

naughty

adjective

When something is **naughty**, it behaves badly.

*The **naughty** puppy chewed up this slipper.*

navigate

verb

You **navigate** when you use a map or tool to find the way to travel.

*Sailors can use the stars to **navigate** across the seas.*

neat

adjective

When something is **neat**, it is clean and orderly.

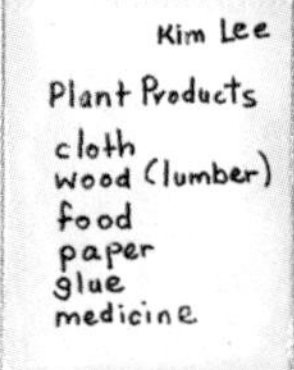

neat

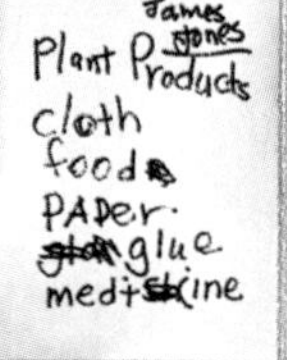

messy

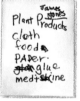

***Neat** papers are easier to read.*

necessary

adjective

Something is **necessary** when you must have it.

*The right equipment is **necessary** for rock climbing.*

needle
noun

A **needle** is a sharp metal tool for sewing.

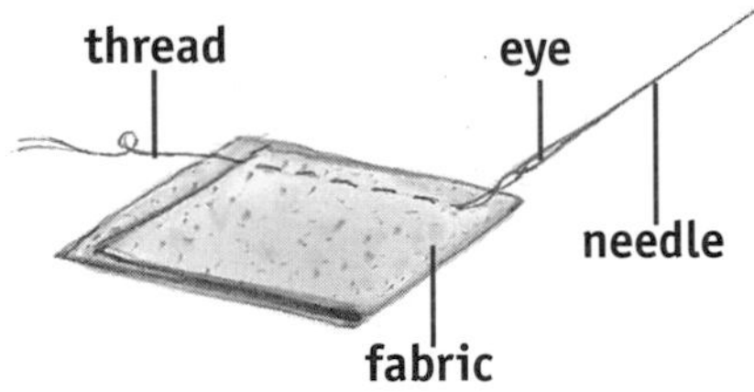

*You use a **needle** to pull thread through fabric.*

negative
adjective

A **negative** number is a number that is less than zero.

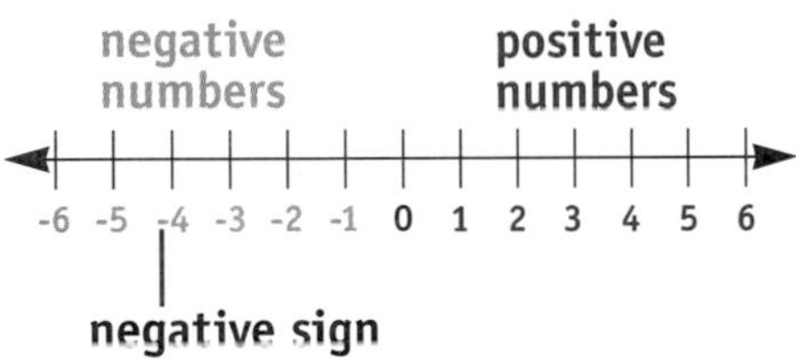

*On a number line, the **negative** numbers are all to the left of zero.*

neighbor
noun

A **neighbor** is a person who lives near you.

*These **neighbors** chat on the steps.*

nephew
noun

A **nephew** is the son of your brother or sister.

*Uncle John enjoys listening to his **nephew**.*

nervous system
noun

In the **nervous system**, the brain, spinal cord, and nerves work together to tell the body what to do.

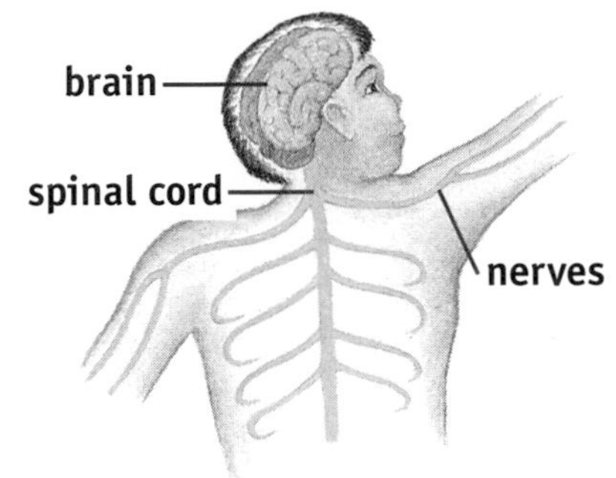

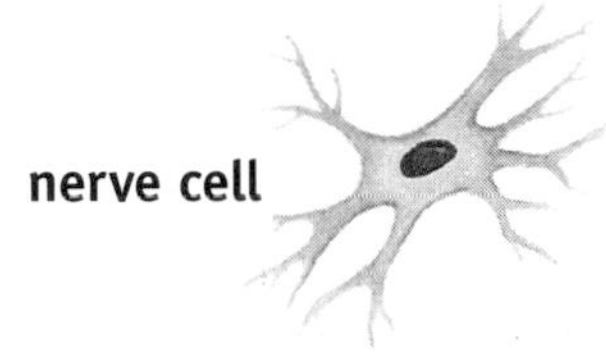

*In the **nervous system**, nerves carry messages between the brain and other parts of the body.*

See also: ***brain***, page 15

network
1 *noun*

A **network** is a system with many parts that work together.

*Your body has a nerve **network** about 50 miles long!*

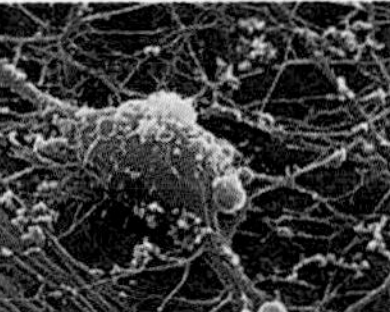

2 *noun*

A computer **network** allows people who are working on different computers to communicate with each other.

*The computers in the lab are on a **network**.*

new
adjective

Something that is freshly made or bought is **new**.

*I like to wear my **new** sneakers!*

news
noun

The **news** is any report of what has happened in the recent past.

*You can watch the **news** from around the world on TV every day.*

newspaper
noun

A **newspaper** is a written report of what happened in the recent past.

name — Your Town Daily
August 11, 2002
headline — New School Ready for Students
article — After a summer of very busy construction, the new West Side Middle School is finally ready for the fall opening.

*Most towns and cities publish a daily **newspaper**.*

niece
noun

A **niece** is the daughter of your brother or sister.

*Gina is Laura's **niece**.*

no

1 *adverb*

You say "**no**" when you do not agree with what someone else says or does.

2 *adjective*

No means not any.

*There are **no** cookies left in this package.*

*More words that mean **no** (not any):*

no person = **nobody**
no thing = **nothing**
no place = **nowhere**
no amount = **none**

Nobody is home today.
There is **nothing** to do.
There is **nowhere** to go.
None of my friends have called.

nonfiction

adjective

Nonfiction books are about real people, places, things, and events.

*This **nonfiction** book has information about farming.*

See also: *fiction*, page 38

note

1 *noun*

A **note** is a short message or letter.

Dear Kate,
You are a great writer.
Your story is scary!
Keep up the good work.
Mrs. Osaki

*Here's the **note** Kate's teacher wrote about her story.*

2 *noun*

A **note** is a way of writing down a musical sound.

*You can play these **notes** on the piano.*

notice

verb

You **notice** something when you pay attention to it.

*What do they **notice** in the water?*

noun

noun

A **noun** is a word that names a person, place, or thing.

*Boy and bench are **nouns** that name what you see in this photo.*

nutrition

noun

Nutrition is the study of the way our bodies use the food we eat.

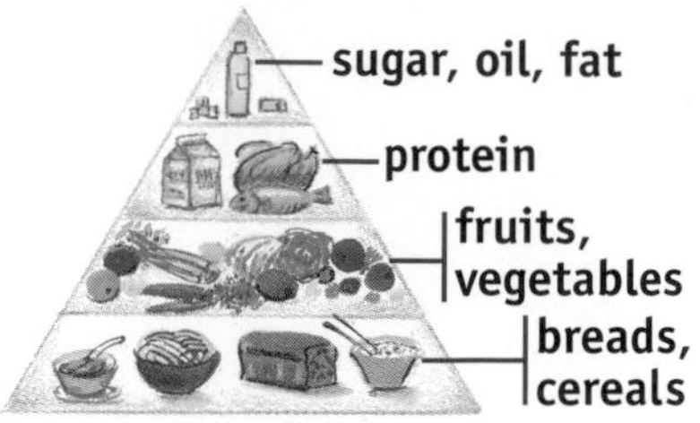

*The shape of this chart helps show how much of each food to eat for good **nutrition**.*

Protein

Our bodies use protein from foods like fish, cheese, and beans to build bones and muscles.

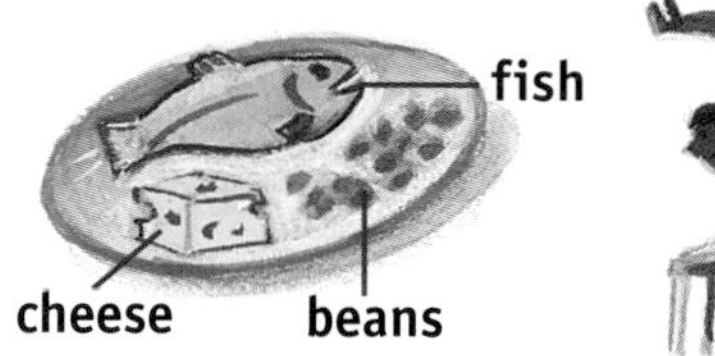

Fruits and Vegetables

The vitamins and minerals in fruits and vegetables help us stay healthy.

Breads and Cereals

Our bodies use the carbohydrates in breads and cereals for quick energy.

Sugar, Fat, Oil

Our bodies do not need very much sugar, fat, or oil.

Oo

observe
verb

You **observe** something when you watch it in a careful way.

*You can **observe** ocean birds from the seashore.*

obtain
verb

When you **obtain** something, you get it.

*You can **obtain** information about the ocean at the library.*

occur
verb

Something occurs when it happens.

*Sometimes huge storms **occur** near the ocean.*

ocean
noun

The **ocean** is the salt water that covers almost three-fourths of Earth.

*The **oceans** are visible from outer space.*

*There are big waves in the **ocean** today.*

See also: ***tide*, page 107**

octopus
noun

An **octopus** is a sea animal that has eight arms, or tentacles.

often
adverb

When something happens **often**, it happens many times.

*My cat **often** follows me to school.*

oil
noun

Oil is a fatty liquid used for food preparation. Oil can come from plants or animals.

*You can fry potatoes in cooking **oil**.*

Idiom:
burn the midnight oil

You **burn the midnight oil** when you stay up very late to work.

on-line
adjective

An **on-line** service is a connection to a network of computers.

*You can use **on-line** information to write a report.*

opinion
noun

Your **opinion** is what you believe about something.

*What is your **opinion** of this movie?*

A B C D E F G H I J K L M N O P Q R S T U V W X Y Z

opposite

adjective

Two things are **opposite** when they are completely different from each other.

back

front

curved

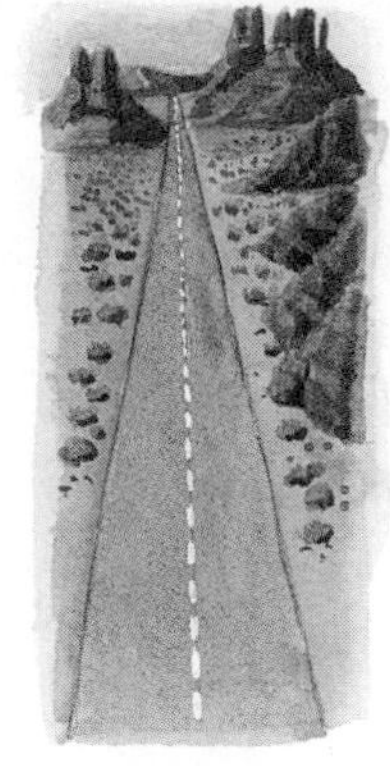
straight

hard

soft

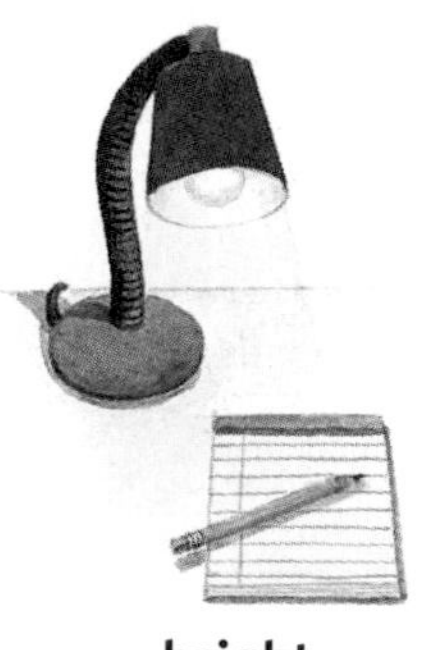
bright

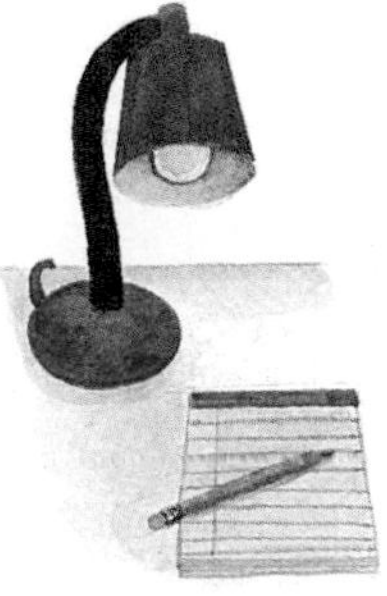
dim

different

same

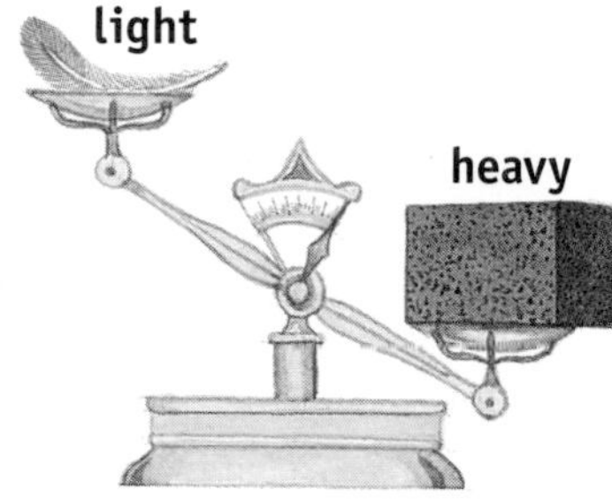
light

heavy

clean

dirty

empty

full

high

low

rough

smooth

few

many

inside

outside

liquid
solid
open
closed
add
subtract
long
short
sharp
dull
break
fix
GLUE
light
dark
huge
tiny
male
female
narrow
wide
thick
thin
enter
exit

orbit

verb

In space, something orbits when it moves around a sun, a moon, or a planet in a predictable path.

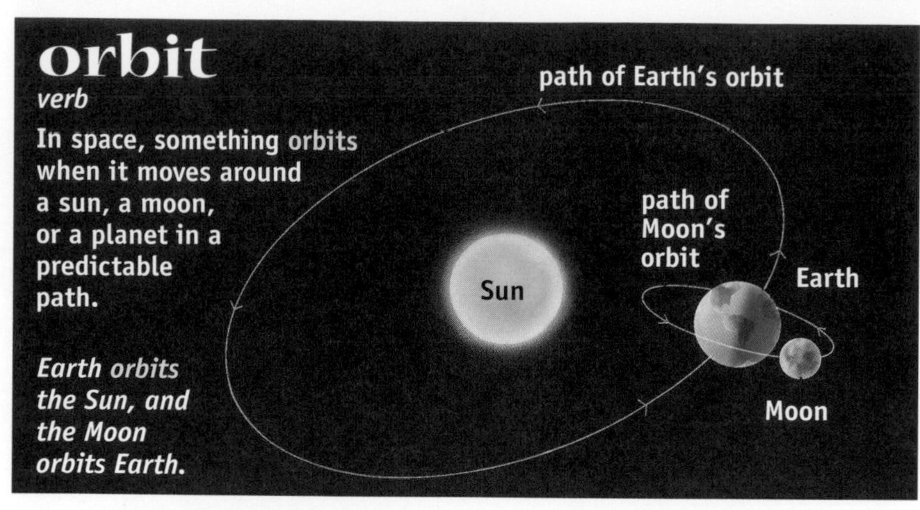

Earth orbits the Sun, and the Moon orbits Earth.

orchestra

noun

An **orchestra** is a group of people who play musical instruments together.

Symphony Orchestra in Chicago, USA

Gamelan Orchestra in Java, Indonesia

order

❶ *noun*

Order is a way to arrange things according to one or more features.

*These piñatas are in **order** by size from small to large.*

❷ *verb*

When you **order** something in a restaurant, you ask for it.

*I would like to **order** a tuna sandwich, please.*

organ

❶ *noun*

An **organ** is a part of a plant or animal. It is made of different types of cells and has a special purpose.

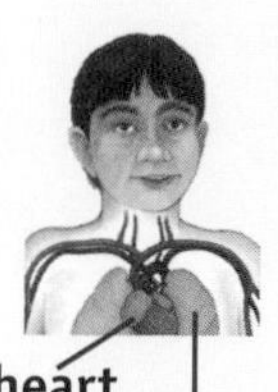

*The heart and lungs are **organs** that work together in the human body.*

See also: ***blood*, page 14; *digestion*, page 28**

❷ *noun*

An **organ** is a musical instrument. It has keyboards and pipes that produce sounds.

organize

verb

When you **organize** something, you put it together in an orderly way.

Facts About Human Organs

ORGAN	LOCATION	SIZE	PURPOSE
heart	middle of chest	size of your fist	pumps blood
lungs	inside chest cavity	size of a balloon	exchange gases

*This chart **organizes** facts about the body's organs.*

owe

verb

When you **owe** money, it means you have to pay for something.

*Tom **owes** Alex a quarter.*

Pp

pack

1 *noun*

A **pack** is a bag for carrying things on your back.

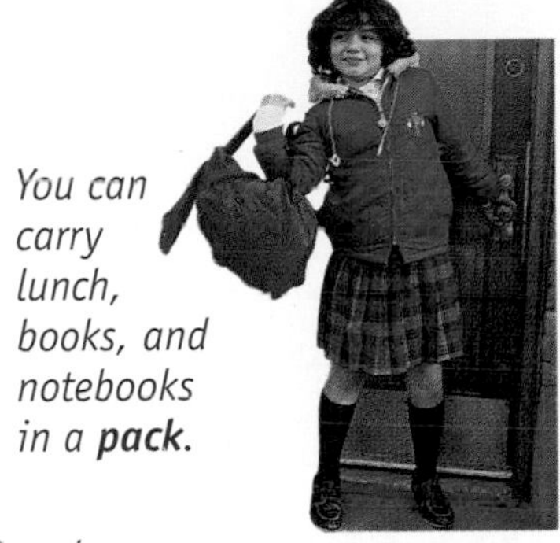

*You can carry lunch, books, and notebooks in a **pack**.*

2 *verb*

When you **pack**, you put things in a suitcase.

*If I **pack** tonight, I'll be ready to go in the morning.*

package

noun

A **package** is a box or bag that is packed and then closed up.

*Miguel will send a **package** to his grandmother in Mexico.*

paint

1 *noun*

Paint is a liquid you can use to change the color of something.

*He uses bright **paint** for the mural.*

2 *verb*

When you **paint** something, you use paint to color it.

*This artist likes to **paint** outdoor scenes.*

pair

noun

A **pair** is a set of two things that match or belong together.

*This **pair** of socks will go nicely with this pair of shoes.*

paragraph

noun

A **paragraph** is a piece of writing. It includes sentences about the same idea.

indent

Turtles have shells and lay eggs. Some turtles live in the sea. Some turtles live in fresh water. All turtles are reptiles.

*This **paragraph** is about turtles.*

parallel

adjective

Parallel lines are straight and always the same distance apart.

*The two sides of this ladder are **parallel**. So are the rungs.*

parent

noun

A **parent** is a father or a mother.

***Parents** love to hold a new baby.*

partner

noun

A **partner** is someone who works with one or more other people.

*The **partners** are selling lemonade.*

passenger

noun

A **passenger** travels in a vehicle that someone else is driving.

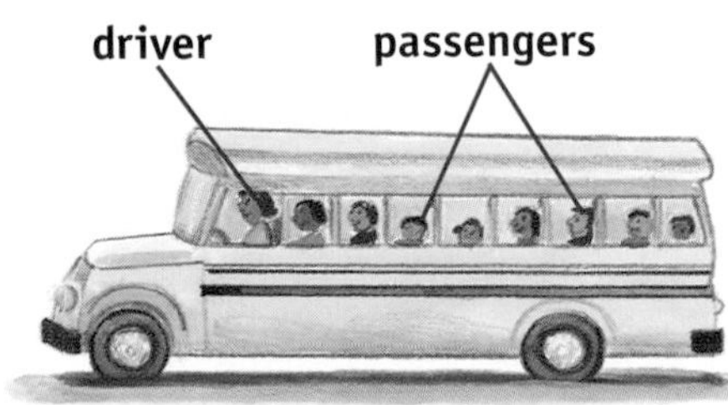

*This bus holds many **passengers**.*

past

noun

The **past** is the time that has already gone by.

*In the **past**, dinosaurs lived on Earth.*

pasture

noun

A **pasture** is a field of grass. Animals graze, or eat grass in a pasture.

pattern

❶ *noun*

A **pattern** is a design that is repeated more than once.

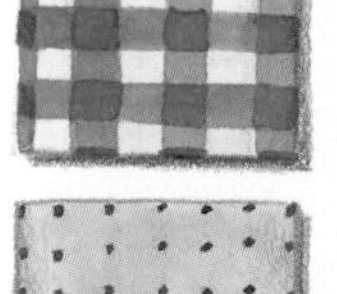

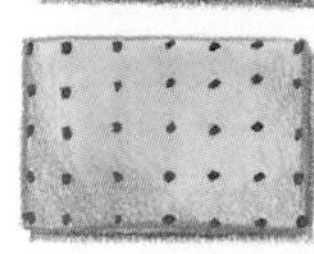

*Each piece of cloth has a different **pattern**.*

❷ *noun*

A **pattern** is a model to be followed.

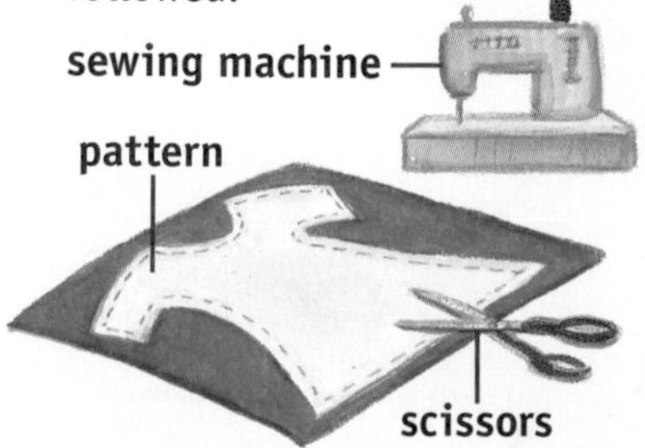

*You can use a **pattern** to cut out cloth for a dress.*

peace

noun

There is **peace** when there is no war or fighting.

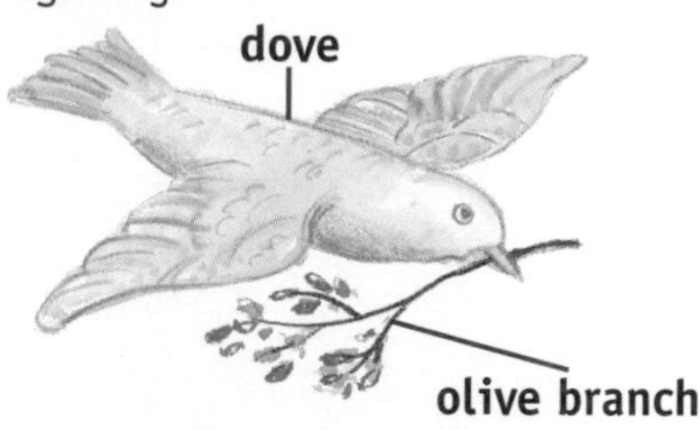

*A dove with an olive branch is a symbol of **peace**.*

percent

noun

A **percent** is one part of 100. The symbol for percent is %.

*Twenty **percent** of this grid is red.*

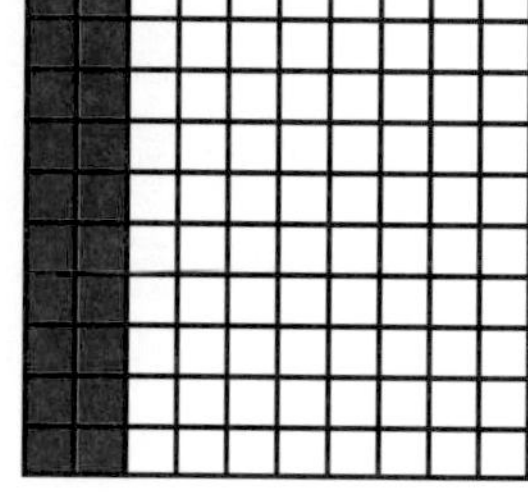

perfect

adjective

When something is **perfect**, it has no mistakes.

*Maria is proud of her **perfect** score on the test.*

perform

verb

You **perform** when you put on a show for other people.

*These students will **perform** for the school.*

period

❶ *noun*

A **period** is a dot used as a mark of punctuation.

Use a period at the end of a sentence.

❷ *noun*

A **period** is a particular time in history.

*You can learn about the colonial **period** on a field trip to Colonial Williamsburg.*

See also: ***colony*, page 21**

permanent

adjective

When something is **permanent**, it lasts forever.

*This is a **permanent** memorial to the Civil War.*

permission

noun

When you have **permission**, you are allowed to do something.

*They all have **permission** to go on the roller coaster.*

persuade

verb

You **persuade** when you give a good reason for doing something.

Editorials

Time For a New School

by José López

Our classrooms are too crowded. Our science labs are out of date. Our football field has no room for spectators. It is time to start planning a new school.

*An editorial tries to **persuade** you to agree with the writer's opinion.*

petition

noun

A **petition** is a written request that is sent to a decision-maker. It is signed by many people.

Town of Concord
Petition for New School

1. Susan Clark
2. [illegible]
3. [illegible] Williams
4. [illegible]

*This **petition** asks the mayor for a new school.*

phase

noun

A phase is one stage of development or growth.

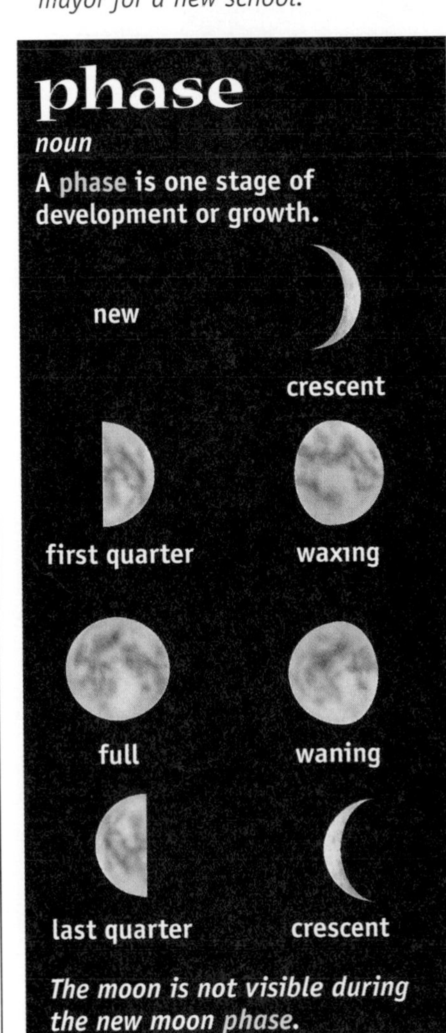

The moon is not visible during the new moon phase.

photosynthesis

noun

Photosynthesis is the process that plants use to make food and oxygen from light, carbon dioxide, water, and chlorophyll.

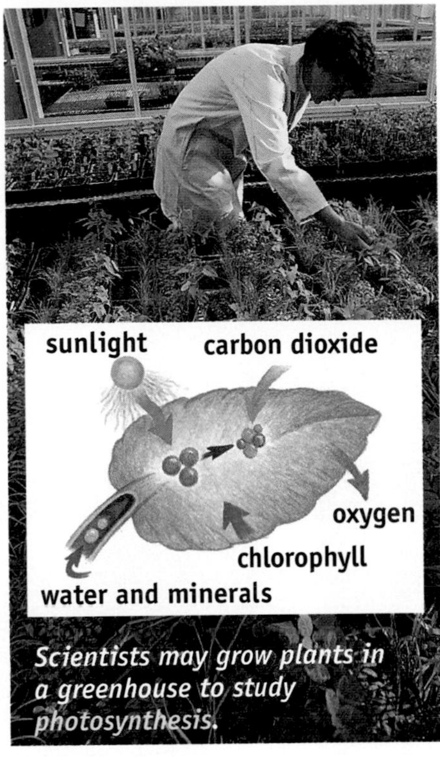

Scientists may grow plants in a greenhouse to study photosynthesis.

phrase

noun

A **phrase** is a group of words that do not make a complete sentence.

phrase — to school on Fridays

subject **verb**

complete sentence — We go to school on Fridays.

*A **phrase** needs a subject and a verb to become a sentence.*

physical

adjective

Something **physical** has to do with the body.

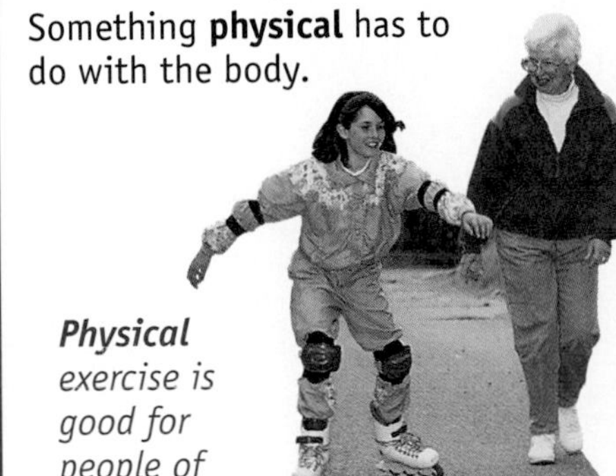

***Physical** exercise is good for people of all ages.*

pick

verb

When you **pick** something, you choose it.

*You can **pick** what you want from the menu.*

Idiom:

to pick up

When you **pick up** something, you learn it.

*She **picked up** knitting from her aunt.*

picture

noun

A **picture** is an image of a person, an object, or a scene.

drawing

photograph

painting

*A **picture** may be a drawing, a painting, or a photograph.*

pilgrim

noun

A **pilgrim** is a person who goes on a religious journey.

the *Mayflower*

The Pilgrims in America

The **Pilgrims** were a group of people who left England to look for religious freedom. They arrived in North America in 1620. They started a community called Plimoth Plantation, located in an area now called Plymouth, Massachusetts.

chopping wood

building homes for shelter

a Pilgrim village

cooking

sewing

growing crops

carrying water

a Pilgrim family

A B C D E F G H I J K L M N O P Q R S T U V W X Y Z

pilot

noun

A **pilot** is a person who flies an aircraft.

*You must study hard to become a **pilot**.*

pioneer

noun

A **pioneer** is one of the first people to explore and settle an area.

*In the 19th century, **pioneers** headed west in covered wagons. Pioneer life involved hard work.*

See also: *frontier*, **page 41;** *settler*, **pages 96–97**

pipe

noun

A **pipe** is a tube that carries gases or liquids from one place to another.

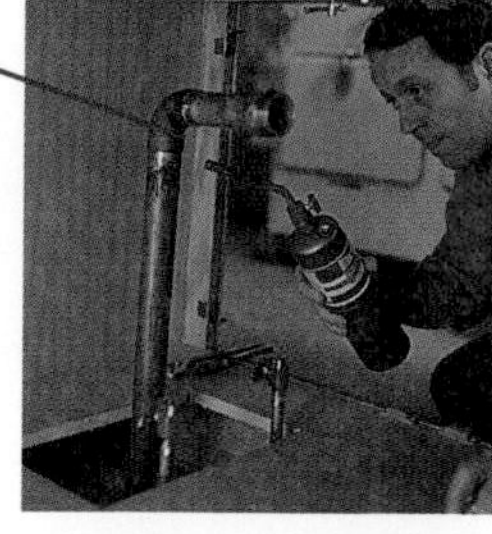

*In a home, water often flows through copper **pipes**.*

pirate

noun

A **pirate** is a person who robs ships at sea.

*It's fun to read make-believe stories about the adventures of **pirates**.*

plain

❶ *noun*

A **plain** is a large area of flat, nearly treeless land.

*Bison, or buffalo, live on America's Great **Plains**.*

❷ *adjective*

When something is **plain**, it has no marks or decoration on it.

*He is wearing a **plain** white shirt.*

plan

❶ *noun*

A **plan** is a set of organized ideas that will help you reach a goal.

My Plan
1. Make bed.
2. Put away clothes.
3. Throw away junk.
4. Clean desk.
5. Relax!

*This is a **plan** for cleaning a bedroom.*

❷ *verb*

When you **plan**, you decide how you will do something.

*It is a good idea to **plan** all the steps before doing a job.*

planet

noun

A planet is a large body that orbits around the sun or another star.

Saturn is one of nine planets in our solar system.

See also: ***orbit*, page 76; *solar system*, page 103**

plankton

noun

Plankton are tiny plants and animals that float in the sea.

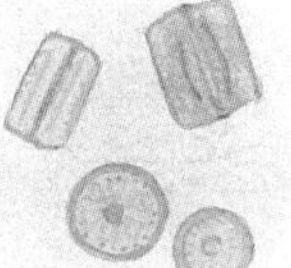

***Plankton** are at the bottom of the food chain in the ocean.*

See also: *food chain*, **page 39**

plant

noun

A **plant** is a living thing that can make its own food by photosynthesis. Many plants have roots, stems, and leaves.

See also: *growth*, page 46; *photosynthesis*, page 79; *seed*, page 94

Types of Plants

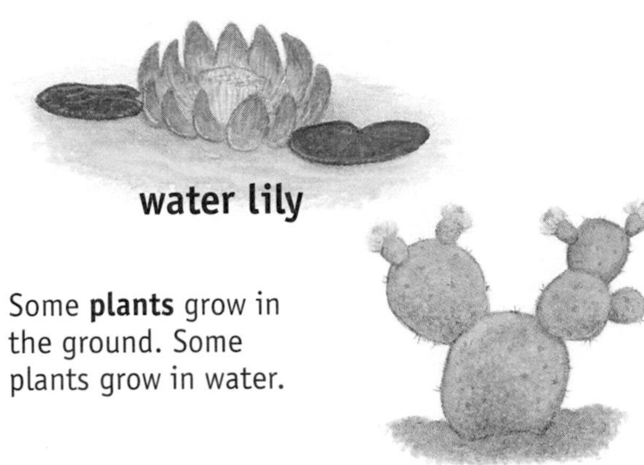

water lily

Some **plants** grow in the ground. Some plants grow in water.

cactus

pine tree

How Plants Grow

sunflower

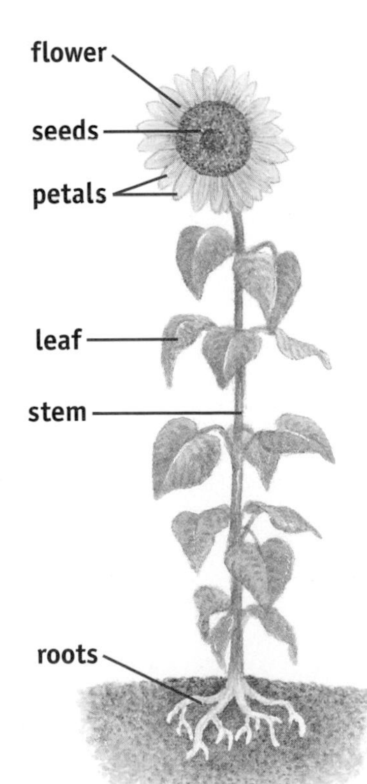

Some **plants**, like flowers, grow from seeds.

pine cone

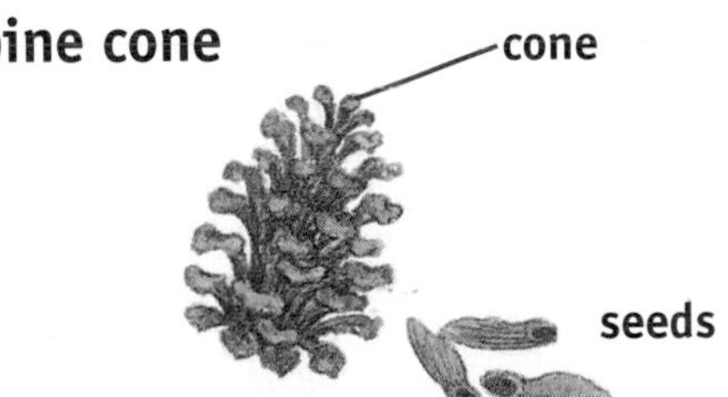

Seeds for some **plants**, like pine trees, are made inside cones.

fern

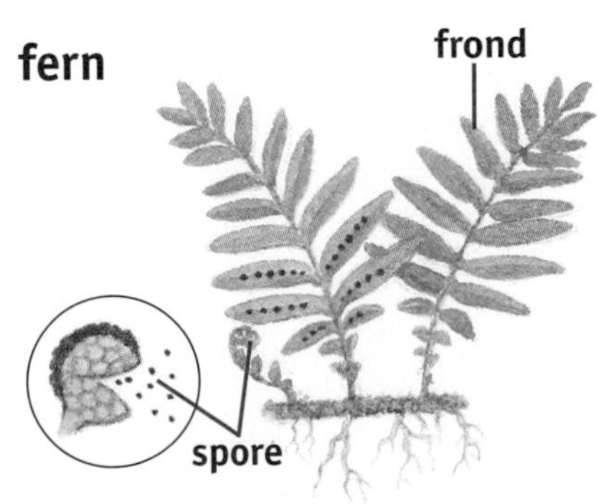

Some **plants**, like ferns, have no seeds. New plants grow from spores. This fern has spores on the underside of its fronds.

play

❶ *verb*

When you **play**, you take part in a game.

*Julio and Vera like to **play** checkers after school.*

❷ *noun*

A **play** is a story that is acted out on a stage.

*Our class **play** is "The Wizard of Oz."*

plot

noun

A **plot** is the story in a book, a play, or a film.

*The **plot** of this play is about a girl who dreams of a journey to a magical land.*

poem

noun

A **poem** is a piece of creative writing arranged in verses.

Question

Do you love me
Or do you not?
You told me once
But I forgot.

—*Anonymous*

*I like to read **poems** that rhyme.*

A B C D E F G H I J K L M N O P Q R S T U V W X Y Z

pollution

noun

Pollution makes our air, water, and soil dirty.

See also: *environment*, page 32; *landfill*, page 57

How Pollution Happens

Factories and cars send harmful gases into the air. This causes air **pollution**. Garbage and other harmful wastes cause soil and water pollution. If we stop pollution, the air, soil, and water can become clean and pure again.

Before Cleanup

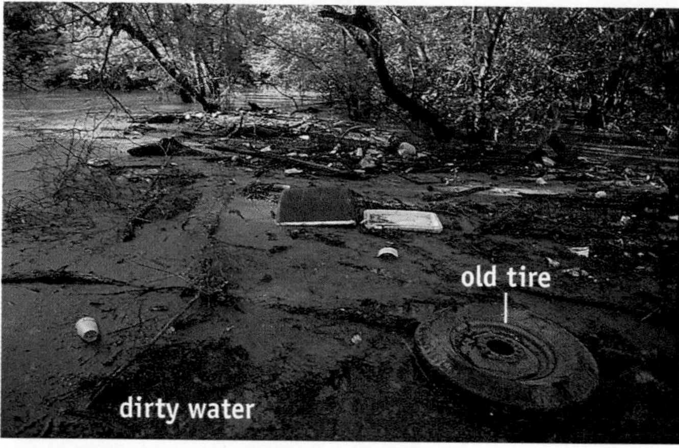

Garbage floats in a bayou.

Trash gets dumped into a landfill.

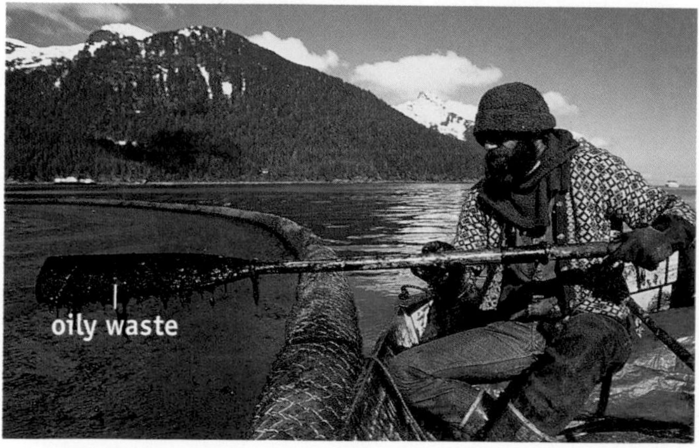

A worker cleans up an oil spill.

After Cleanup

Clean water flows through the bayou.

A man-made garden covers the landfill area.

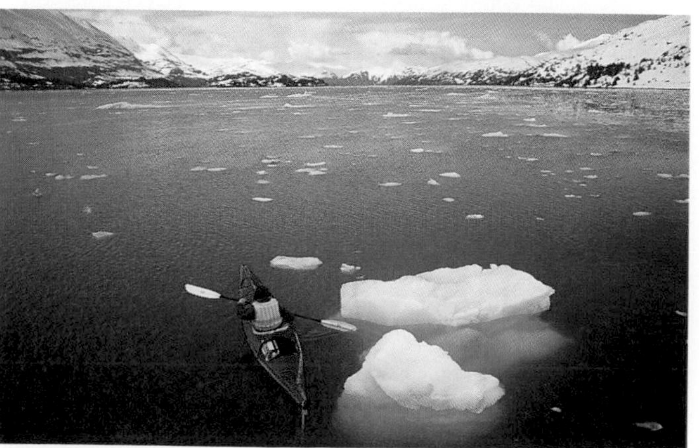

A kayaker enjoys the beauty of the bay.

possession

noun

A **possession** is something that you own.

*This kitten is her most prized **possession**.*

possible

adjective

Something is possible when it can or might happen.

It is possible that it will rain today.

powerful

adjective

When you are **powerful**, people listen to what you say.

*Martin Luther King, Jr. was a **powerful** leader.*

powwow

noun

A **powwow** is a ceremonial meeting of Native Americans.

*There is usually music and dancing at a **powwow**.*

predict

verb

You **predict** when you tell what you think will happen.

*The picture will help her **predict** what happens next.*

pretend

verb

When you **pretend**, you make believe something is true.

*He **pretends** to be an astronaut on the moon.*

price

noun

The **price** is the amount of money you must pay to buy something.

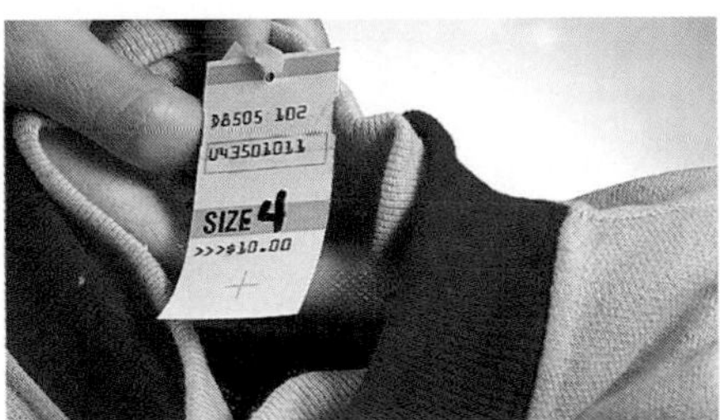

*The **price** of this shirt is $10.*

prince

noun

A **prince** is the son of royal parents, such as a king, queen, emperor, or another prince or princess.

*Crown **Prince** Naruhito of Japan is the son of Emperor Akihito.*

process

noun

A **process** is a set of steps that happen in a certain order.

Making Candles

1. Melt wax.

2. Pour wax.

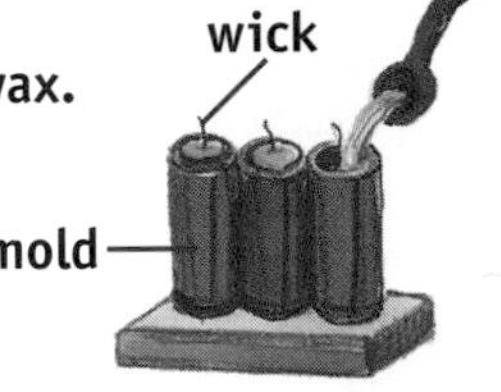

3. Let candles cool.

4. Unmold candles.

*These pictures show the **process** of making a candle.*

product

1 *noun*

A **product** is anything that is made or grown.

*Candles are the **product** sold by this candlemaker.*

2 *noun*

A **product** is the number that results when you do a multiplication problem.

```
   1 2 8 — multiplicand
 ×   7 2 — multiplier
 -------
   2 5 6
 8 9 6
 -------
 9,2 1 6 — product
```

program

1 *noun*

A **program** is a list of items or events set down in order.

Spring Concert

Zuni Hymn to the Sun
Mexican Hat Dance
Harlem Nocturne

*The first act on this **program** is a song by the chorus.*

2 *noun*

A **program** is a set of orders for a computer to perform.

```
<H3>Contents</H3> <MENU
COMPACT>
<LI><A HREF="#G31">FTP</A>
<LI><A HREF="
#G32">GOPHER</A> <LI><A
HREF="#G33">...</A> </MENU>
<H3> <A NAME
="G31".3.1FTP>
```

*A computer **program** is written in a special language.*

pronoun

noun

A **pronoun** is a word used in place of a noun.

*The **pronoun** it takes the place of the noun book.*

protect

verb

You **protect** something when you guard it against harm.

*Some whales are endangered. Laws can **protect** them.*

proverb

noun

A **proverb** is an old saying that gives advice about life.

A Stitch in time saves nine.

*This **proverb** means that doing a job now will save you a bigger job later.*

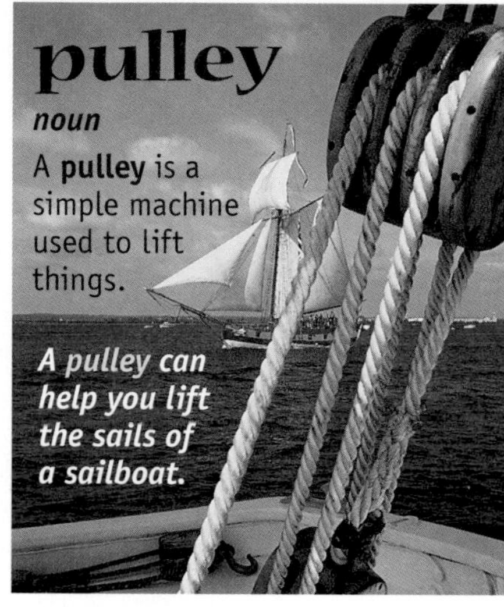

pulley

noun

A **pulley** is a simple machine used to lift things.

A pulley can help you lift the sails of a sailboat.

pump

verb

You **pump** when you use a machine to push a liquid or a gas through something.

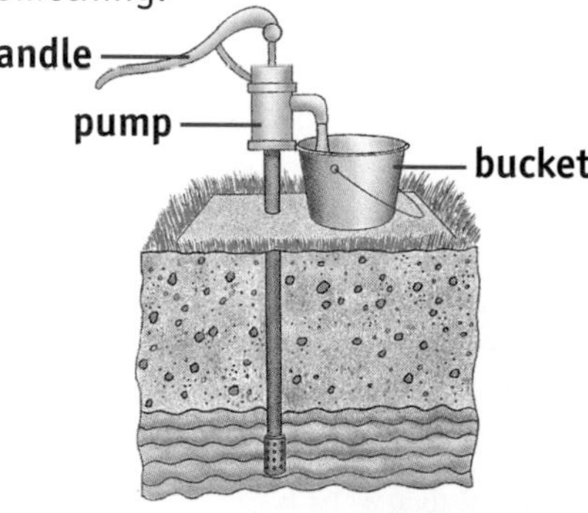

*You can **pump** water from the well into a bucket with a water pump.*

Idiom:
pumped up

You get **pumped up** when you get yourself ready for a game or an event.

Qq

quality

noun

A **quality** is a characteristic that makes something special.

*Loyalty is a **quality** that people appreciate in dogs.*

quest

noun

A **quest** is a search or a hunt.

*His **quest** for a book about famous inventions took him to the library.*

question

noun

A **question** is what you ask when you want to know something.

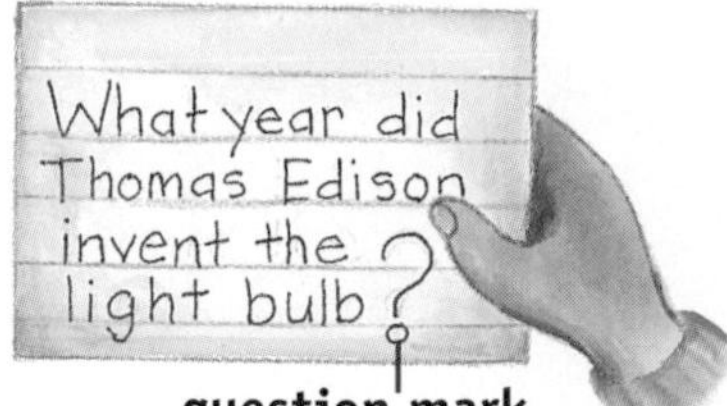

What year did Thomas Edison invent the light bulb?
question mark

*A **question** ends with a question mark.*

quickly
adverb

Something happens **quickly** when it happens with great speed.

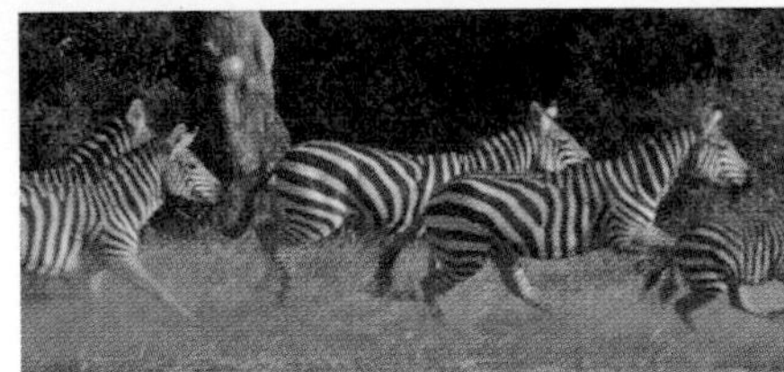

*Zebras run **quickly** when they are startled or afraid.*

quit
verb

To **quit** means to stop doing something.

*You **quit** a computer program when you have finished using it.*

Idiom:
call it quits

You **call it quits** when you decide to stop something.

*He was ready to **call it quits** after the long practice.*

quotient
noun

The **quotient** is the result you get when you divide one number into another.

```
            91 — quotient
divisor — 5|455 — dividend
            45
             05
              5
              0
```

Rr

railroad
noun

A **railroad** is a system of tracks, trains, and stations used for transportation.

*The **railroad** helped open the western United States to settlers.*

reach
verb

You **reach** when you stretch your arm out to get something.

*They **reach** to get their markers.*

reaction
noun

A **reaction** is something that happens because of another action.

action

reaction

*When you push the first domino, the **reaction** of the others is to fall.*

See also: ***chemical reaction***, page 19

recipe
noun

A **recipe** is a set of directions you follow to make something to eat.

title — Fruit Salad (for two)

1 orange	1 banana
1 apple	1 peach
1 box dried raisins	

Cut the fruit into small pieces.
Sprinkle the raisins over the fruit.

ingredients **directions**

recycle
verb

When you **recycle** something, it is used again instead of being thrown away.

*Machines can **recycle** old newspapers into other kinds of paper.*

See also: ***landfill,*** page 57

a b c d e f g h i j k l m n o p q r s t u v w x y z

A B C D E F G H I J K L M N O P Q R S T U V W X Y Z

region

noun

A **region** is an area that has similar features.

Regions of the Continental United States

The United States has five geographical regions.

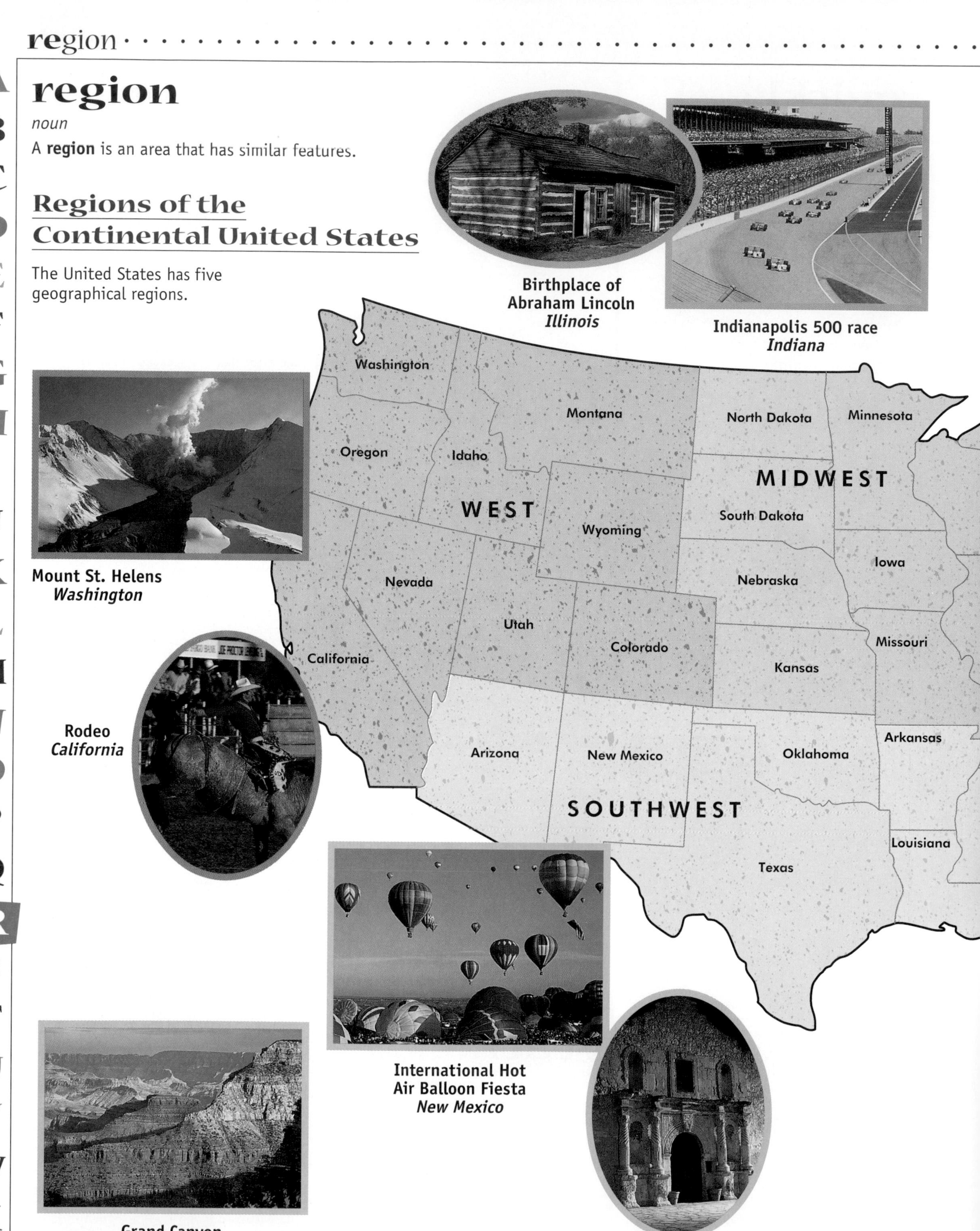

Birthplace of Abraham Lincoln
Illinois

Indianapolis 500 race
Indiana

Mount St. Helens
Washington

Rodeo
California

International Hot Air Balloon Fiesta
New Mexico

Grand Canyon
Arizona

Alamo
Texas

Lake Superior
Michigan

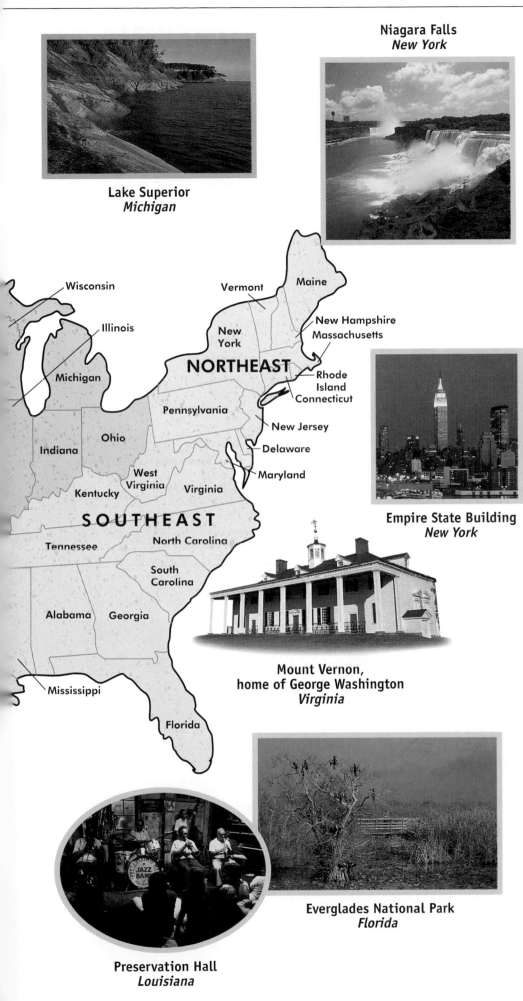

Niagara Falls
New York

Wisconsin
Illinois
Michigan
Vermont
Maine
New Hampshire
Massachusetts
New York
NORTHEAST
Rhode Island
Connecticut
Pennsylvania
New Jersey
Delaware
Maryland
Indiana
Ohio
West Virginia
Kentucky
Virginia
SOUTHEAST
Tennessee
North Carolina
South Carolina
Alabama
Georgia
Mississippi
Florida

Empire State Building
New York

Mount Vernon,
home of George Washington
Virginia

Everglades National Park
Florida

Preservation Hall
Louisiana

What special foods do people eat in each region?

In Massachusetts, people like to eat lobster and clam chowder.

This meal in Virginia features fried chicken and mashed potatoes.

In Texas, a favorite food is barbecue.

Americans everywhere like these thin round cakes, called *flannel cakes* in Eastern Pennsylvania, *hot cakes* in the Southwest, *flapjacks* in the Midwest, and *pancakes* in many places.

A B C D E F G H I J K L M N O P Q R S T U V W X Y Z

relative
noun

Relatives are people who are part of the same family.

*This family has many other **relatives**.*

remind
verb

When you **remind** someone, you help them remember something.

Thursday -
dentist 1:00

*Mom wrote this note to **remind** us about my appointment.*

rent
verb

When you **rent** something, you pay money to use it for a certain amount of time.

For Rent

ONE-BEDROOM APARTMENT, HEAT AND HOT WATER INCLUDED: $400/MONTH

TWO-BEDROOM APARTMENT, NO UTILITIES: $695/MONTH

repair
verb

When you **repair** something, you fix it.

*She can **repair** her own bicycle.*

repeat
verb

When you **repeat** something, you say or do it again and again.

*When you **repeat** new words, it helps you to learn them.*

reply
verb

When you **reply**, you use words or actions to answer someone or something.

*Tonya likes to **reply** to a letter right away.*

report
noun

A **report** is writing that describes what you have learned about a topic.

Ravi's Report

title — Reptiles

body — Reptiles may look scary, but most of them do no harm to people.

Reptiles have dry, scaly skin. They lay eggs like birds do. Their body temperature stays about the same as the air temperature. That is why some reptiles only come out at night.

conclusion — Snakes, turtles, and lizards are examples of reptiles.

represent
verb

When you use a symbol to take the place of another thing, it **represents** that thing.

*The 50 stars in the U.S. flag **represent** the 50 states.*

reptile
noun

A **reptile** is an animal with dry, scaly skin. Reptiles lay eggs.

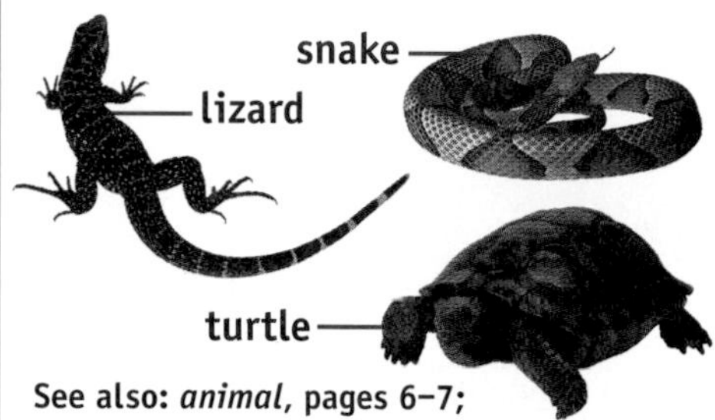

See also: ***animal*, pages 6–7; *vertebrate*, page 114**

research
❶ *noun*

Research is a careful study to find facts about a topic.

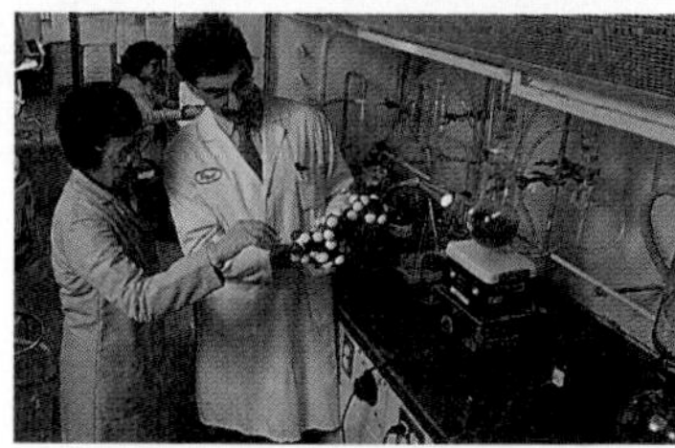

*The **research** done by these scientists may help keep people healthy.*

❷ *verb*

When you **research** a topic, you hunt carefully for facts about it.

*Ravi had to **research** facts about reptiles for his report.*

revolution

noun

During a **revolution**, people change their government. They often use violence or war to make this change.

The Revolutionary War

In the 1700s, British colonists in North America became unhappy with the government in England. They started a **revolution** to win their freedom. The Revolutionary War lasted from 1775 to 1783. The first battles of the war were fought at Lexington and Concord, Massachusetts, on April 19, 1775.

See also: *battle*, pages 10–11; *colony*, page 21; *United States*, page 113

minuteman

colonial woman

Every year, people in Lexington and Concord act out the battles that took place on April 19, 1775.

Battle of Lexington

At Lexington, a band of about 70 minutemen faced 700 British soldiers. The minutemen were farmers and local citizens. They had agreed to be ready in "just one minute" to defend their property. The British, called *redcoats* because of their bright red uniforms, killed 8 Americans and wounded 10 before they moved on to Concord.

drummer

British soldier

Battle of Concord

In Concord, the British searched houses for weapons and burned some buildings. Americans kept British troops away at the North Bridge. It was the first day of the Revolutionary War.

revolve
verb

To revolve means to move in a circle around an object.

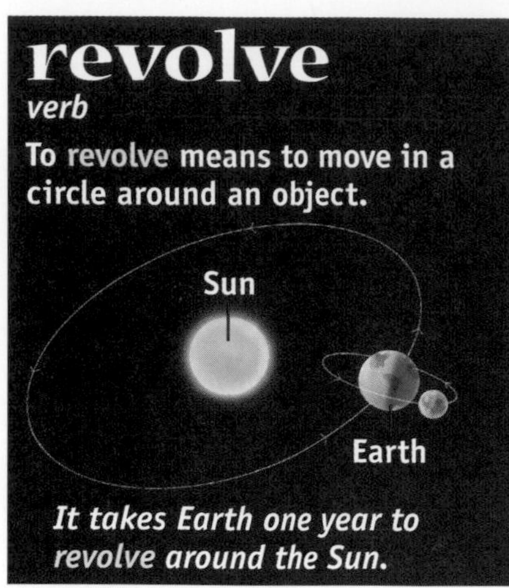

It takes Earth one year to revolve around the Sun.

rhyme
noun

A **rhyme** is a poem. Sets of lines in the poem end with the same final sound.

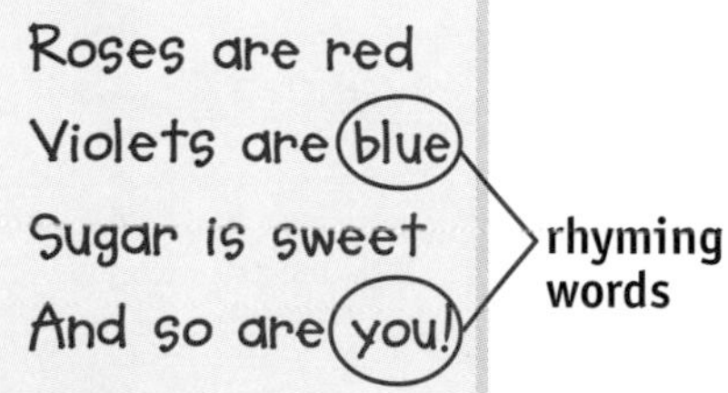

Roses are red
Violets are blue
Sugar is sweet
And so are you!
rhyming words

rhythm
noun

Rhythm is created by repeating sounds or movements.

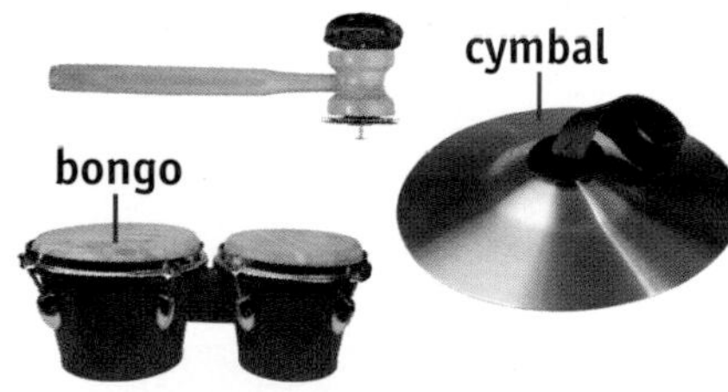

*These instruments help set the **rhythm** of the music.*

riddle
noun

A **riddle** is a word puzzle that is hard to answer.

What's black and white
and read all over?

(a newspaper)

*Can you figure out the answer to this **riddle**?*

ripe
adjective

When fruit is **ripe**, it is ready to be picked or eaten.

*A **ripe** peach is soft, juicy, and very sweet.*

rock
noun

Rock is the hard mineral material that helps form the Earth.

*There are three basic types of **rocks**.*

rotate
verb

When something **rotates**, it turns around an invisible central point, called an *axis*.

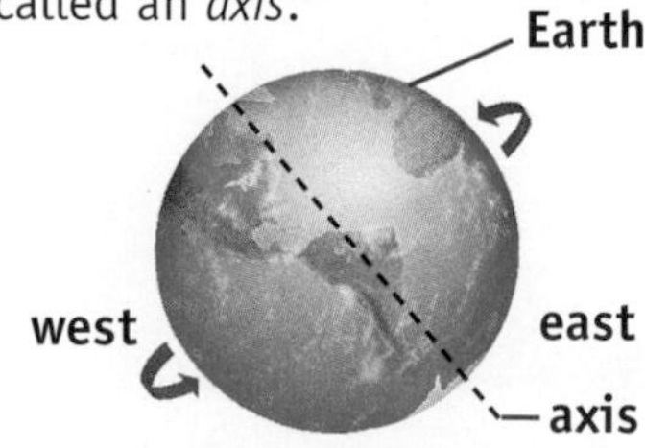

*Earth **rotates** on its axis as it revolves around the Sun.*

rude
adjective

When people are **rude**, they are impolite to other people.

*It's **rude** to think only of yourself.*

ruins
noun

Ruins are the remains of buildings that were once whole.

*It's very interesting to visit the ancient Mayan **ruins** in Mexico.*

rule
verb

The person who **rules** is the one who governs a state or nation.

*A king named Alexander the Great used to **rule** much of the ancient world.*

Idiom:

rule the roost

When someone **rules the roost**, that person is in charge.

*When our parents go out, I **rule the roost**.*

Ss

safe
adjective

When something is **safe**, it is protected from harm or danger.

*The yard is a **safe** place to play.*

same
adjective

When two or more things match exactly, they are the **same**.

*Carlos and Sandy got the **same** grade on their math homework—100%!*

satellite
noun

A satellite is a natural or man-made object in space that orbits around a larger object.

Communication satellites like this one help people on Earth communicate.

See also: *orbit*, page 76

save
1 *verb*

When you **save**, you set something aside to use later.

*Tim will **save** his money to pay for college.*

2 *verb*

When you **save** someone, you rescue that person from danger.

*His neighbor will **save** him from the freezing water.*

Idiom:
saved by the bell

When you are **saved by the bell**, you are rescued just in time.

scatter
verb

When something **scatters**, it spreads out in many directions.

*She **scatters** the bird seed all around the yard.*

scent
noun

A **scent** is something you can smell.

*A rose has a pleasant **scent**.*

scientist
noun

A **scientist** is a person who studies the natural world.

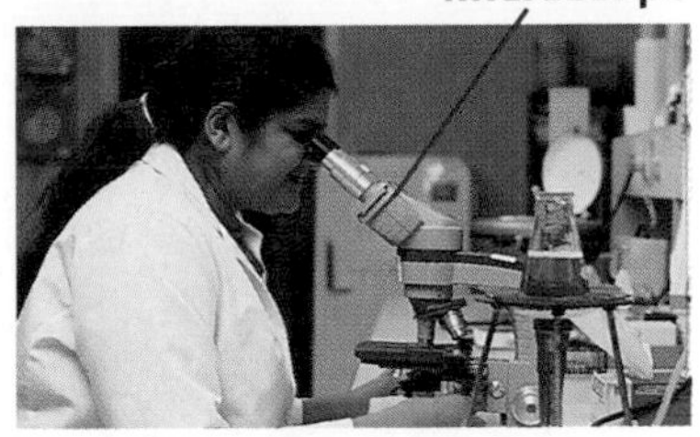

*This **scientist** is examining cells under a microscope.*

scratch
verb

You can **scratch** something by moving a sharp object over it.

*All cats like to **scratch** things with their claws.*

scroll
1 *noun*

A **scroll** is a roll of paper or parchment with writing on it.

*Jewish teachings, called the Torah, are written on a **scroll**.*

2 *verb*

You **scroll** when you move up and down through a document on a computer screen.

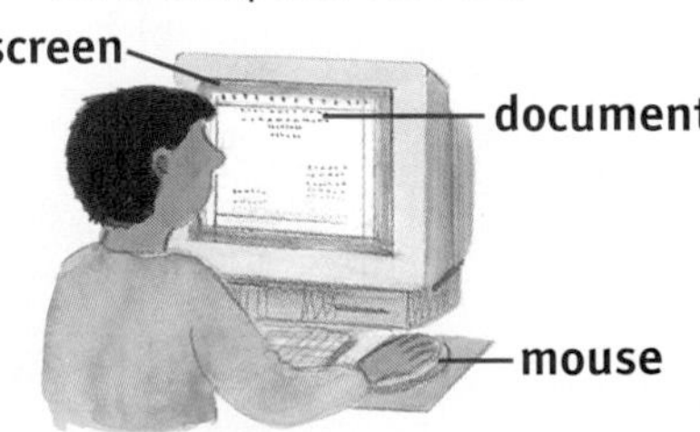

*You can use the mouse to **scroll** to the end of a document.*

A B C D E F G H I J K L M N O P Q R S T U V W X Y Z

scrub

verb

You **scrub** something when you rub it hard to clean it.

*He **scrubs** the cutting board with a sponge.*

search

verb

You **search** when you make a careful effort to find something.

*She will **search** the room to find her favorite ring.*

season

noun

The year is divided into four **seasons**, each with a different kind of weather.

section

noun

A **section** is a part of a larger whole.

*What is your favorite **section** of the newspaper?*

seed

noun

A **seed** is the part of a plant that can grow to become a new plant.

See also: ***growth*, page 46; *life cycle*, page 61; *plant*, page 83**

*Each plant develops from its own kind of **seed**.*

*When a **seed** begins to grow, you can watch it change over time.*

sense

noun

A **sense** is the body's ability to be aware of what is all around us. The body uses five senses: sight, hearing, smell, taste, and touch.

smell

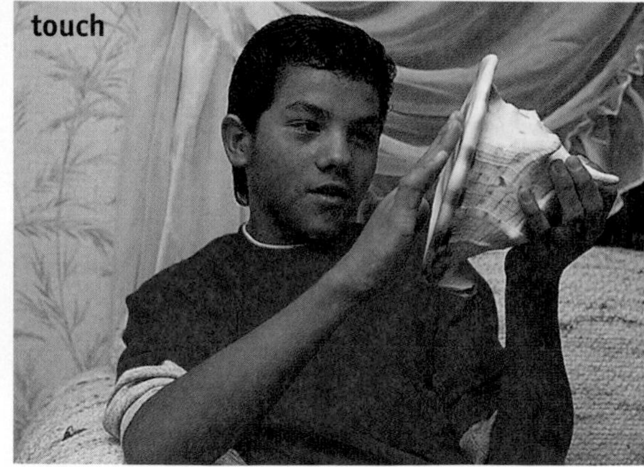

sentence
noun

A **sentence** is a group of words that expresses a complete thought.

capital letter

sentence

A sentence always begins with a capital letter and ends with a punctuation mark.

period

separate
verb

You **separate** things when you keep them apart.

*It's a good idea to **separate** a pet cat from a pet fish.*

sequence
noun

When things are in a **sequence**, one thing follows another in a special order.

January

Sunday	Monday	Tuesday	Wednesday	Thursday	Friday	Saturday
				1	2	3
4	5	6	7	8	9	10
11	12	13	14	15	16	17
18	19	20	21	22	23	24
25	26	27	28	29	30	31

*This is the **sequence** of the days of the week: Sunday, Monday, Tuesday, Wednesday, Thursday, Friday, Saturday.*

A B C D E F G H I J K
L M N O P Q R S T U
V W X Y Z

*This alphabet is made up of a **sequence** of 26 letters.*

series
noun

A **series** is a number of related objects that are created or arranged one after another.

*There are many books in this **series**.*

serious
adjective

You are **serious** when you mean what you say.

*People heard **serious** speeches about civil rights at the 1963 March on Washington.*

serve
verb

You **serve** someone when you offer food to them.

*Dad will **serve** dinner tonight.*

service
noun

A **service** is a business that provides something that people need.

telephone pole

*Workers like this make sure there is telephone **service** for everyone.*

set
1 *noun*

A **set** is a group of objects that belong together.

*This **set** of dolls comes from Eastern Europe.*

2 *verb*

When you **set** something, you put it in a certain place or position.

*Vinnie **set** the glass on the table.*

settle
verb

When something **settles**, it sinks to the bottom.

*After you mix water and sand, the sand will **settle** at the bottom.*

Idiom:
settle down

You **settle down** when you become quiet and calm.

*We tell a story to help us **settle down** at bedtime.*

A B C D E F G H I J K L M N O P Q R S T U V W X Y Z

settler

noun

A **settler** is a person who moves to a new region to live.

See also: ***frontier*, page 41; *journal*, page 55; *pioneer*, page 82**

Settlers on the American Frontier

Since Colonial times, many different groups of **settlers** have moved to parts of the United States where there were no towns or cities. This continued until the whole United States had been explored and settled.

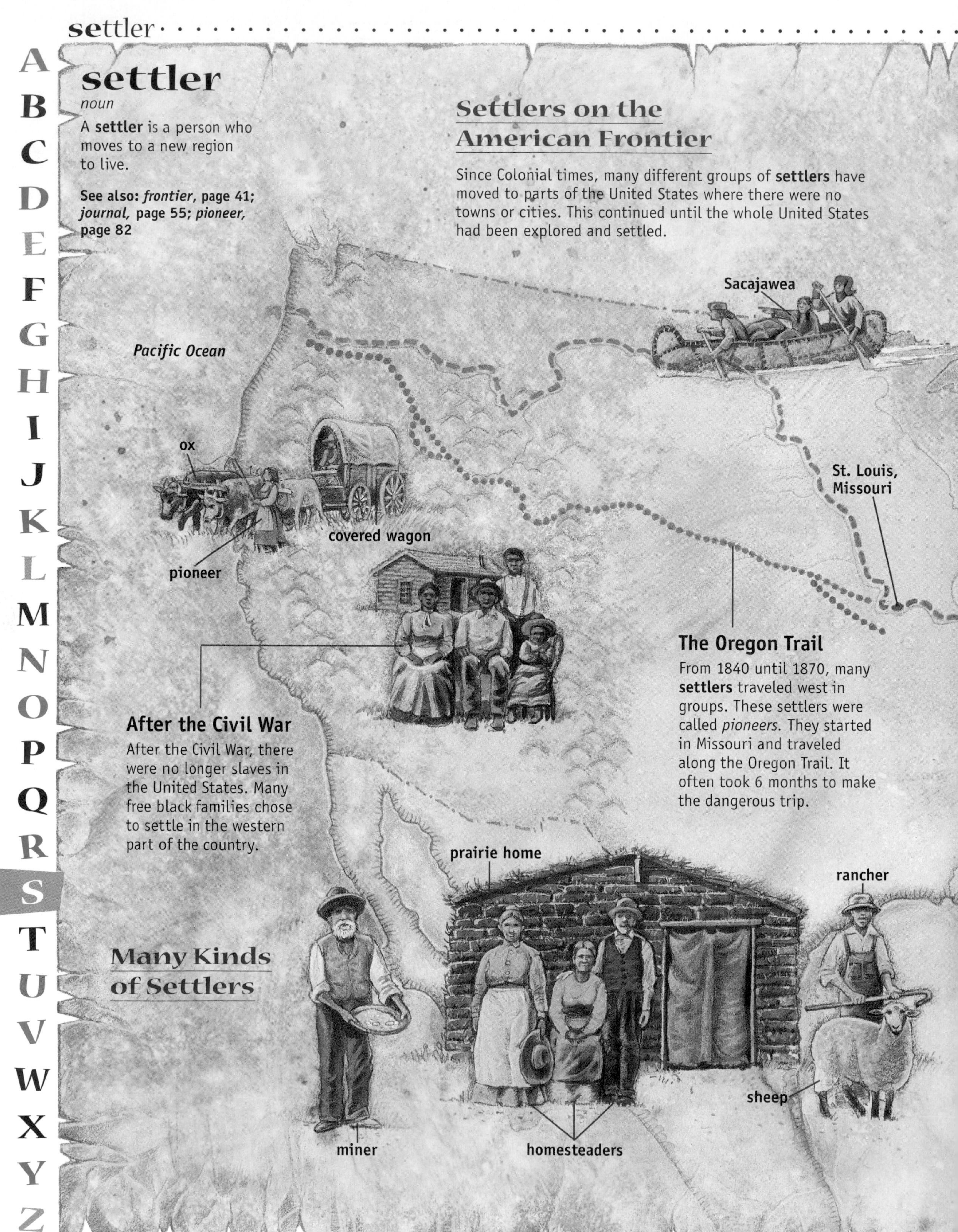

The Oregon Trail

From 1840 until 1870, many **settlers** traveled west in groups. These settlers were called *pioneers.* They started in Missouri and traveled along the Oregon Trail. It often took 6 months to make the dangerous trip.

After the Civil War

After the Civil War, there were no longer slaves in the United States. Many free black families chose to settle in the western part of the country.

Many Kinds of Settlers

The Lewis and Clark Expedition

In 1803, the United States bought the land west of the Mississippi River from France. Meriwether Lewis and William Clark set out to explore the new land. Their guide, a Native American woman named Sacajawea, took them all the way to the Pacific Ocean. Later, **settlers** would follow their trail.

The Wilderness Road

Before 1775, people did not have an easy way to get across the Appalachian Mountains. Then Daniel Boone opened the Wilderness Road. It went through the Cumberland Gap into Kentucky. **Settlers** began moving to Kentucky.

How was the life of a settler different from ours today?

Colorado
The settlers had to grow their food or hunt for it. We can buy food at the store.

Montana
Pioneer women made their own bread. They did not buy bread at the store.

State of Washington
The settlers were not able to buy houses. They had to build them.

several

adjective

Several means more than two things, but not more than five or six.

*On Saturday, **several** children played in the yard.*

shadow

noun

A **shadow** is a dark area made when something blocks the light.

*Your **shadow** can be very long in the afternoon.*

shake

verb

When you **shake** something, you move it up and down or side to side.

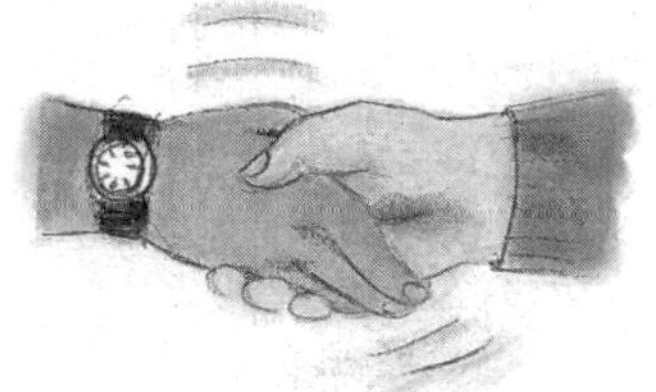

*When you are introduced to someone, it is polite to **shake** hands.*

In the past:
We **shook** hands.
We **have shaken** hands.

Idiom:
shake a leg

You **shake a leg** when you try to do something quickly.

*"We'll be late if you don't **shake a leg**!"*

shape

noun

A **shape** is the outline or form of something.

rectangle

squares

circles

triangles

*These are all geometric **shapes**.*

share

verb

When you **share** something, you give part of it to other people.

*Kim **shares** her grapes with her friends.*

shelter

noun

A **shelter** is a covered place where you are safe from the weather.

Bedouin tent

Plains Indian tepee

Central Asian yurt

*People around the world build different kinds of **shelters**.*

shine

verb

Something shines when it gives off or reflects light.

You can shine your flashlight in the dark to see better.

shrink

verb

When something **shrinks**, it gets smaller.

*Hot water can **shrink** some clothes!*

In the past:
It **shrank**.
It **has shrunk**.

shy

adjective

A **shy** person feels uncomfortable around new people.

*Maddy was **shy** on the first day of school.*

sign

noun

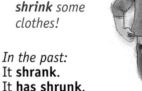

A **sign** has writing or pictures that give information.

*These **signs** tell drivers what to do.*

silently
adverb

Something happens **silently** when it doesn't make any noise.

*The snow fell **silently** all day.*

silk
noun

Silk is a soft, shiny cloth made from threads spun by a silkworm.

***Silk** is used to make beautiful clothes.*

similar
adjective

Two things are **similar** when they are alike but not exactly the same.

baseball **tennis ball**

*A baseball and a tennis ball are **similar**. Both are round and are used to play a sport.*

simple
adjective

Something is **simple** when it is easy to do.

*This is a **simple** problem.*

single
adjective

If there is a **single** thing, there is only one thing.

*There is a **single** coat left on the rack.*

size
noun

Size is a measurement of how big or small something is.

*The popcorn comes in three **sizes**.*

skate
verb

When you **skate**, you slide along the ice or the pavement wearing skates.

ice skates

roller blades

Idiom:
skating on thin ice

You are **skating on thin ice** when you behave in a way that will get you into trouble.

skeleton
noun

A **skeleton** is the set of bones that support the body of a person or animal. Muscles and skin cover the skeleton.

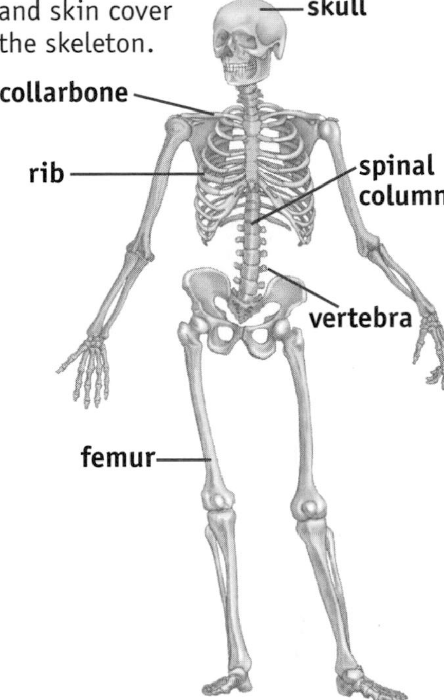

*The human **skeleton** has 206 bones.*

See also: ***bone*****, page 15;** ***spine*****, page 104**

skill
noun

A **skill** is the ability to do something well.

*It takes a lot of **skill** to climb a mountain in winter.*

slam
verb

When you **slam** something, you close it hard, with a loud noise.

*It's not polite to **slam** the door.*

A B C D E F G H I J K L M N O P Q R S T U V W X Y Z

slavery

noun

A person is in **slavery** when he or she is owned by another person. Slaves are forced to work for their owners without being paid.

See also: ***battle*****, pages 10–11;** ***freedom*****, page 40**

Slavery in America

During the Colonial period in the United States, slaves were brought from Africa to work on American farms and plantations. Later, slave traders also brought slaves from Caribbean islands. The slaves lived a hard life. After the Civil War, **slavery** was ended and slaves were freed.

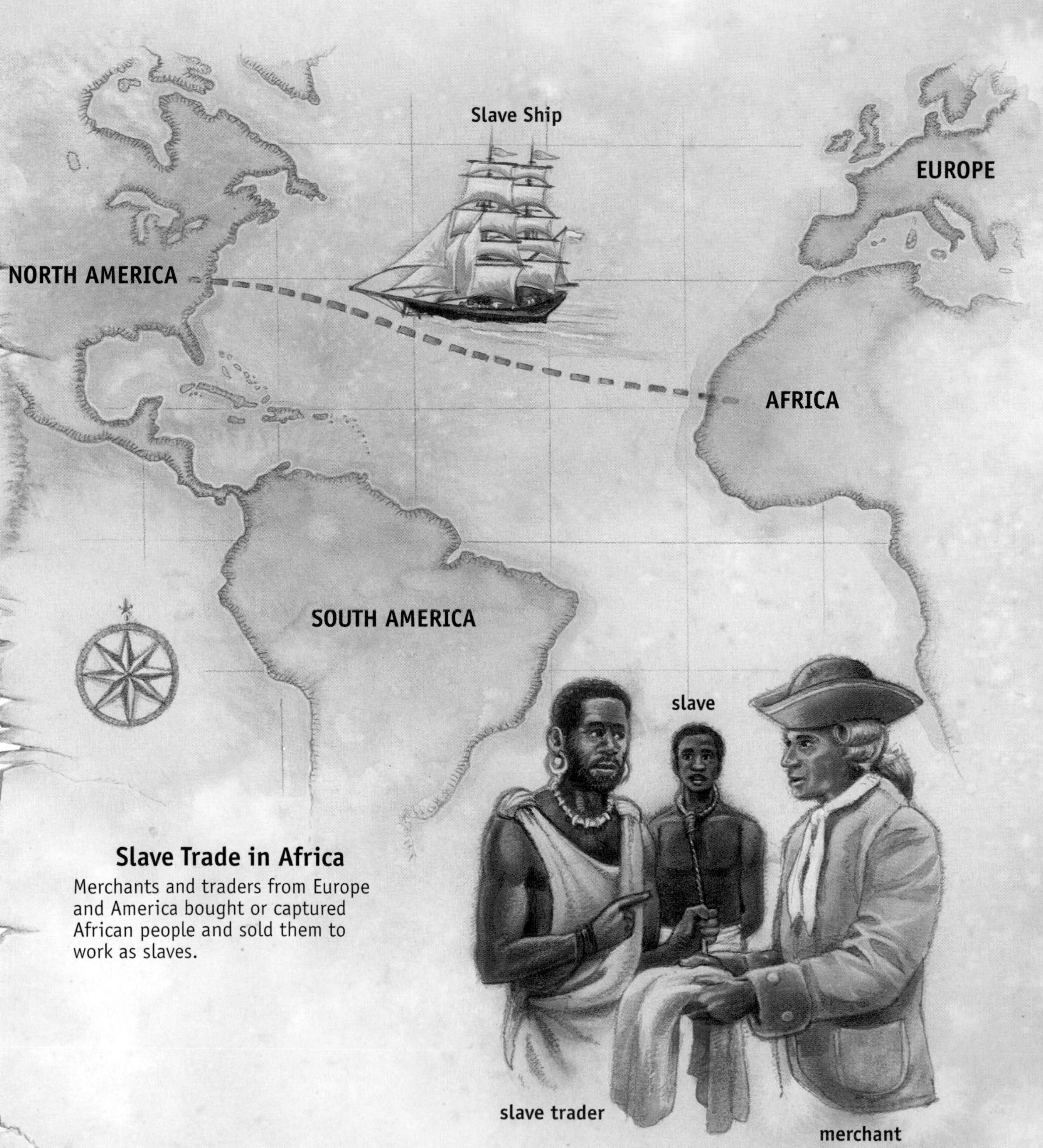

Slave Trade in Africa

Merchants and traders from Europe and America bought or captured African people and sold them to work as slaves.

ship's hold

The Voyage from Africa to the Colonies

Slave ships were very crowded. The slaves could not move. They did not have enough food to eat.

chain

The Auction

In America, slaves were sold at an auction. The person who offered the most money became a slave's owner. Most slaves were bought to work on plantations, or large farms.

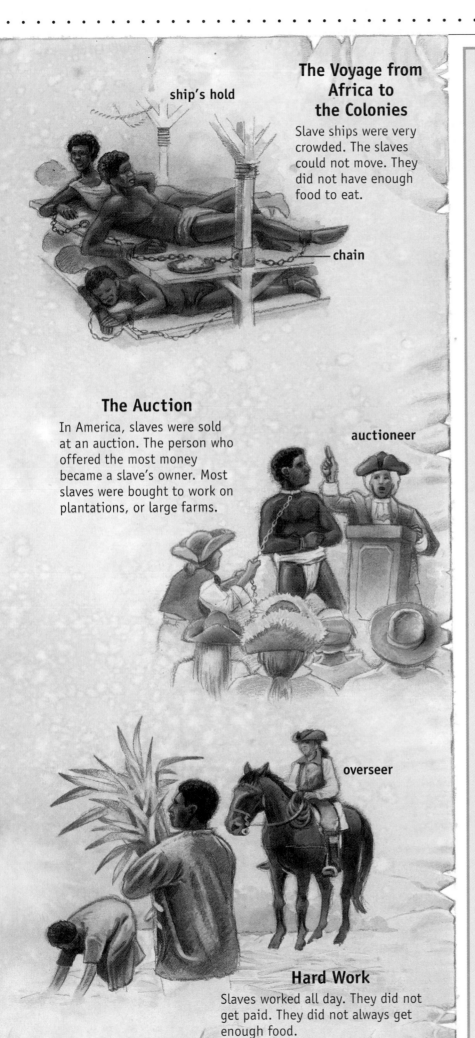

auctioneer

overseer

Hard Work

Slaves worked all day. They did not get paid. They did not always get enough food.

What kind of work did slaves do?

Some slaves worked in the house. They cooked, or took care of children.

Many slaves worked in the fields, under the hot sun. They planted and harvested the crops.

Some slave children worked near their parents in the fields.

sleigh
noun

A **sleigh** is a large vehicle with runners, pulled over the snow by a horse.

slice
noun

A **slice** is a thin piece that has been cut off of something.

*You can use two **slices** of bread to make a sandwich.*

slide
❶ *noun*

A **slide** is a slippery, slanted structure. You can climb up it and then glide down.

*You can go down a **slide** much faster than you climb up!*

❷ *verb*

When something **slides**, it moves smoothly over a surface.

*It's fun to **slide** over the snow on a sled.*

In the past:
They **slid**.
They **have slid**.

slippery
adjective

Something is **slippery** when it makes your hands or feet feel like they are sliding.

*Norma had a hard time holding on to the **slippery** frog.*

smart
adjective

A **smart** person or animal can learn things quickly.

*My dog is so **smart**. He learned how to bring me my shoes.*

smile
noun

A **smile** is a way of moving your mouth that shows you are happy.

*These friends have happy **smiles**!*

sneak
verb

You **sneak** when you move in a secret way so no one will see you.

*Jackie likes to **sneak** into the kitchen to get a cookie.*

soak
verb

When you **soak** something, you make it very wet.

*You can **soak** the muddy clothes in soapy water.*

softly
adverb

When you do something **softly**, you do it quietly and gently.

*Jenna sang **softly** to the baby.*

software
noun

Software is a program of instructions that tells your computer how to use your information.

***Software** can come on a disk or a CD-ROM.*

See also: *computer*, page 24; *disk*, page 29; *program*, page 86

soil
noun

Soil is the dirt plants need in order to grow.

*Plants need to grow in **soil** that is not too hard and dry.*

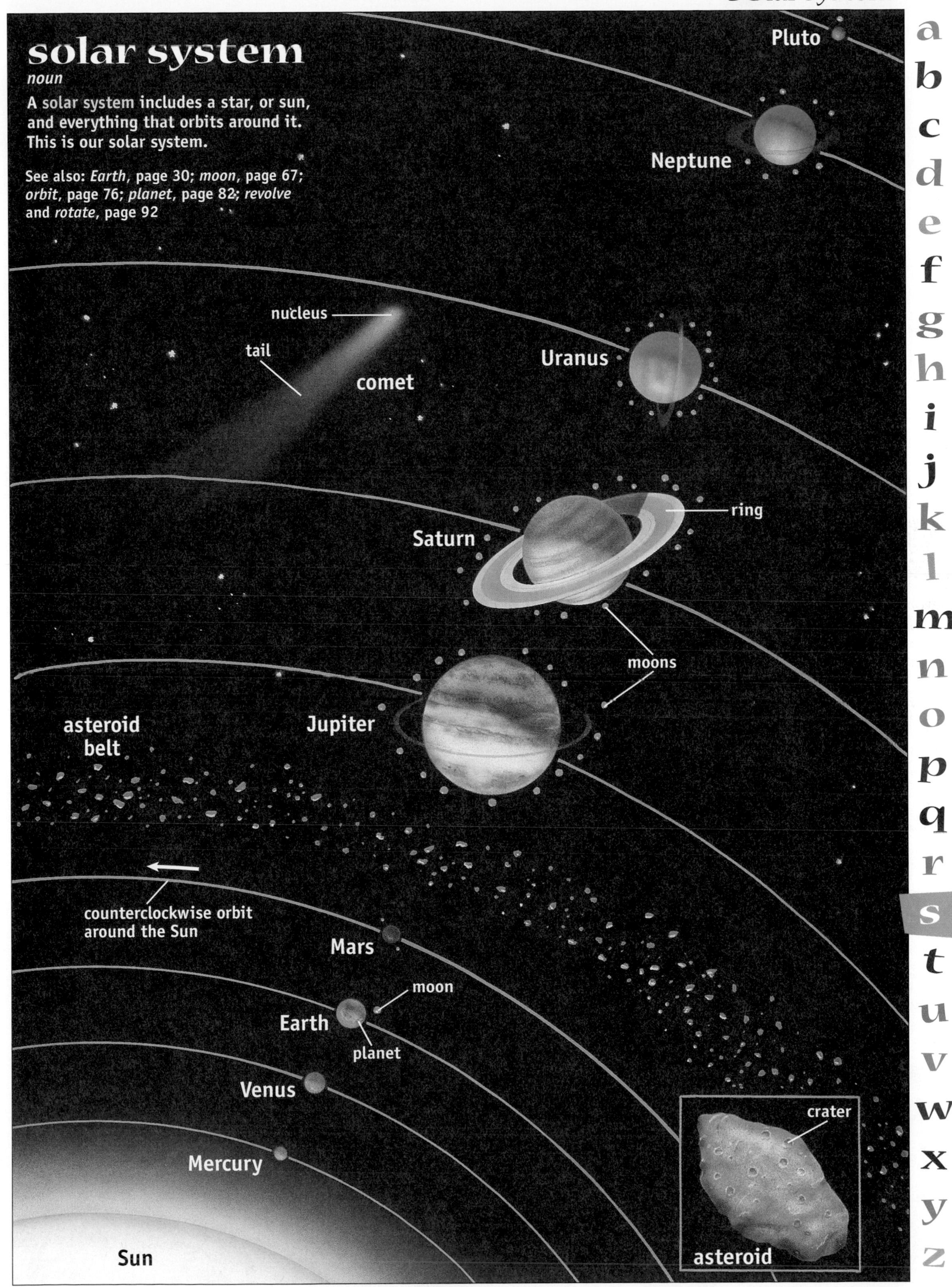

solar system
noun
A solar system includes a star, or sun, and everything that orbits around it. This is our solar system.
See also: Earth, page 30; moon, page 67; orbit, page 76; planet, page 82; revolve and rotate, page 92
Pluto
Neptune
nucleus
tail
comet
Uranus
ring
Saturn
moons
Jupiter
asteroid belt
counterclockwise orbit around the Sun
Mars
moon
Earth
planet
Venus
Mercury
crater
asteroid
Sun

A B C D E F G H I J K L M N O P Q R S T U V W X Y Z

solid

1 *noun*

A **solid** is something that does not change its shape.

*The rock is a **solid**.*

2 *adjective*

A **solid** object has the same hard material all the way through.

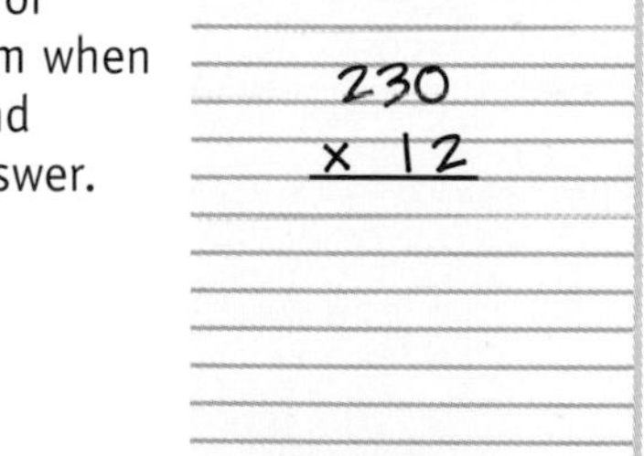

*This plank is **solid** wood.*

solve

verb

You **solve** a puzzle or problem when you find the answer.

230
x 12

*Can you **solve** this math problem?*

son

noun

A **son** is a male child in a family.

sound

noun

A **sound** is a vibration in the air that can be heard through the ear.

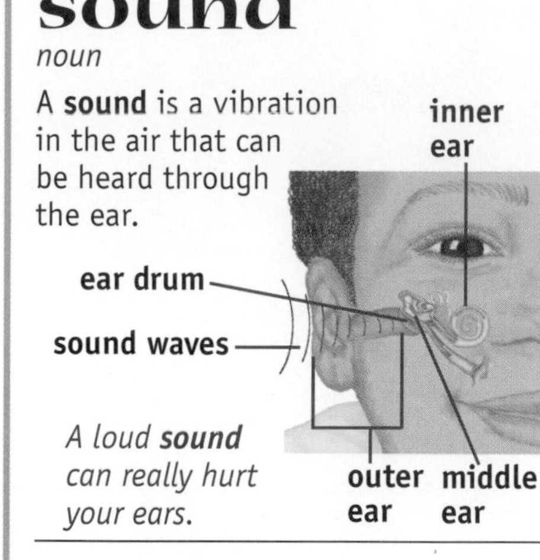

*A loud **sound** can really hurt your ears.*

south

noun

South is one of the four main points on the compass.

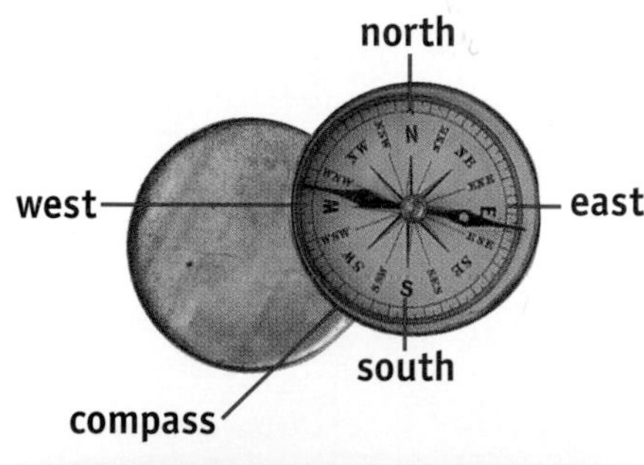

space

noun

Space is the area around Earth. It is full of planets and stars.

spacecraft

noun

A spacecraft is a vehicle used in outer space.

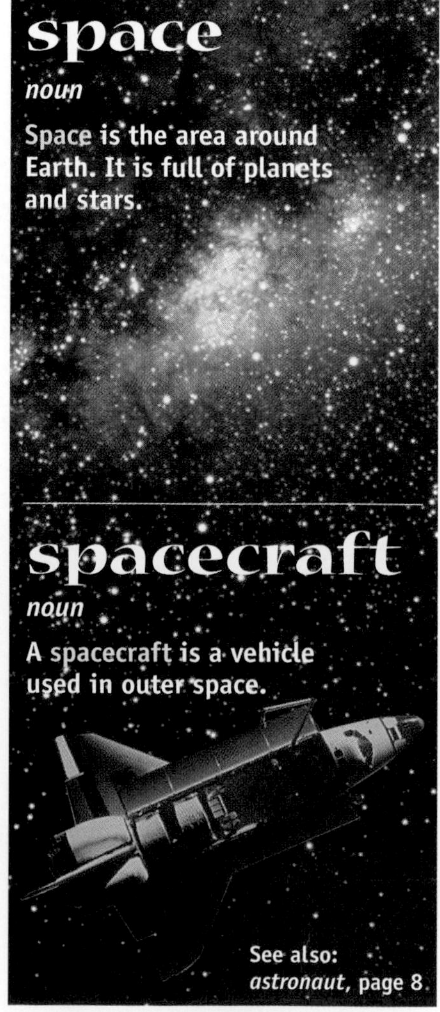

See also: ***astronaut*, page 8**

special

adjective

Something **special** is nicer or more important than other things.

*Rosanna always takes her **special** toy with her on car trips.*

spider

noun

A **spider** is an invertebrate with eight legs, two body parts, and no antennae.

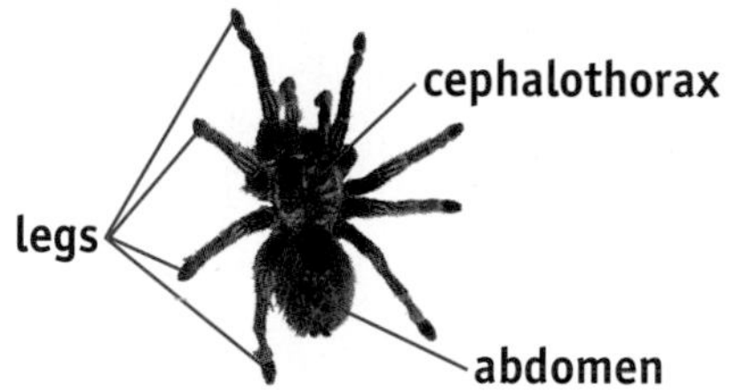

See also: *arachnid*, page 8; *invertebrate*, page 54

spin

verb

When something **spins**, it turns quickly.

In the past:
It **spun**.
It **has spun**.

*A dreidel **spins** easily.*

spine

noun

Your **spine** is made up of many small bones called *vertebrae*. It holds up your back.

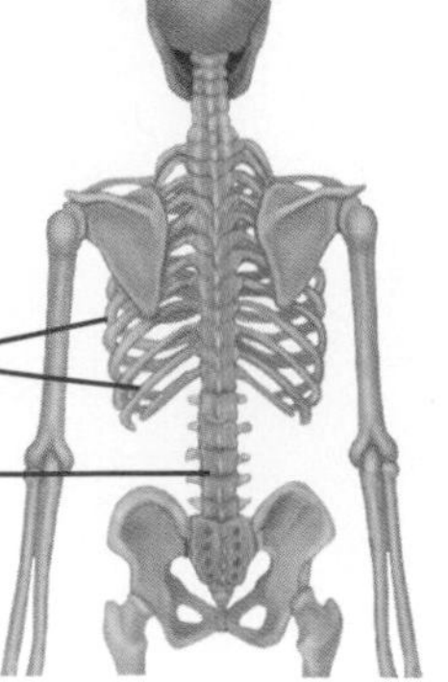

See also: *skeleton*, page 99

spring

1 *noun*

A **spring** is a metal coil. After it is pressed together or pulled apart, it goes back to its own shape.

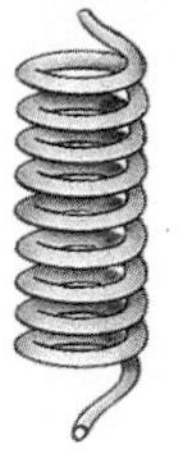

2 *noun*

Spring is the season between winter and summer.

*Plants often begin to grow in the **spring**.*

squeeze

verb

When you **squeeze** something, you press hard on it.

*Juice comes out when you **squeeze** a lemon.*

state

noun

A **state** is a geographic area with its own government.

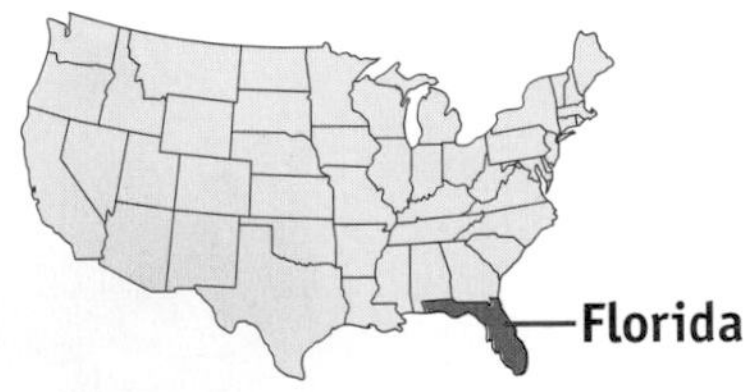

*The **state** of Florida is in the southeastern corner of the United States.*

stripe

noun

A **stripe** is a narrow band of color.

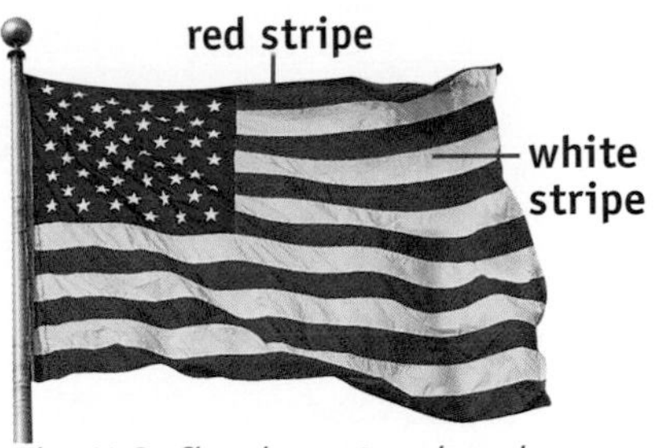

*The U.S. flag has 13 red and white **stripes**.*

subtraction

noun

In math, **subtraction** is the process of taking one number away from another.

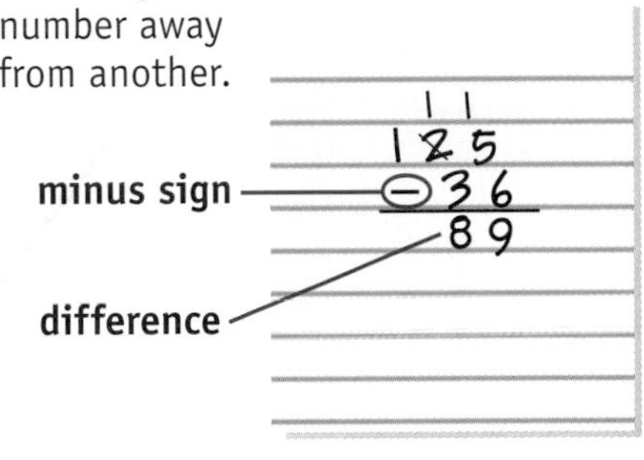

success

noun

Something is a **success** when it turns out well.

*This recipe turned out to be a great **success**!*

summer

noun

Summer is the season between spring and fall.

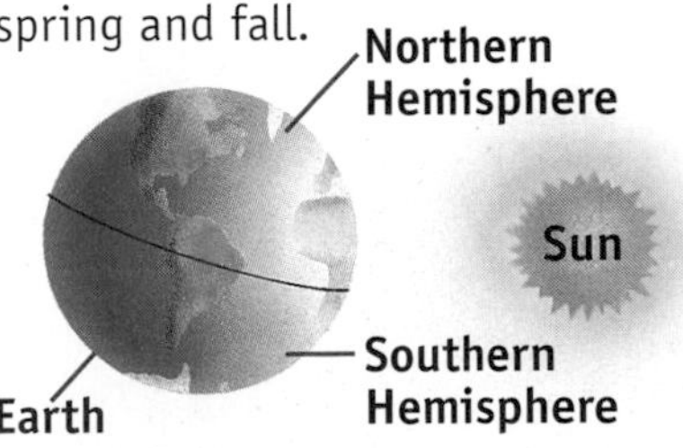

*When it is **summer** in the Northern Hemisphere, it is winter in the Southern Hemisphere.*

supply

verb

When you **supply** something, you give what is needed or wanted.

*Workers help to **supply** food to grocery stores.*

support

verb

Something **supports** another object when it holds that object in place.

*Tall pillars **support** these houses in Kenya.*

surf

1 *verb*

You **surf** when you ride the waves on a surfboard.

*Paco **surfs** ahead of the wave.*

2 *verb*

You **surf** when you search the Internet for information.

*Lin **surfs** the Internet to learn more about John F. Kennedy.*

See also: ***information*** **and** ***Internet*****, page 52**

surface

noun

The **surface** is the outside part of something.

*The **surface** of Mars is covered with dust, sand, and rocks.*

survive

verb

Something **survives** when it stays alive in spite of difficulties.

A spacesuit and helmet help an astronaut survive in space.

swamp

noun

A **swamp** is an area with soft, wet land.

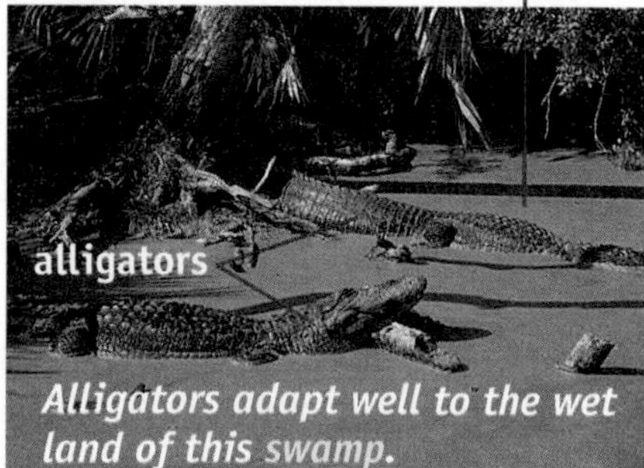

Alligators adapt well to the wet land of this swamp.

swell

verb

Something **swells** when it becomes bigger.

*A balloon **swells** when you blow air into it.*

In the past:
It **swelled.**
It **has swollen.**

swift

adjective

Something is **swift** when it moves very fast.

*The **swift** riders race on their bicycles.*

swim

verb

When you **swim,** you move through the water using your body.

*People and fish **swim** in the ocean.*

In the past:
They **swam.**
They **had swum.**

symbol

noun

A **symbol** is a sign or image that represents an idea or a thing.

Buddhist symbol

Taoist symbol

Hindu symbol

Islamic symbol

Jewish symbol

Christian symbol

*The world's religions each have a special **symbol**.*

Tt

tale

noun

A **tale** is a story.

*A tall **tale** is a funny story with lots of exaggerated details. There are many tall tales about Paul Bunyan and Babe.*

talk

verb

When you **talk,** you use words to communicate with people.

*The students listen when the teacher **talks** to the class.*

tax

noun

A **tax** is money people pay to support a government.

THE SPORT PLACE
YOUR RECEIPT
Rollerblades $159.98
Subtotal $159.98
Tax $7.99
Total $167.97
Thank you for shopping at The Sports Place!
tax

*The government uses money from a sales **tax** to help pay for services.*

technology

noun

Technology is the use of scientific ideas for practical purposes.

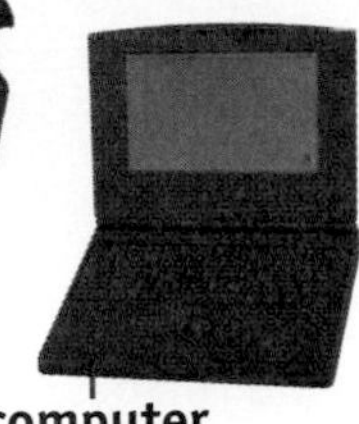

*These machines are examples of modern **technology**.*

tell

verb

When you **tell** about something, you talk about it to others.

*Mr. Lee **tells** the class a story.*

In the past:
He **told** a story.
He **has told** a story.

temperature

noun

Temperature is a measurement of how hot or cold something is.

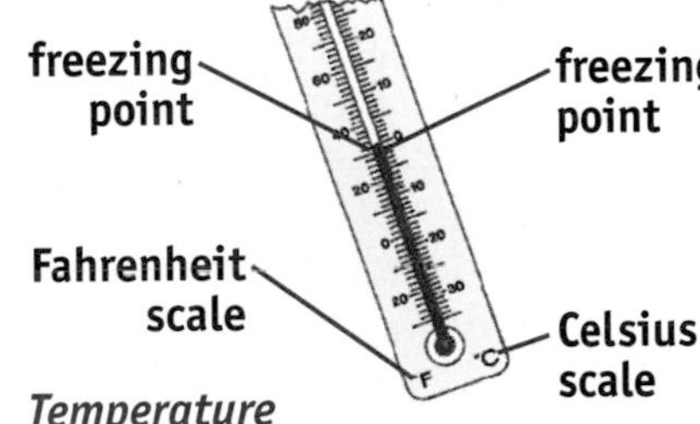

***Temperature** may be measured in degrees Fahrenheit or Celsius.*

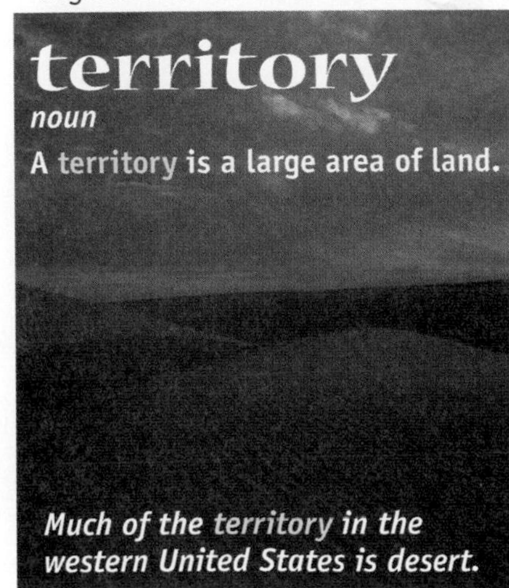

territory

noun

A **territory** is a large area of land.

*Much of the **territory** in the western United States is desert.*

tide

noun

The **tide** is the regular rise and fall of the ocean. It is caused by the pull of the Sun and the Moon.

high tide

low tide

*At high **tide** the boats float, but at low **tide** they sit on the sand.*

time line

noun

A **time line** is a diagram that shows a sequence of events.

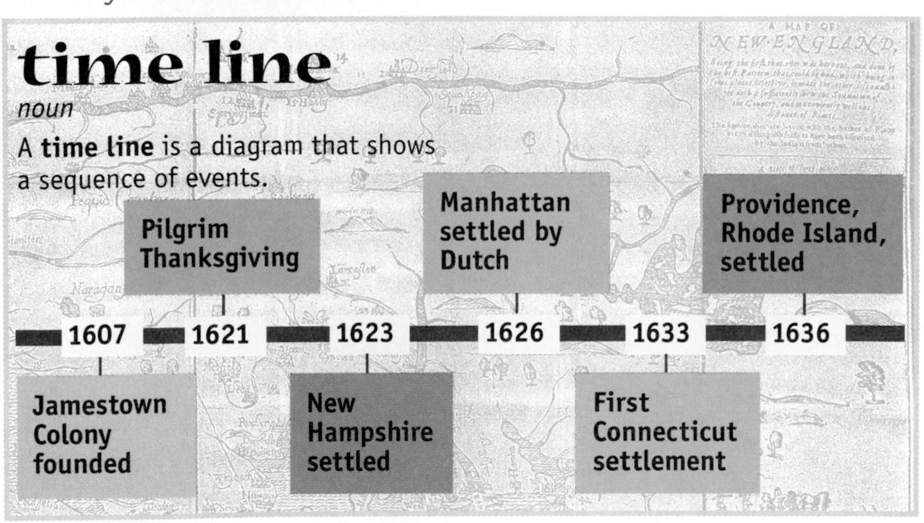

N
O
P
Q
R
S
T
U
V
W
X
Y
Z

tool

noun

A **tool** is something that helps you do a task.

*A hammer is a **tool** that helps you pound nails into wood.*

topic

noun

The **topic** is what a piece of writing is about.

topic—Many animals make good pets. Cats are fun to play with. Fish are interesting to watch. You can teach a dog to do tricks.

*The **topic** of this paragraph is pets.*

tradition

noun

A **tradition** is a custom or belief that is shared by the members of a group of people.

*It's a **tradition** to dress up to celebrate the Chinese New Year.*

*Celebrating the Day of the Dead is a **tradition** from Mexico.*

transport

verb

You **transport** something when you move it from one place to another.

Ways to Transport Goods

Cars, ships, airplanes, trucks, and trains are all used to **transport** goods that will be bought or sold.

Airplanes are the fastest form of transportation for delicate foods like fresh pineapple. Refrigerated airplanes **transport** pineapples from Hawaii to cities all over the world.

How do these strawberries get from California to New Jersey?

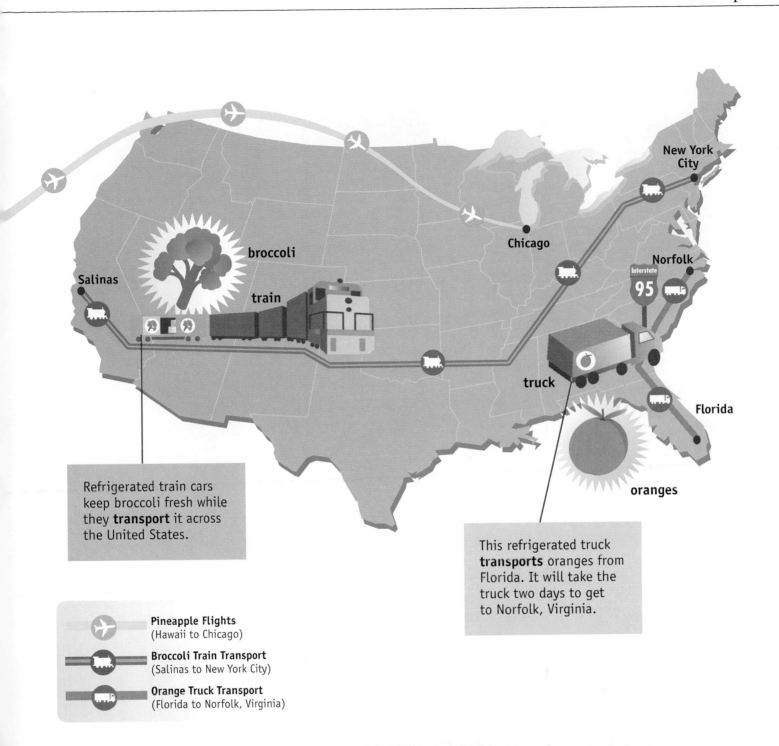

New York City
Chicago
Norfolk
Interstate 95
broccoli
Salinas
train
truck
Florida
oranges

Refrigerated train cars keep broccoli fresh while they **transport** it across the United States.

This refrigerated truck **transports** oranges from Florida. It will take the truck two days to get to Norfolk, Virginia.

Pineapple Flights
(Hawaii to Chicago)

Broccoli Train Transport
(Salinas to New York City)

Orange Truck Transport
(Florida to Norfolk, Virginia)

First, workers in California will pick the strawberries and pack them in boxes.

Next, the strawberries will be taken by truck from the field to the main warehouse.

Then, the strawberries will be loaded onto a refrigerated truck and delivered to a produce market in New Jersey.

trap

❶ *noun*

A **trap** is used for catching animals.

*This fisherman uses a **trap** to catch crabs in the ocean.*

❷ *verb*

When you **trap** something, it cannot get away.

*You can **trap** fish in a net.*

trash

noun

Trash is whatever people throw away.

*A truck comes once a week to collect the **trash**.*

travel

verb

When you **travel**, you go from one place to another.

*You can **travel** around Alaska in a bus.*

tray

noun

A **tray** is a flat object used to carry dishes and food.

*You can use a **tray** to carry your lunch in the school cafeteria.*

treasure

noun

A **treasure** is a collection of jewels, money, or other valuable items.

*Gold coins were part of the **treasure** in this chest.*

treat

noun

A **treat** is a special pleasure.

*Eating ice cream is a **treat** on a hot summer day.*

treatment

noun

A **treatment** is a way to care for an illness or injury.

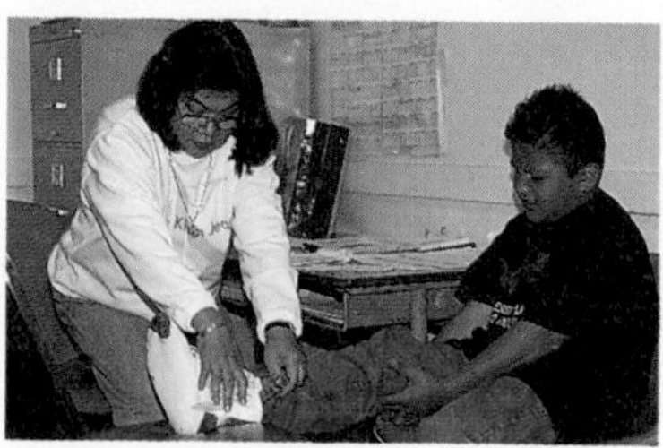

*An ice pack is a good **treatment** for a twisted ankle.*

tree

noun

A **tree** is a tall plant with branches, leaves, and a main stem called a *trunk*.

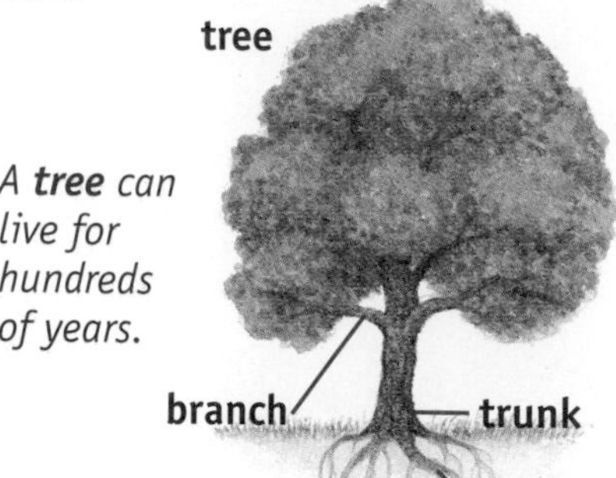

*A **tree** can live for hundreds of years.*

Idiom:
bark up the wrong tree

When you **bark up the wrong tree**, you waste your time looking for something in the wrong place.

*This man is fishing in sand. He is **barking up the wrong tree**.*

tremble

verb

When you **tremble**, you shake with fear, cold, or excitement.

*Crissy got so cold in the water that she started to **tremble**.*

tremendous

adjective

When something is **tremendous**, it is either very large or very beautiful.

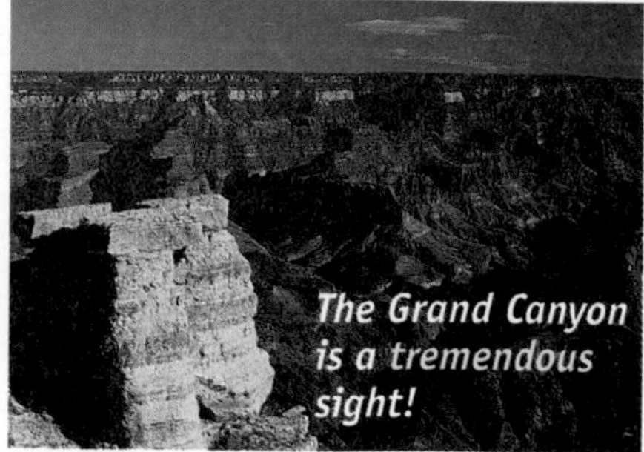

The Grand Canyon is a tremendous sight!

tribe

noun

A **tribe** is a group of people with common ancestors who share similar values, customs, and social organization. Members of a tribe usually live near each other and speak the same language.

See also: ***Native Americans*****, pages 68–69**

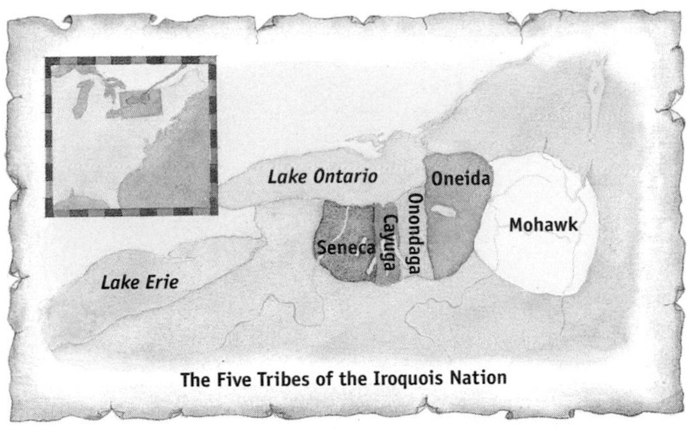

The Five Tribes of the Iroquois Nation

The Iroquois Nation

In the mid-1500s, five **tribes** of Native Americans, living in what is now upper New York State, decided to join together to form a federation, or union. They called this federation the Iroquois Nation.

Over 20,000 descendants of Iroquois nation tribes live today as citizens of the United States or Canada. Many live near their capital of Onondaga, New York.

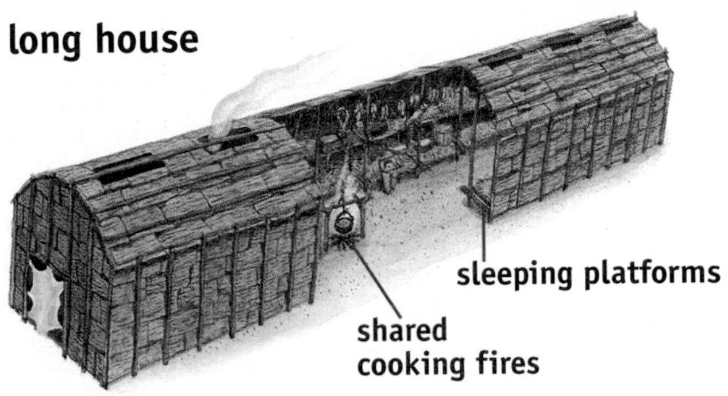

Iroquois families lived in structures called *long houses.* All families in a long house were related through their mothers and grandmothers. Each family shared a fire with a family on the other side of the house.

Each **tribe** sent leaders to the Great Federation Council. The members voted on all decisions. Some historians say that the democratic organization of the Federation was a model for the writers of the United States Constitution.

Iroquois men cleared the fields so the women could grow corn, beans, and squash. The men also hunted and fished to provide food for their families.

Women played an important part in Iroquois life. An Iroquois woman was the head of her family. She made sure everyone had food, clothing, and a place to live. Women chose all the leaders for the tribal council. The tribal council made every important decision about life in the **tribe**.

A B C D E F G H I J K L M N O P Q R S T U V W X Y Z

Uu

trouble
noun

Trouble is a problem or a difficult situation.

*A hot day can lead to car **trouble**.*

true
adjective

Something is **true** when it is real and correct.

*It is not **true** that the world is flat. The truth is that the world is round.*

try
verb

When you **try**, you make an effort to do something.

*He will **try** to ride the bicycle.*

twice
adverb

When something happens **twice**, it happens two times.

*I called my mother **twice**, but she was not home.*

under
preposition

When something is **under**, it is below something else.

*These girls hide **under** the blanket.*

Idiom:
under the weather

When you are **under the weather**, you don't feel well.

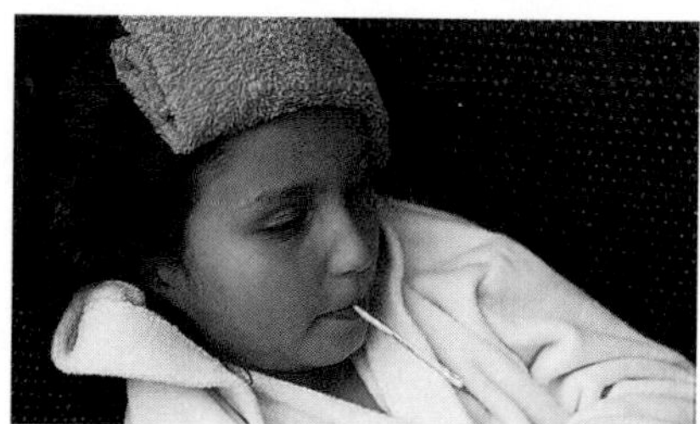

*Stay in bed and rest when you are **under the weather**.*

understand
verb

When you **understand** something, you know what it means.

*Mr. Ngo helps the students to **understand** the lesson.*

unicorn
noun

A **unicorn** is an imaginary animal with one horn on its forehead.

*You can read about **unicorns** in fairy tales and myths.*

uniform
noun

A **uniform** is a set of clothes worn for a special job or purpose.

*Everyone in this band wears the same **uniform**.*

unit
noun

A **unit** is an amount used in measuring or counting.

Unit of Length

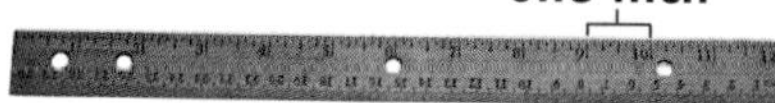

Unit of Time

unite
verb

When things or people **unite**, they join together.

*People from many nations **unite** to discuss world problems at the United Nations in New York City.*

United States

noun

The **United States** is a nation of fifty states, located mostly in North America. The United States began as a group of 13 colonies.

The original 13 English colonies became the first 13 states of a new nation called the **United States**.

Some of the colonies had claimed new lands before the Revolutionary War. This land became part of the new nation when the war was over.

1776

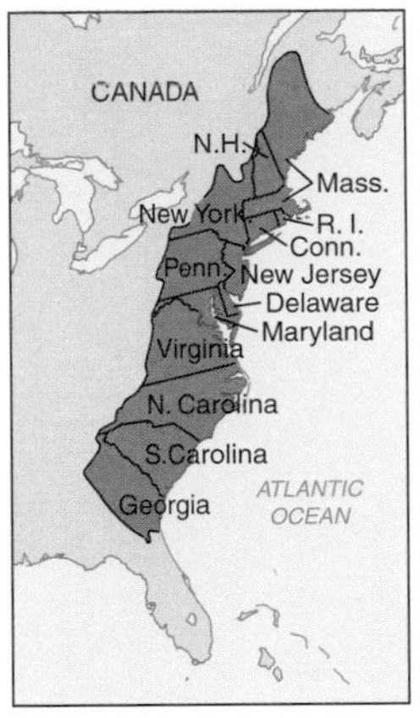

1790

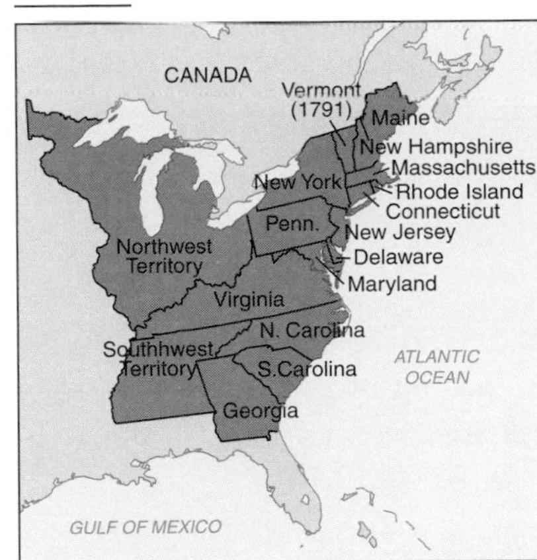

1803 and 1819

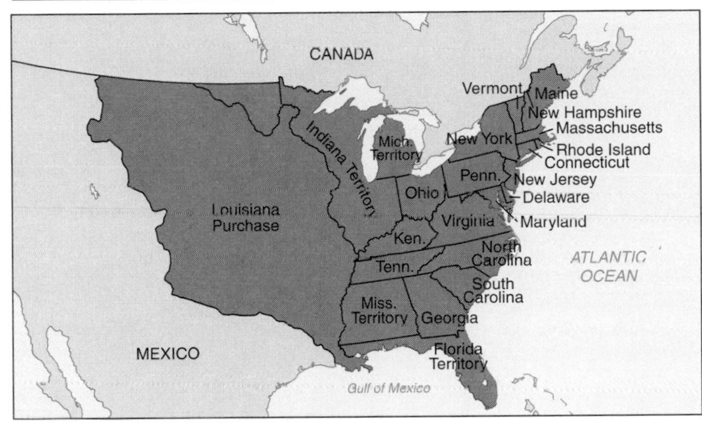

More states were created between 1787 and 1830. In 1803, President Thomas Jefferson bought land from France. It was called the Louisiana Purchase. The Florida Territory was granted to the **United States** by Spain in 1819.

1845 and 1846

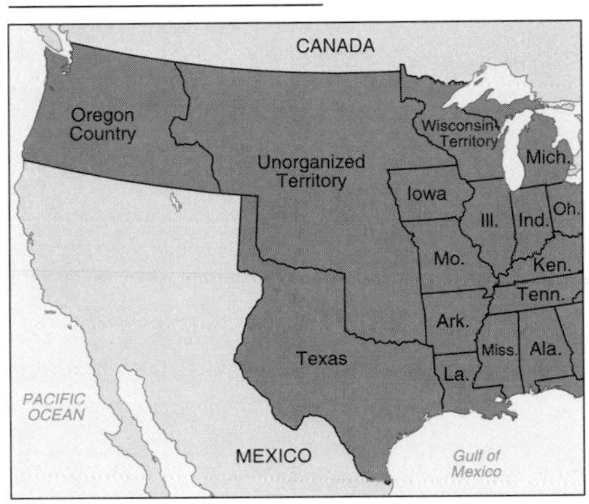

Texas became a state in 1845. The **United States** and Great Britain both wanted the Oregon Country. In 1846, they agreed to divide up the land.

1848

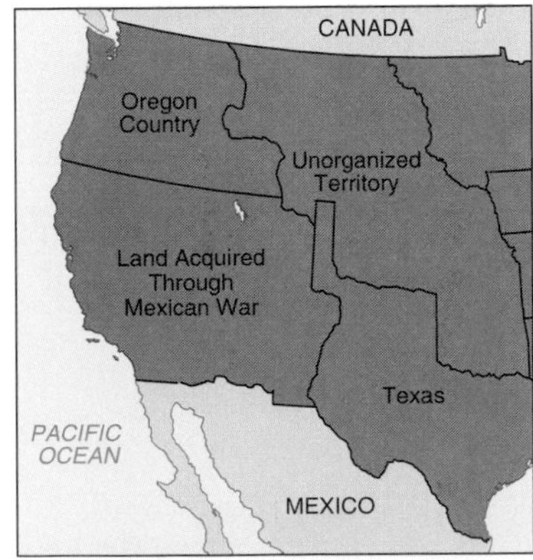

American settlers in the Mexican Territory of California wanted to be free. The **United States** helped them fight Mexico. In 1848, Mexico was forced to give up California and the Southwest for 15 million dollars.

1959

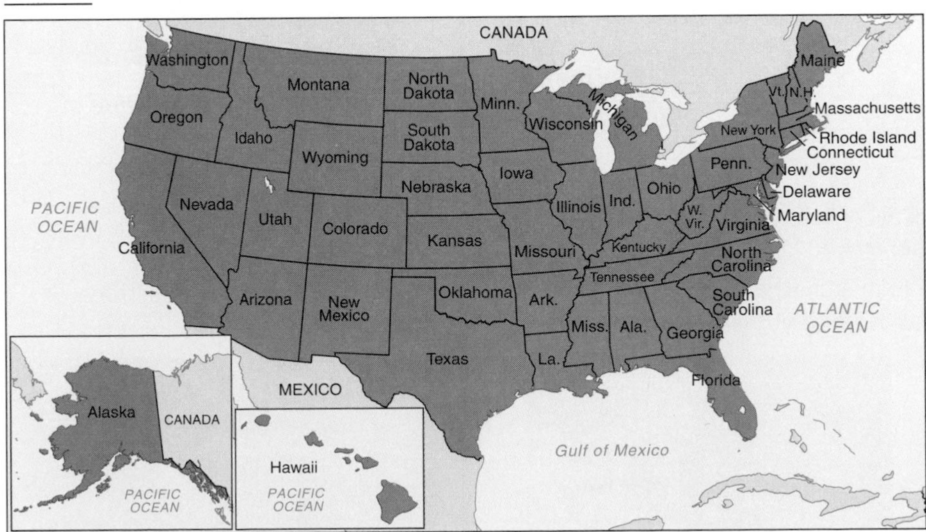

The **United States** bought Alaska from Russia in 1867 and acquired Hawaii in 1893. The territories of Alaska and Hawaii became the 49th and 50th states in 1959.

A B C D E F G H I J K L M N O P Q R S T U V W X Y Z

universe
noun

The **universe** includes everything that exists on Earth and in space.

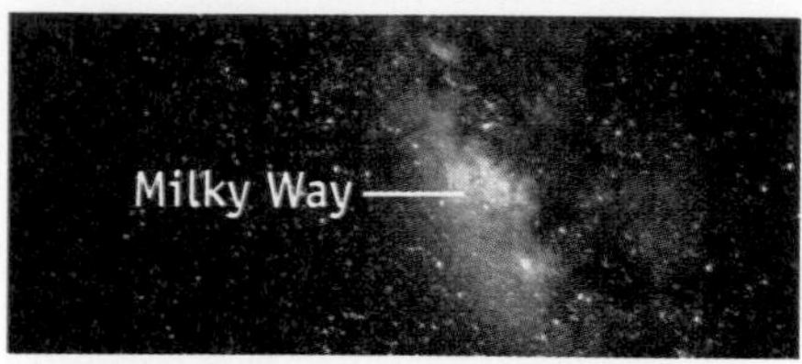

*The Milky Way is just one of the large groups of stars in the **universe**.*

university
noun

A **university** is a place to study for a career or a profession.

*After you graduate from high school, you can study at a **university**.*

See also: *college*, page 21

upward
adverb

When something goes **upward**, it moves to a higher place.

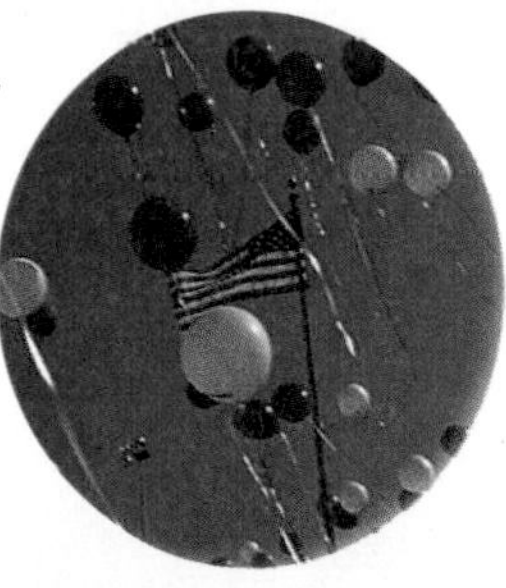

*The pretty balloons float **upward** into the sky.*

usual
adjective

When something is **usual**, it is something you are used to.

*My **usual** breakfast is milk and cereal.*

Vv

vacation
noun

A **vacation** is a time of rest from work or school.

*You can relax and have fun during a **vacation**.*

value
noun

The **value** of something is its worth or usefulness.

*Experts will decide the **value** of these jewels.*

verb
noun

A **verb** is a word that describes an action.

*The words roll and push are **verbs**.*

verse
noun

A **verse** is a poem, or one section of a longer poem.

Do you ever wonder
What makes the sky so blue?
Or how bees make
their honeycombs?
I do.

*This **verse** has five lines.*

vertebrate
noun

A **vertebrate** is an animal that has a backbone.

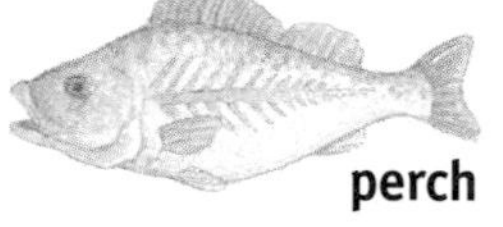

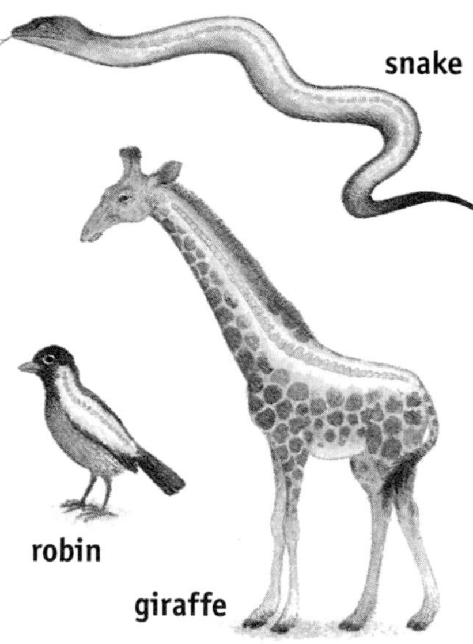

*Fish, birds, reptiles, and mammals are all **vertebrates**.*

See also: *invertebrate*, page 54

village
noun

A **village** is a small community of people.

*In this **village** in China, people of all ages live and work together.*

Ww

visible

adjective

Something is **visible** when you can see it.

*The sun is **visible** behind the trees.*

visit

verb

You **visit** people when you go to see them.

*I like to play the trumpet when we **visit** my grandparents.*

volcano

noun

A **volcano** is a mountain made by hot melted rock from inside the earth.

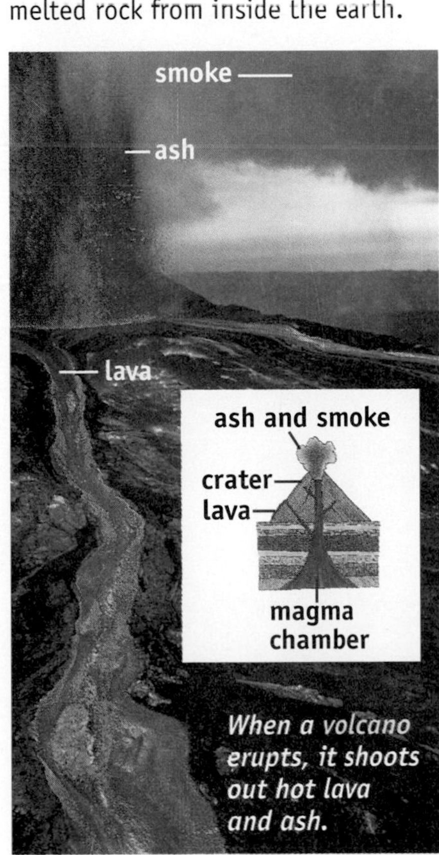

When a volcano erupts, it shoots out hot lava and ash.

wage

noun

A **wage** is money paid to a person for doing work.

*Anna is paid a **wage** of $5 an hour for babysitting.*

warehouse

noun

A **warehouse** is a large building used to store things.

*The cargo in the trailer is moved into the **warehouse**.*

See also: ***transport*****, pages 108–109**

warn

verb

You **warn** someone when you tell them something bad may happen.

*This sign **warns** drivers that rocks may fall on the road.*

warrior

noun

A **warrior** is a person who fights bravely in a war or battle.

*Red Cloud was a Sioux **warrior**. He defended his land and people in the 1860s.*

waste

noun

Waste is material that has been left over or thrown away.

*Our school recycles paper and metal **waste**.*

watch

❶ *noun*

A **watch** is a small clock you wear on your wrist.

❷ *verb*

When you **watch**, you look at something for a period of time.

*These space campers **watch** a rocket launch.*

Idiom:

Watch out!

You can say, "**Watch out!**" to warn someone of danger.

a b c d e f g h i j k l m n o p q r s t u v w x y z

water

noun

Water is the clear liquid that falls from the clouds as rain. Water makes up Earth's oceans, lakes, and rivers. All living things need water to survive.

See also: ***dam*****, page 26;** ***environment*****, page 32;** ***landform*****, pages 58–59**

The Water Cycle

The amount of **water** on Earth doesn't change. The water is reused again and again. This process is called the water cycle.

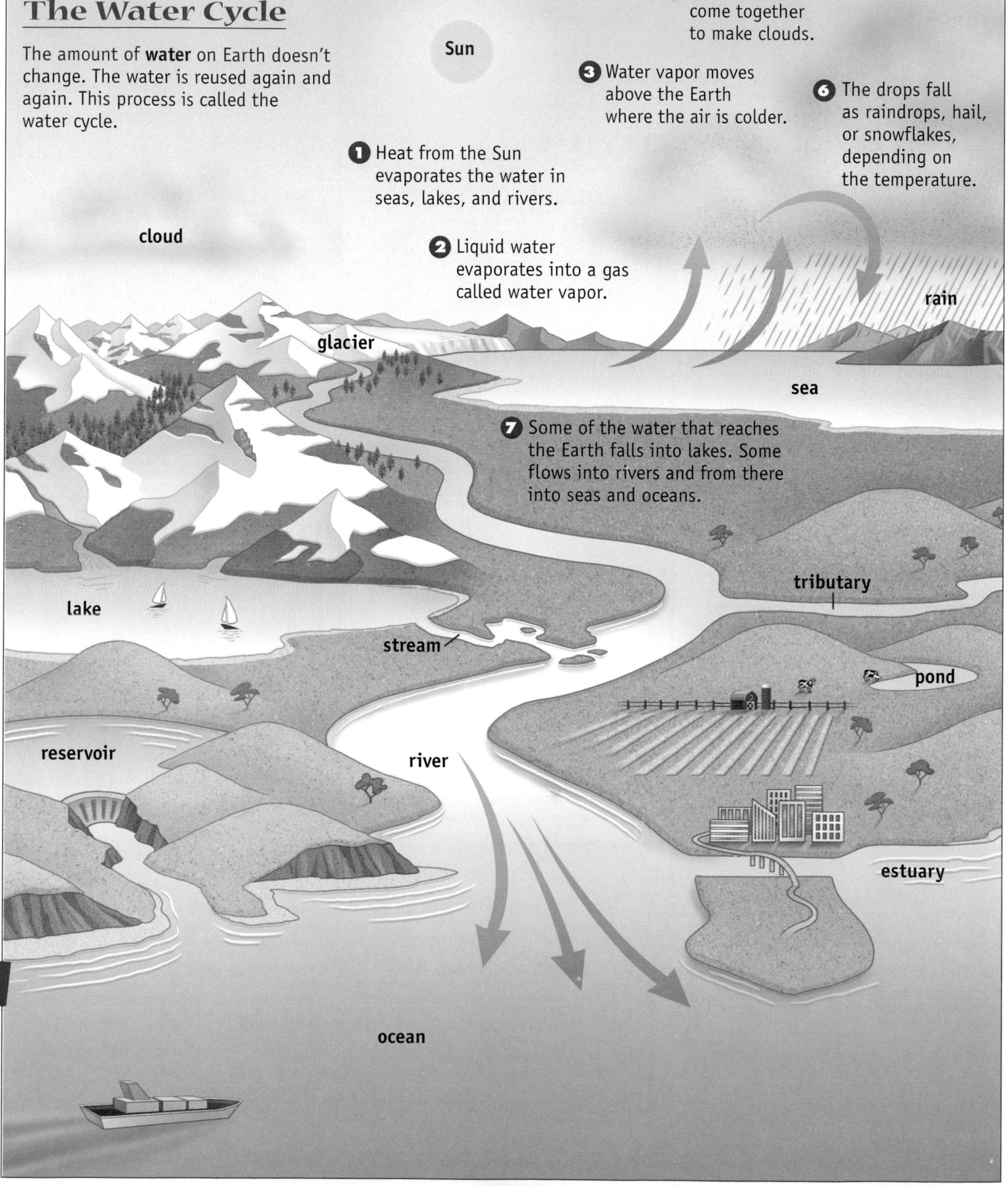

Sun

1. Heat from the Sun evaporates the water in seas, lakes, and rivers.
2. Liquid water evaporates into a gas called water vapor.
3. Water vapor moves above the Earth where the air is colder.
4. Water droplets come together to make clouds.
5. When there are millions of water droplets in the clouds, they fall to the Earth.
6. The drops fall as raindrops, hail, or snowflakes, depending on the temperature.
7. Some of the water that reaches the Earth falls into lakes. Some flows into rivers and from there into seas and oceans.

cloud

glacier

rain

sea

tributary

lake

stream

pond

reservoir

river

estuary

ocean

weather

noun

Weather is the condition of the air, or atmosphere, at a certain place and time. It includes the temperature and the amount of wind, rain, snow, sun, or clouds.

See also: ***blizzard*****, page 13;** ***drought*****, page 29;** ***fierce*****, page 38;** ***ocean*****, page 73;** ***temperature*****, page 107;** ***water*****, page 116**

Some Types of Weather

thunderstorm

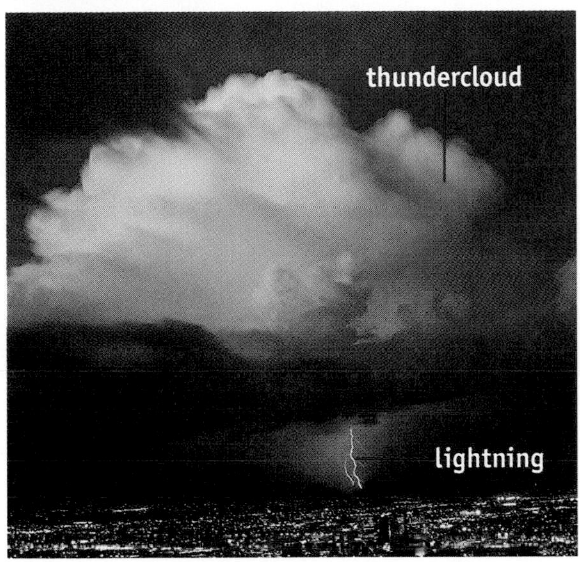

Lightning is electricity in a thundercloud. Air heated quickly by lightning can cause the booming noise of thunder. Rain, thunder, and lightning create a **thunderstorm**.

blizzard

A **blizzard** is a snowstorm with strong winds. The winds drive the snow sideways and make it very difficult to drive or to see. The heavy snow and wind can also knock down branches and power lines.

hurricane

A **hurricane** is a storm that has a lot of rain and very strong winds. Hurricanes usually begin over the ocean. In tropical climates a hurricane may be called a *typhoon*.

tornado

A **tornado** is a spinning column of air that comes from a thundercloud. The part that reaches the earth is a funnel cloud. A tornado can cause terrible destruction to homes and roads.

fog

Fog is a cloud that settles close to the ground or water. The cloud is full of drops of water. Fog makes it very hard for drivers to see where they are going, and this sometimes causes traffic accidents.

A B C D E F G H I J K L M N O P Q R S T U V W X Y Z

weave

verb

When you **weave**, you lace threads, grass, or other materials together in a pattern.

*She **weaves** thread into beautiful cloth.*

In the past:
She **wove**.
She **has woven**.

web

1 *noun*

A **web** is the network of threads a spider weaves.

*A spider catches insects in its **web**.*

2 *noun*

A **web** is a network of locations, or sites, on the Internet.

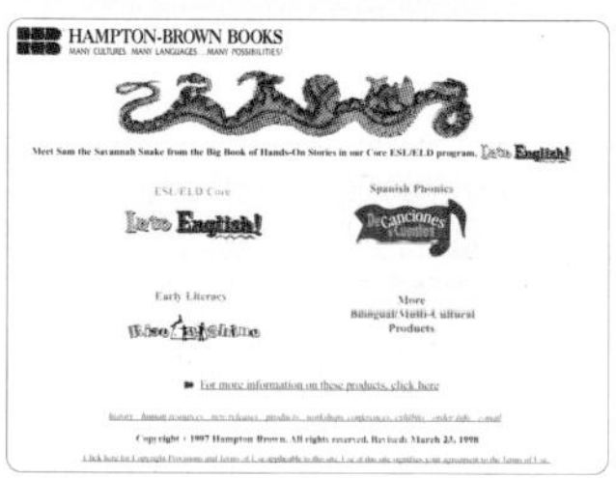

*This **web** page tells about books for students and teachers.*

See also: ***Internet*****, page 52;** ***network*****, page 71**

weep

verb

When you **weep**, tears roll down your face.

*She **weeps** for her lost dog.*

In the past:
She **wept**.
She **has wept**.

weigh

verb

When you **weigh** something, you measure how heavy it is on a scale.

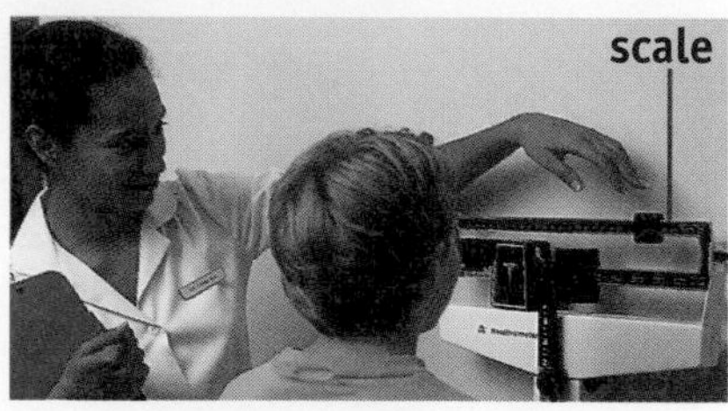

*He **weighs** ten pounds more than last year.*

wharf

noun

A **wharf** is a platform in a harbor where ships load and unload cargo.

*This ship is docked at the **wharf**.*

whistle

noun

A **whistle** is a small object. It makes a high, shrill sound when you blow air into it.

*The referee blows a **whistle** to get the players' attention.*

Idiom:
as clean as a whistle

Something is **as clean as a whistle** when it is very neat and clean.

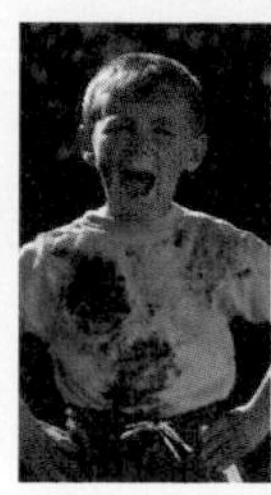

*The boy on the right is **as clean as a whistle**.*

whole

adjective

Something is **whole** when it is complete. It is not divided or cut into pieces.

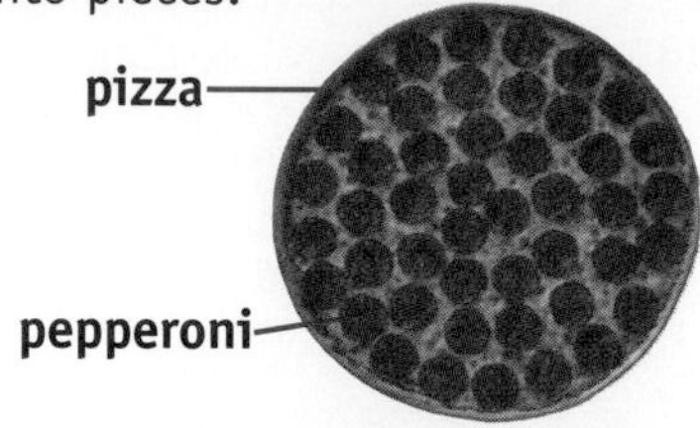

*I ordered a **whole** pepperoni pizza for dinner.*

wick

noun

A **wick** is the string inside a candle. It burns when you light it with a match.

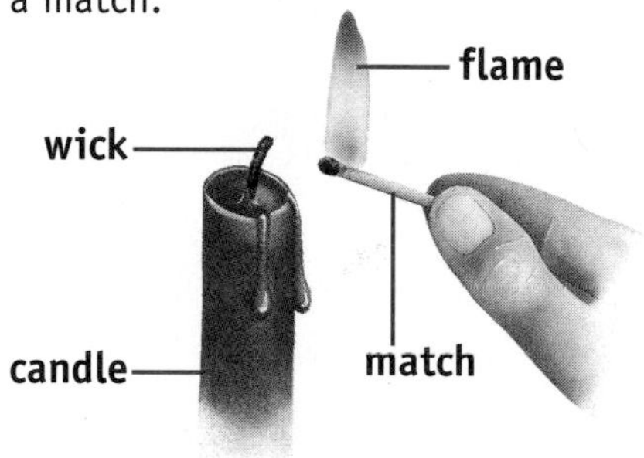

width

noun

Width is a measurement of how wide an object is.

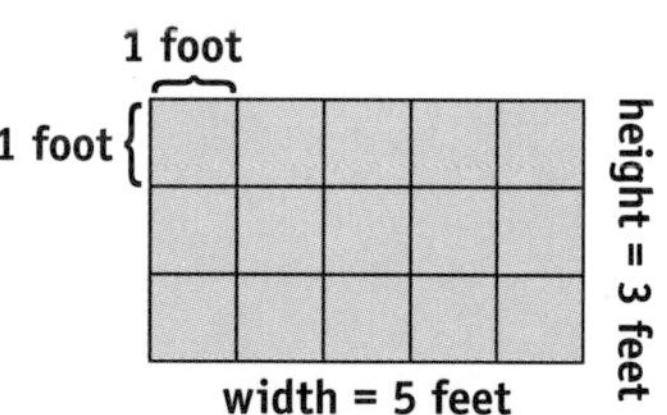

*The **width** of this rectangle is 5 feet wide.*

wild

adjective

Something is **wild** when it lives or grows in nature.

***Wild** zebras live on the grasslands of Africa.*

winter
noun

Winter is the coldest season of the year.

rays
Northern Hemisphere
Earth
Sun

*It is **winter** in the Northern Hemisphere when that part of Earth tilts furthest away from the Sun.*

wipe
verb

You **wipe** something when you clean it or dry it by rubbing.

*They **wipe** the windshield.*

wisdom
noun

Wisdom is an understanding about life. It usually comes with age and experience.

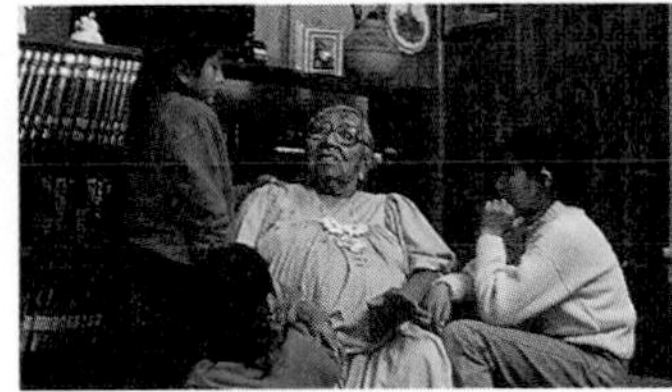

*The stories our grandmother tells are full of **wisdom**.*

wonderful
adjective

Something is **wonderful** when it is amazing or very good.

*The new aquarium is a **wonderful** place to visit.*

wooden
adjective

Something that is **wooden** is made out of wood.

*You can learn to make **wooden** furniture in school.*

worker
noun

A **worker** is a person who works at a job.

*This **worker** is building a house.*

worth
noun

The **worth** of something is its value.

*The age of this doll increases its **worth**.*

wrap
verb

You **wrap** something when you fold something around it.

*A gift looks more special when you **wrap** it nicely.*

wreck
noun

A **wreck** is something that is broken or ruined.

*The cars in this junkyard are **wrecks**.*

wring
verb

You **wring** something when you twist it to get water out of it.

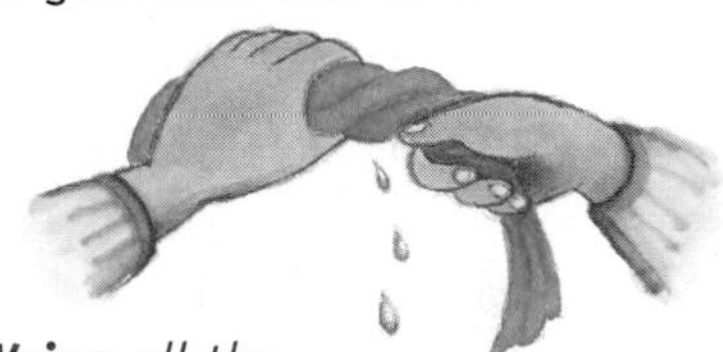

***Wring** all the water out of the washcloth before you hang it up.*

In the past:
He **wrung.**
He **has wrung.**

write
verb

You **write** something when you form letters, words, or numbers in order to communicate.

***Write** in a journal to remember your feelings.*

In the past:
She **wrote.**
She **has written.**

wrong
adjective

Something is **wrong** when it is not correct.

*These shoes are the **wrong** size!*

Xx

X-ray
noun

An **X-ray** is a picture that shows the bones inside your body.

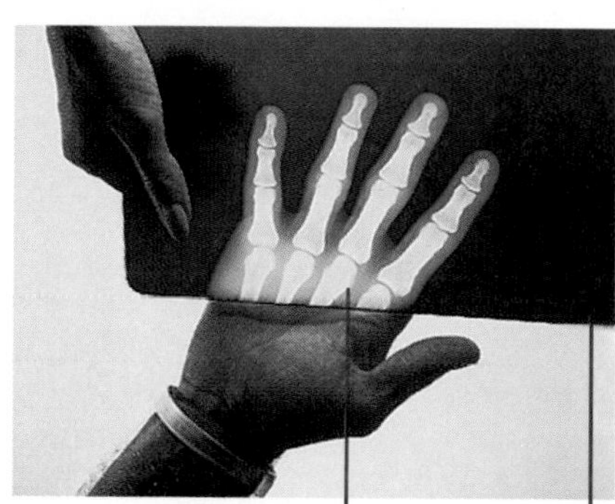

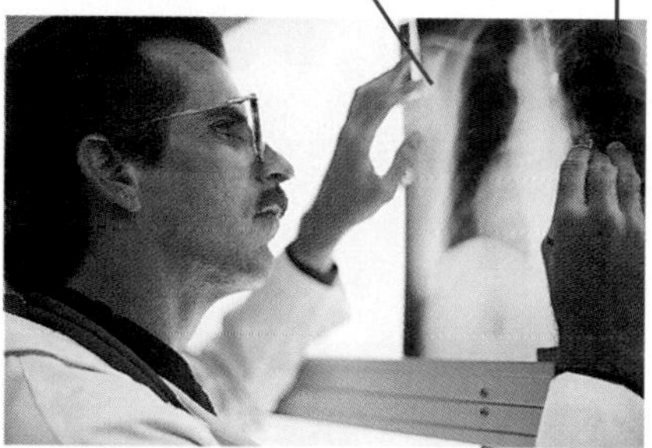

*On an **X-ray**, a doctor can see if a bone is broken.*

See also: *skeleton*, page 99

xylophone
noun

A **xylophone** is a musical instrument with a row of wooden or metal bars. You hit the bars to make music.

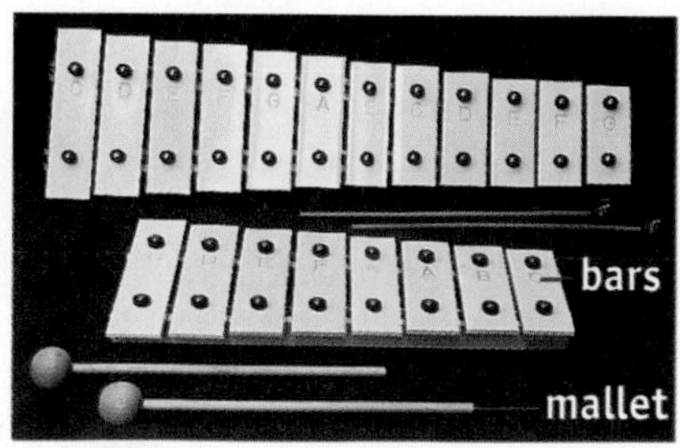

Yy

yell
verb

You **yell** when you shout very loudly.

*People **yell** as the parade goes by.*

youth
❶ *noun*

A **youth** is a young person.

*These **youths** are checking their team line-up.*

❷ *noun*

Youth is the time of life when a person is young.

*This man was a football player in his **youth**.*

Zz

zero
noun

Zero is the word for the number 0.

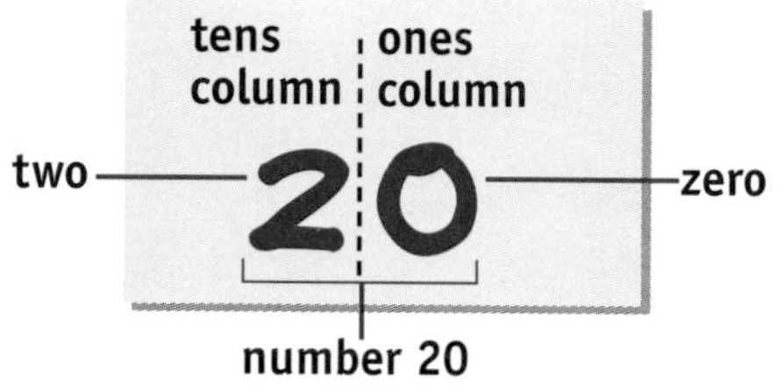

*You write the number 20 with a two in the tens place and a **zero** in the ones place.*

zone
noun

A **zone** is an area used for something special.

*There is a no-parking **zone** outside our school.*

zoom
verb

Something that **zooms** moves very fast.

*You can feel a gust of air when a bike **zooms** by.*

The Basics

Basic Vocabulary for Beginning English Learners

Contents

The Body

Parts of the Body

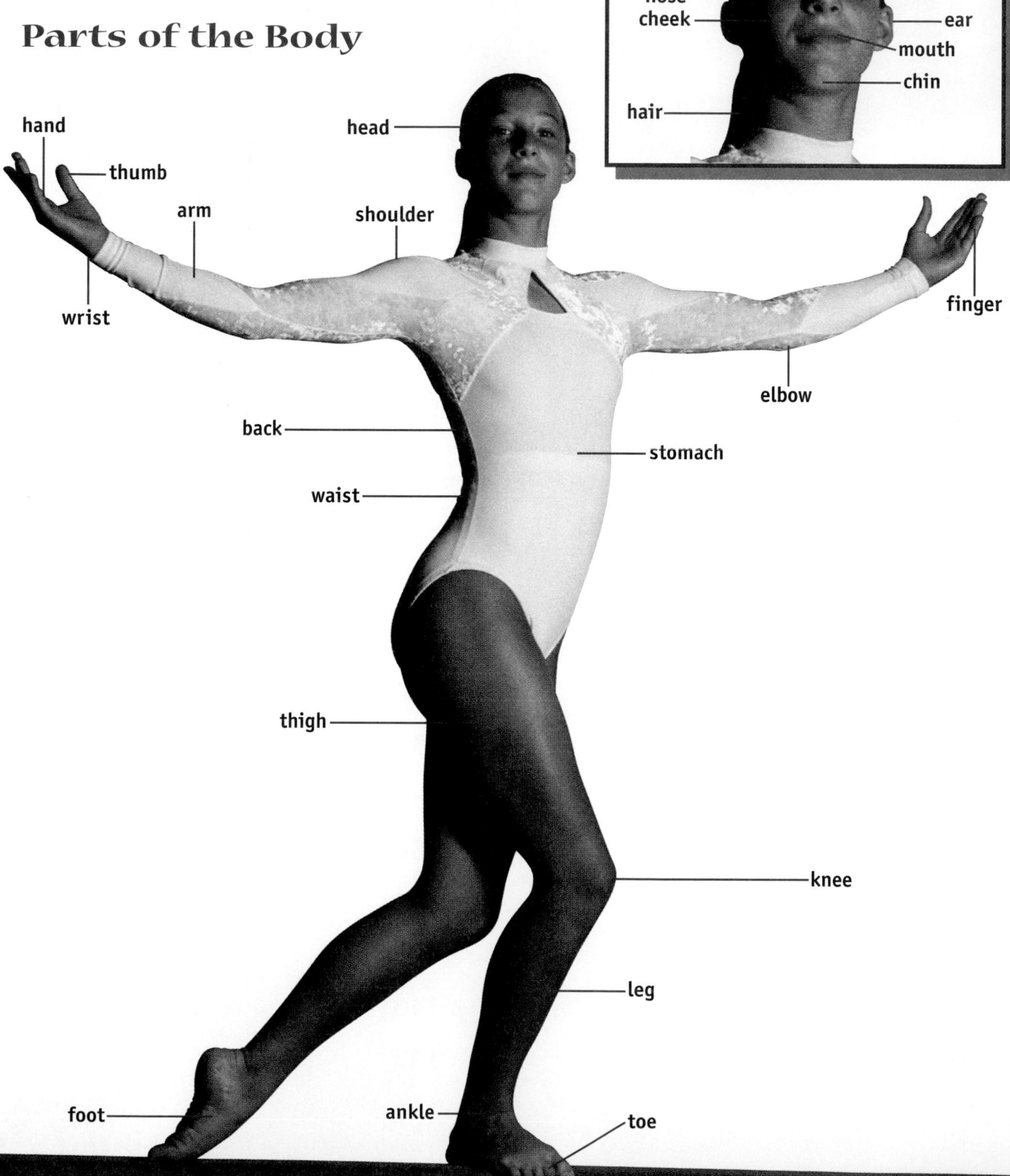

Get Exercise

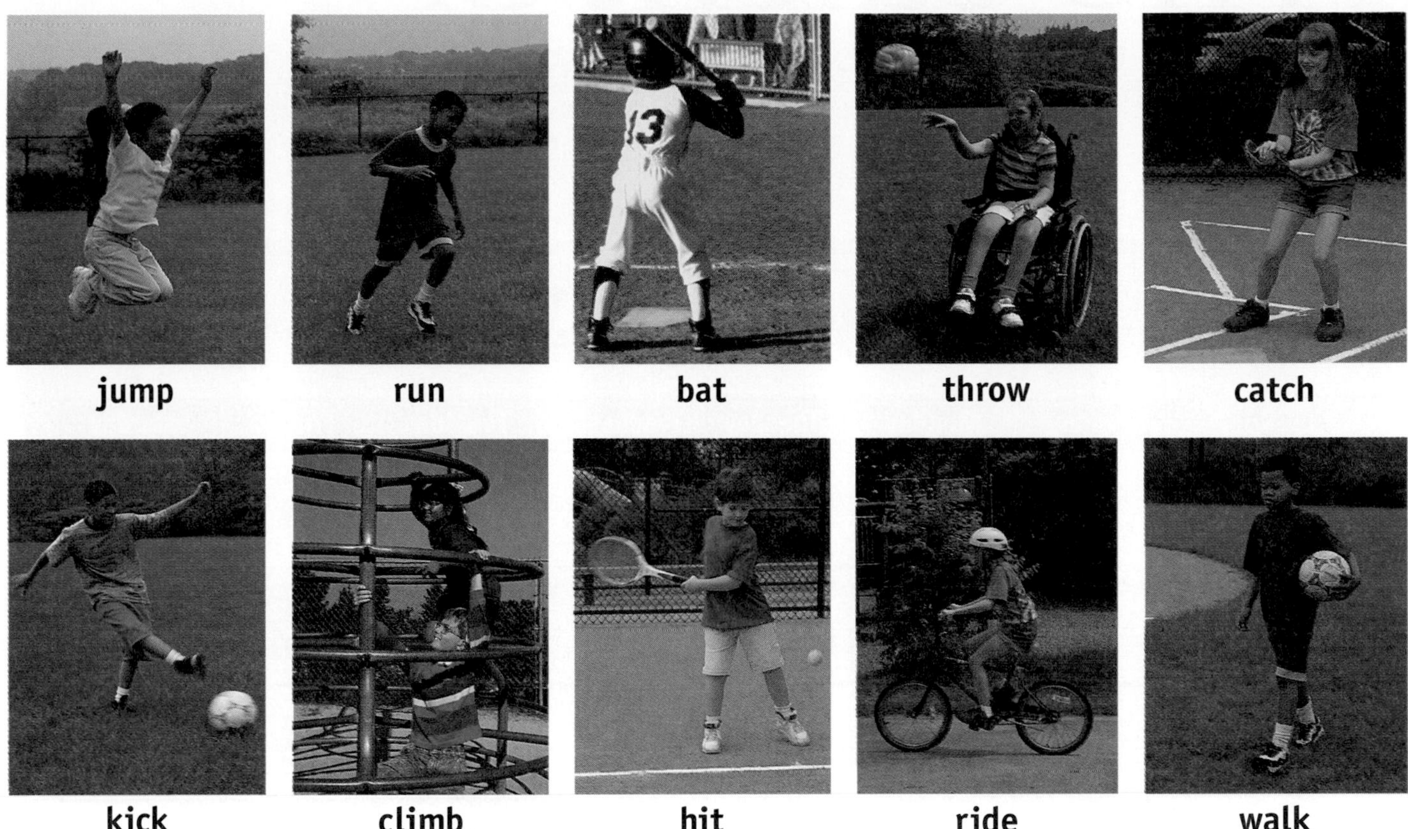

Stay Healthy

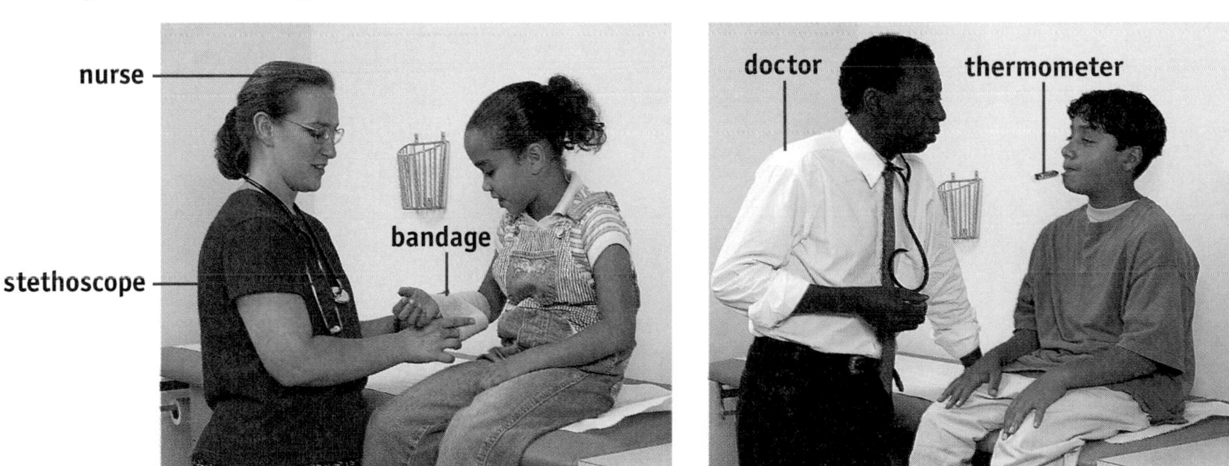

Stay Clean

take a shower

brush teeth

wash hands

brush hair

The Calendar

day · month · year

days of the week

January 2001

Sunday	Monday	Tuesday	Wednesday	Thursday	Friday	Saturday
	1	2	3	4	5	6
7	8	9	10	11	12	13
14	15	16	17	18	19	20
21	22	23	24	25	26	27
28	29	30	31			

Seasons and Months of the Year

December
January
February

March
April
May

June
July
August

September
October
November

Colors and Shapes

Colors

red

green

yellow

blue

black

brown

purple

orange

white

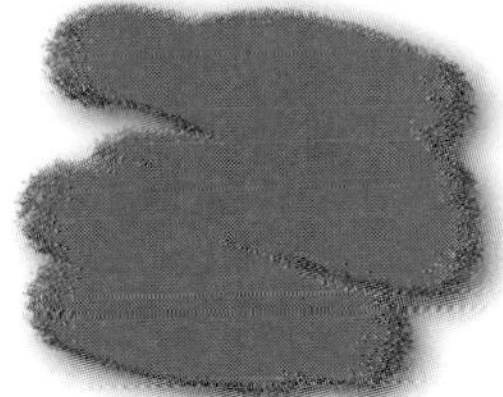
pink

tan

gray

Shapes

square

circle

triangle

rectangle

cube

cone

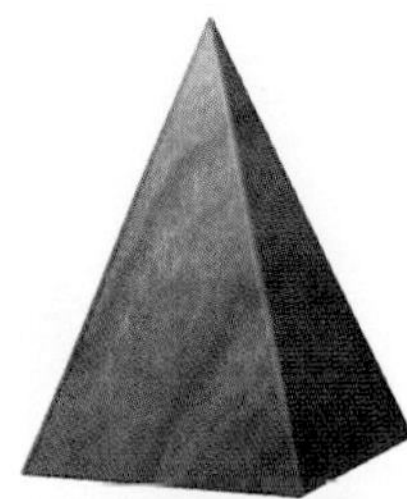
pyramid

sphere

Clothing

cap
jacket
T-shirt
jeans
sneaker
polo shirt
sunglasses
shorts
sandal
umbrella
raincoat
rainboot
backpack
sweater
blouse
belt
skirt
sock
loafer
robe
pajamas
slipper
undershirt
sweatshirt
sweatpants
sneaker

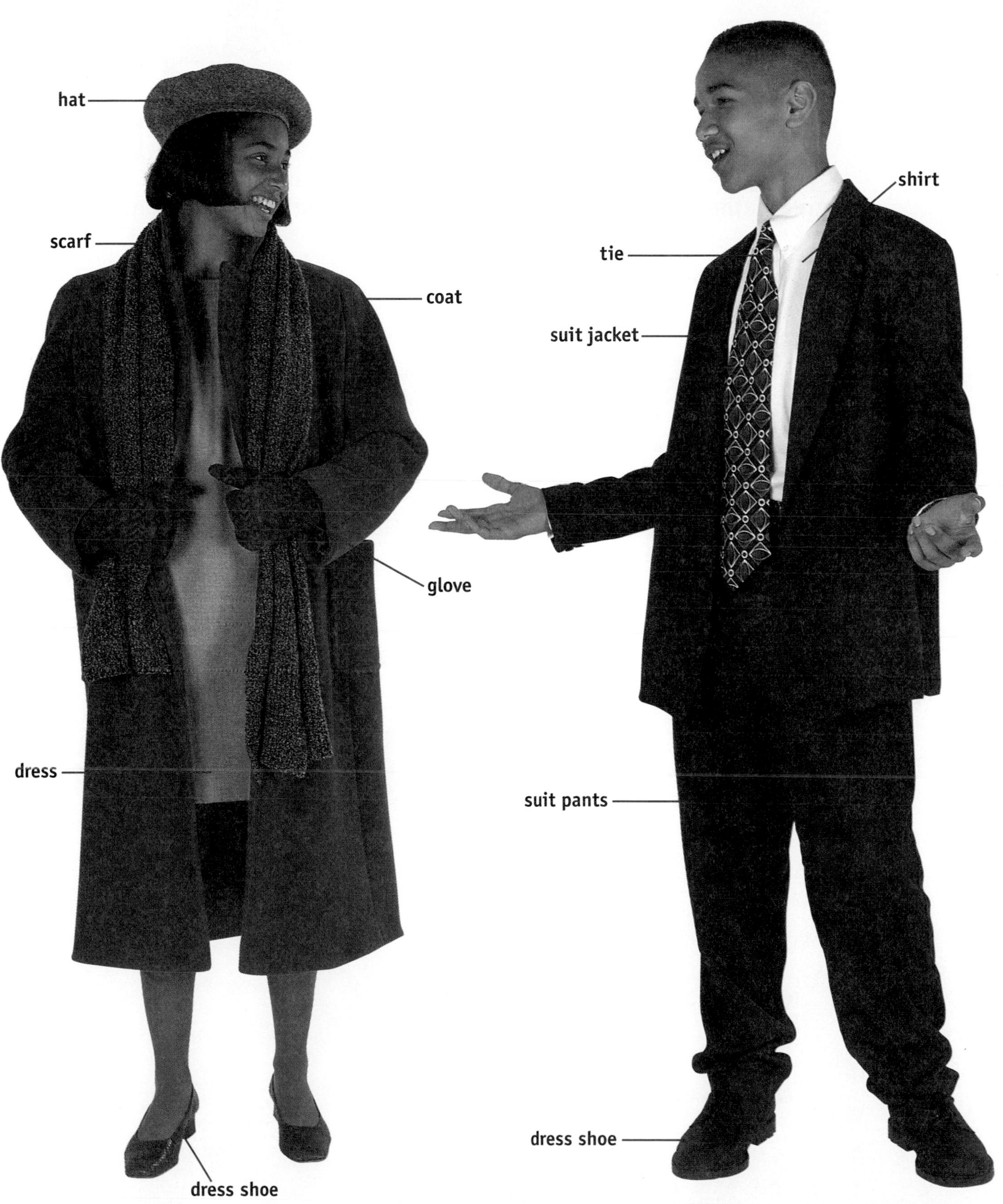
hat
scarf
coat
glove
dress
dress shoe
shirt
tie
suit jacket
suit pants
dress shoe

Family

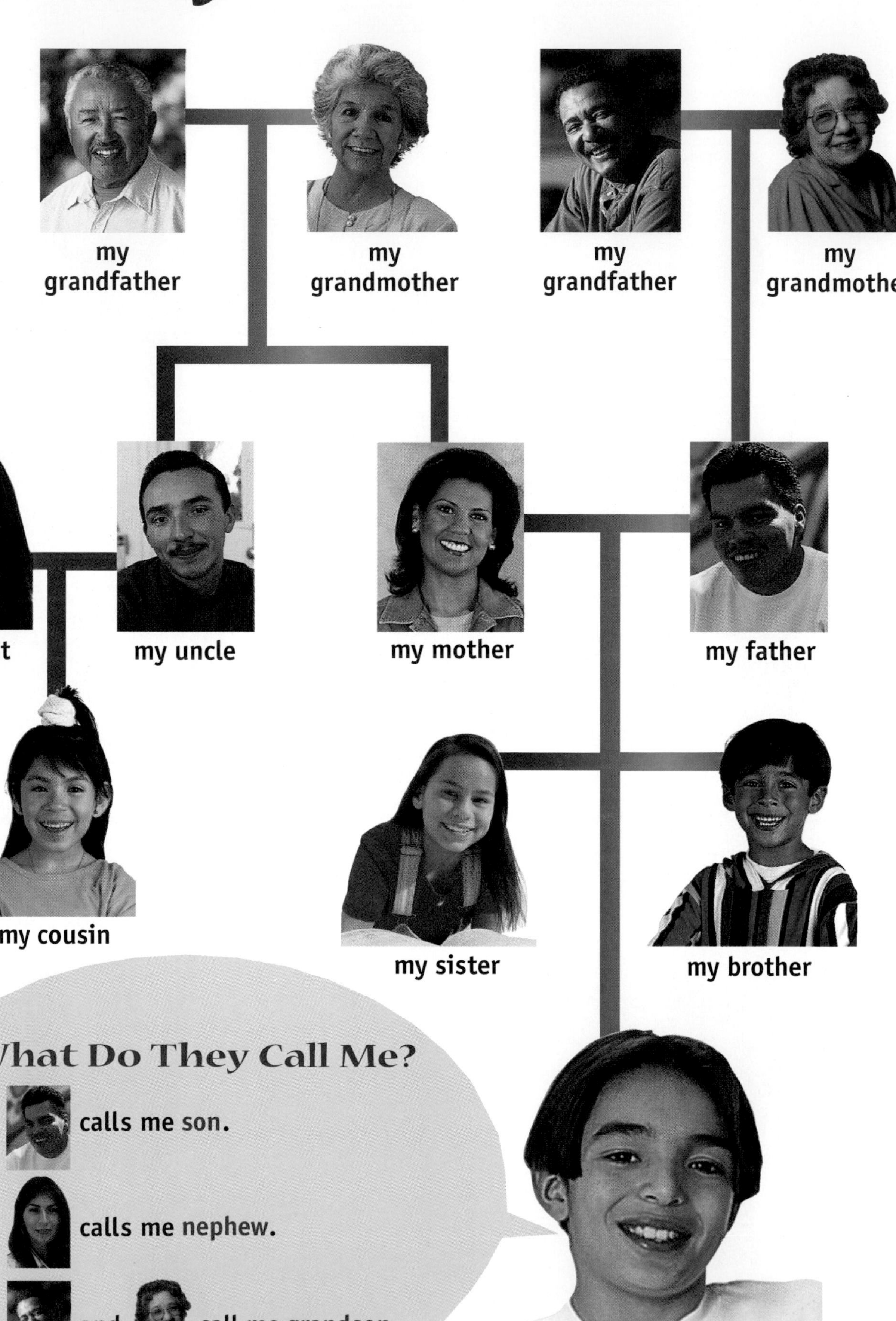

What Do They Call Me?

calls me son.

calls me nephew.

and call me grandson.

Feelings

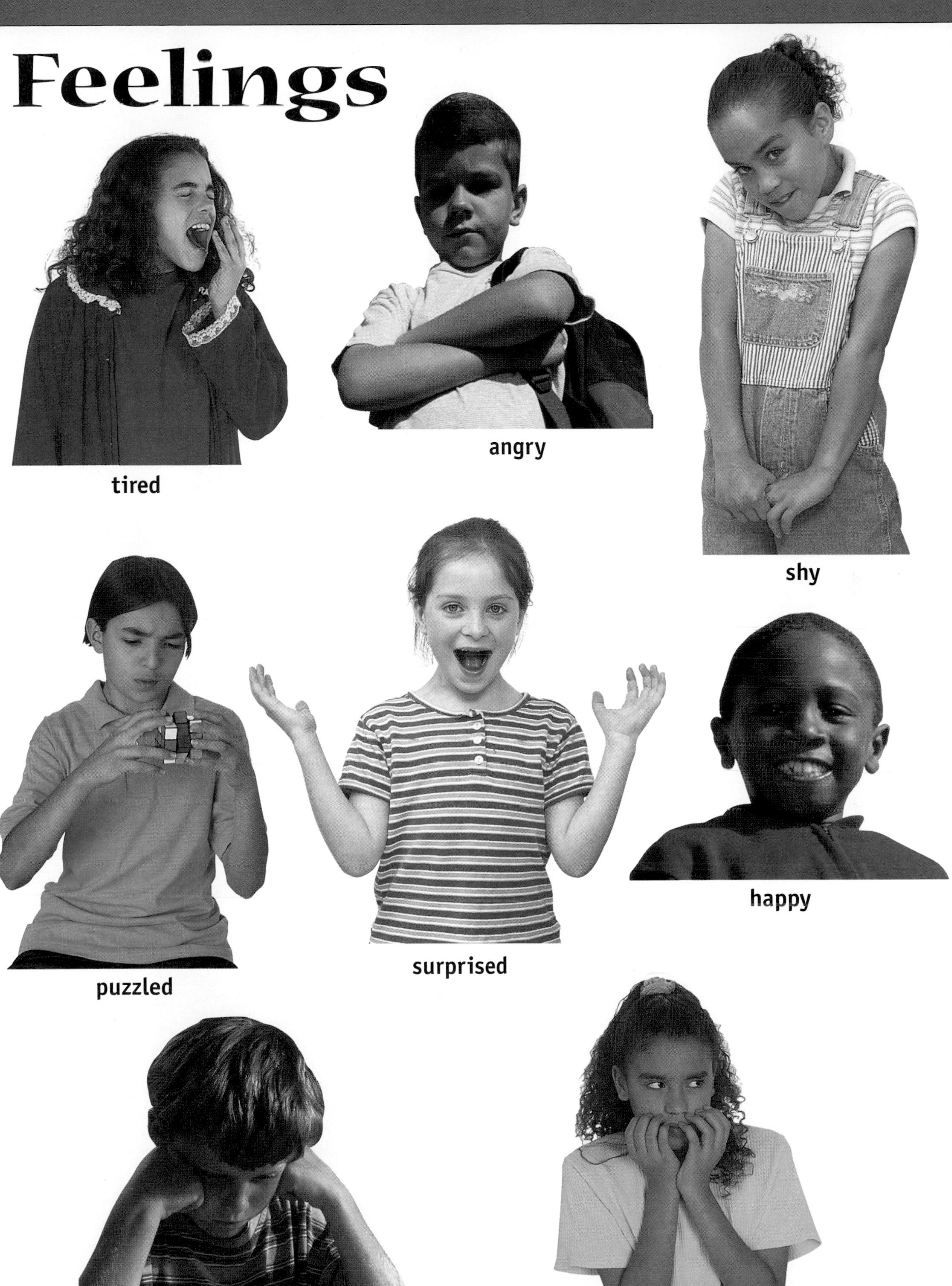

tired

angry

shy

puzzled

surprised

happy

sad

scared

Food

What's for breakfast?

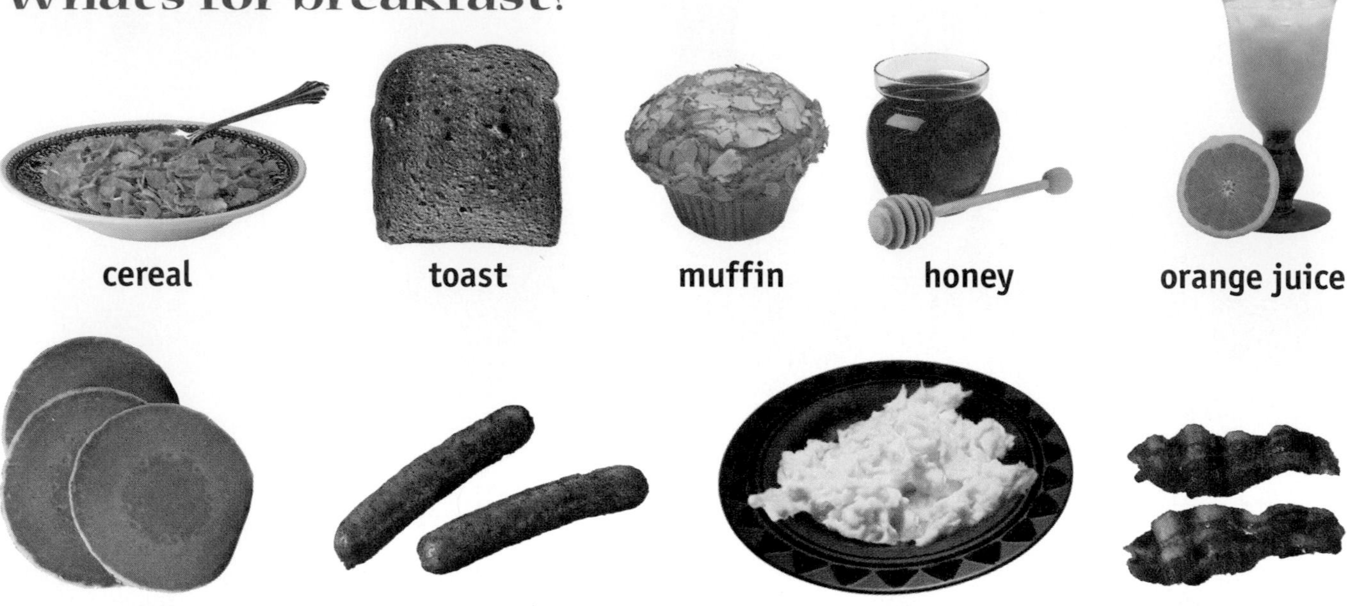

cereal toast muffin honey orange juice

pancakes sausages eggs bacon

What's for lunch?

sandwich  burrito  pizza  hamburger  hot dog

corn-on-the-cob  apple 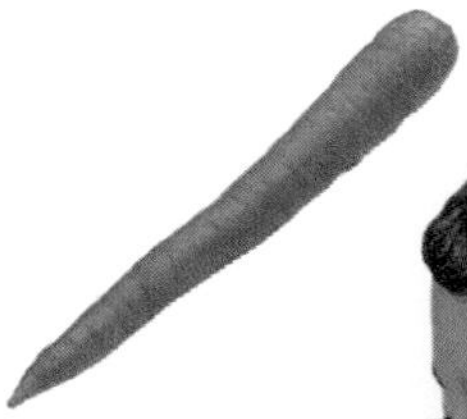 carrot

banana

milk

a place setting

What's for dinner?

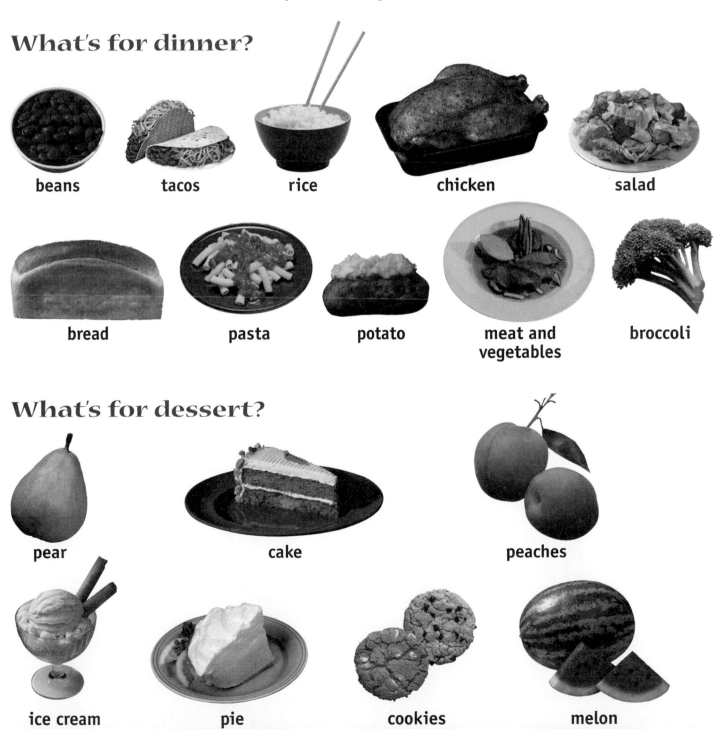

beans

tacos

rice

chicken

salad

bread

pasta

potato

meat and vegetables

broccoli

What's for dessert?

pear

cake

peaches

ice cream

pie

cookies

melon

Homes

house

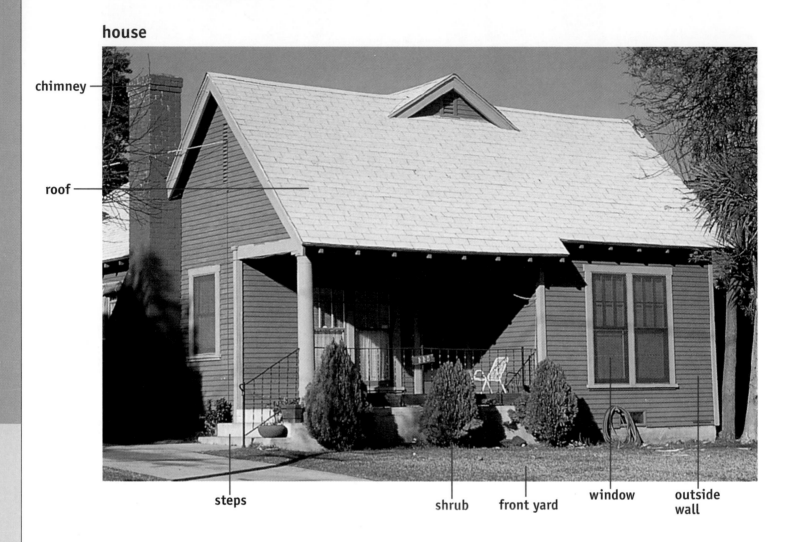

chimney
roof
steps
shrub
front yard
window
outside wall

apartment building

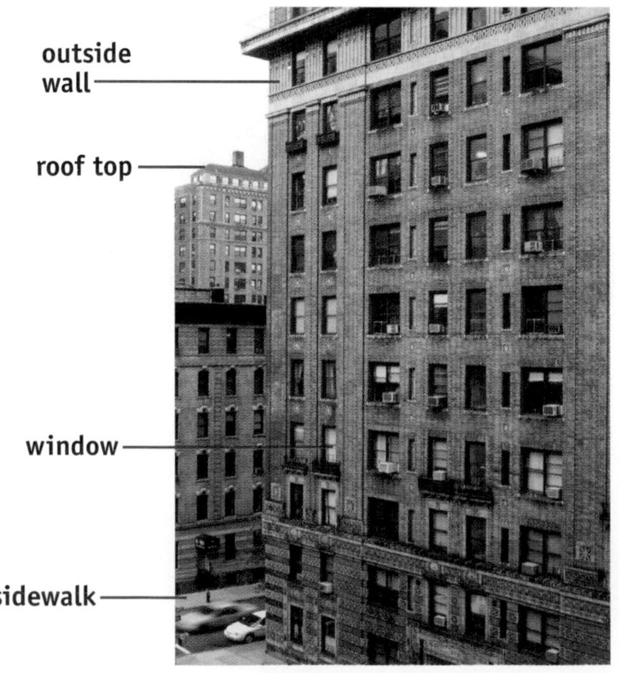

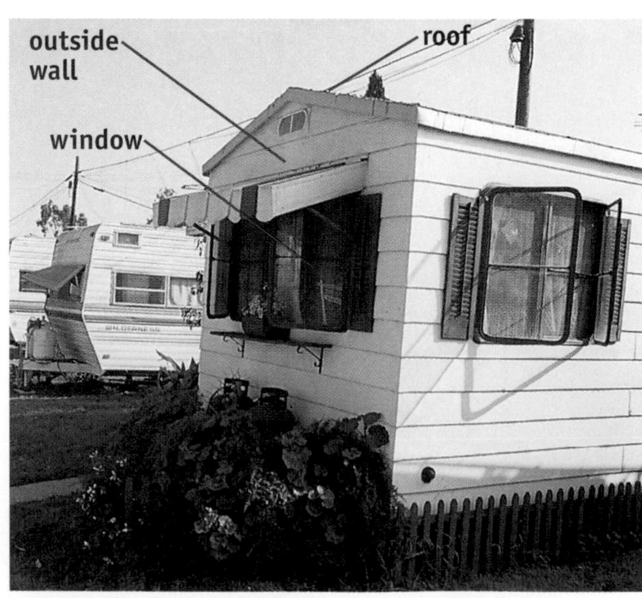

mobile home

kitchen

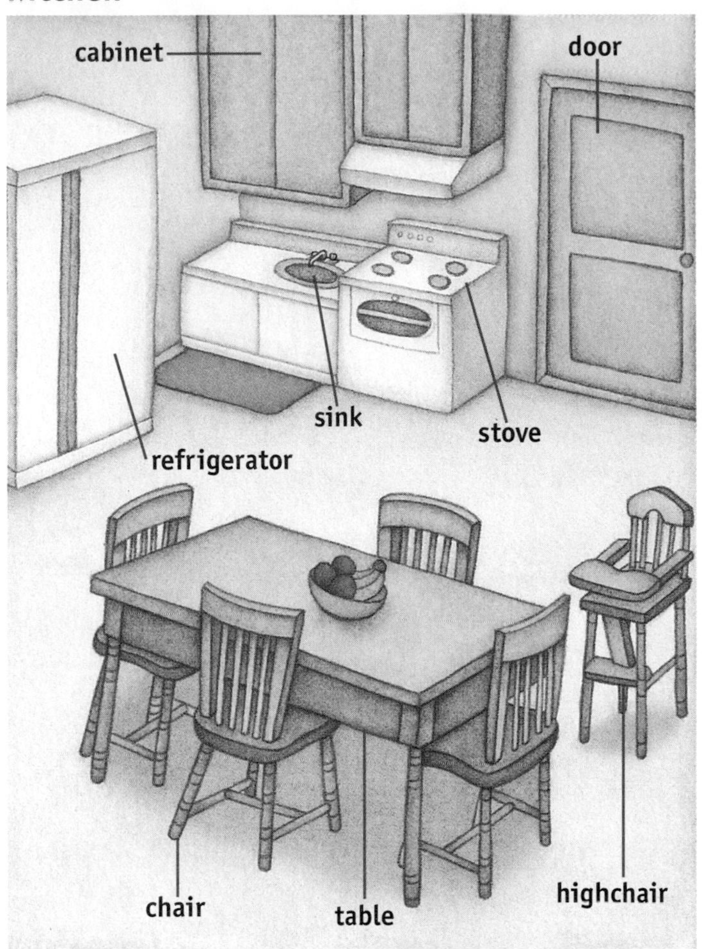

living room

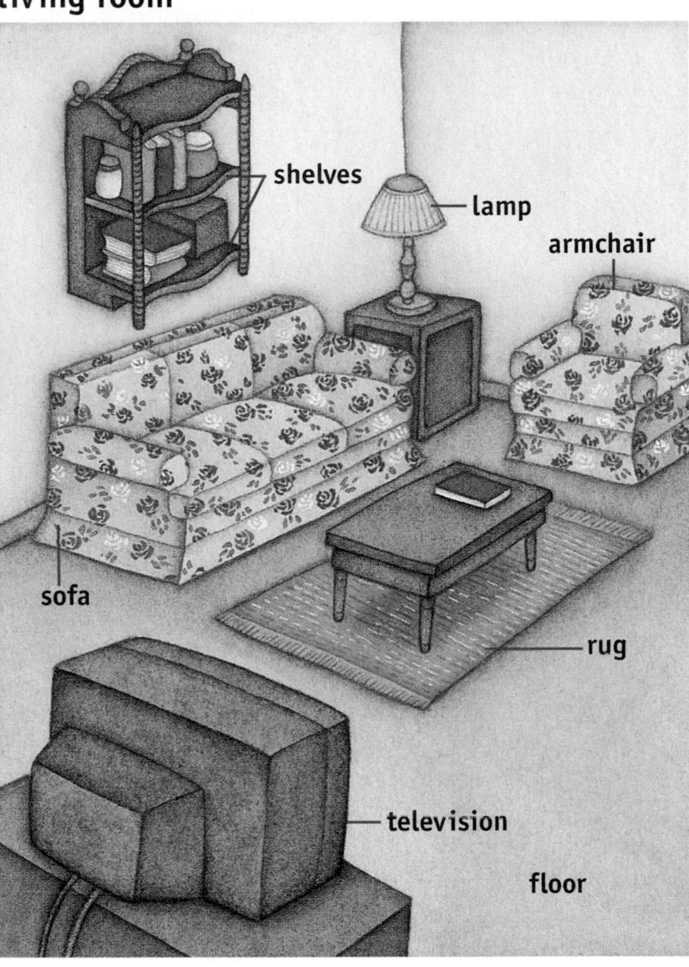

bedroom

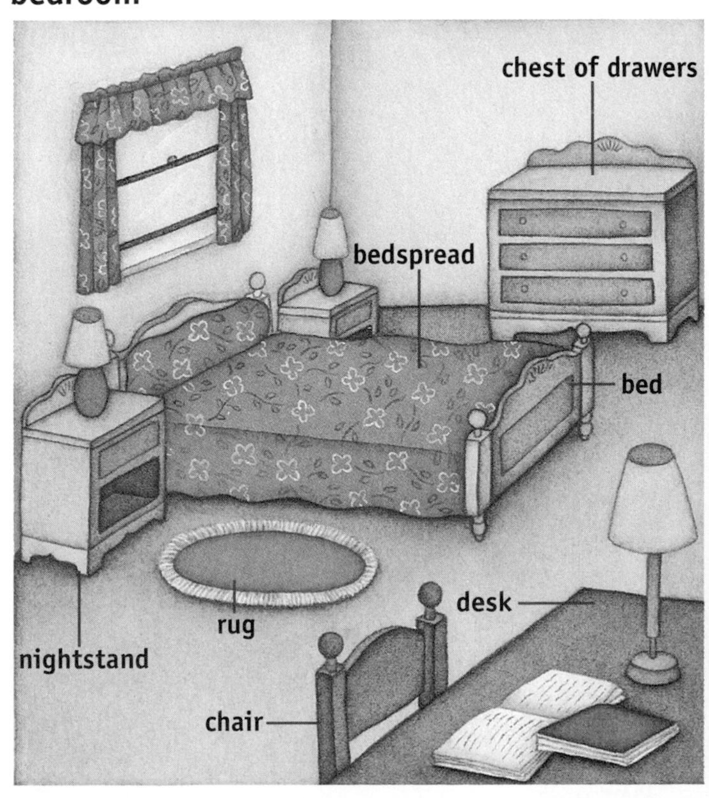

bathroom

The Neighborhood

patrol car

police station

fire truck

fire station

row houses

office building

hospital

ambulance

car

onvenience store

library

place of worship

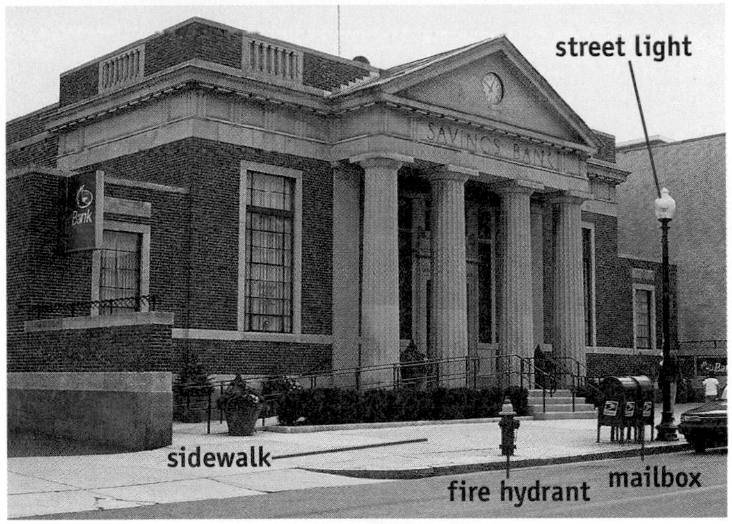

bank

clothing store

playground

post office

shoe repair shop

garden shop

basketball court

gas station

Numbers and Money

0 zero

1 one

2 two

3 three

4 four

5 five

6 six

7 seven

8 eight

9 nine

10 ten

11 eleven
12 twelve
13 thirteen
14 fourteen
15 fifteen
16 sixteen
17 seventeen
18 eighteen
19 nineteen
20 twenty

21 twenty-one
22 twenty-two
23 twenty-three
24 twenty-four
25 twenty-five
26 twenty-six
27 twenty-seven
28 twenty-eight
29 twenty-nine

30 thirty
40 forty
50 fifty
60 sixty
70 seventy
80 eighty
90 ninety
100 one hundred
1000 one thousand

$ .01
penny

$ .05
nickel

$ .10
dime

$ .25
quarter

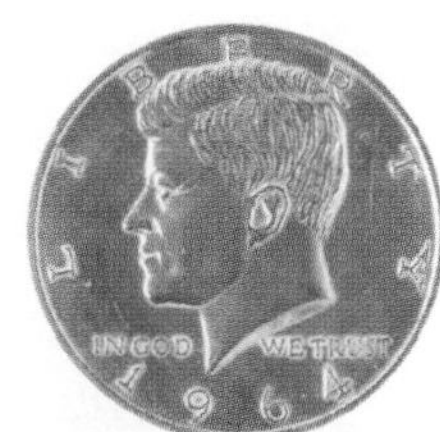

$ .50
half dollar

$1.00
one dollar

$5.00
five dollars

$10.00
ten dollars

$20.00
twenty dollars

On the Playground

on top of the tube slide

between the swings

across the bars

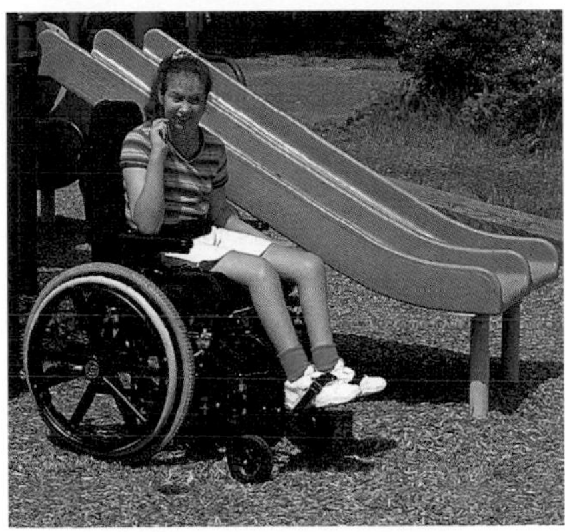
next to the slide

through the tunnel

behind the tree

above the ground

in front of the tree

under the foot bridge

on the swing

in the tube slide

with my brother

School

Classroom

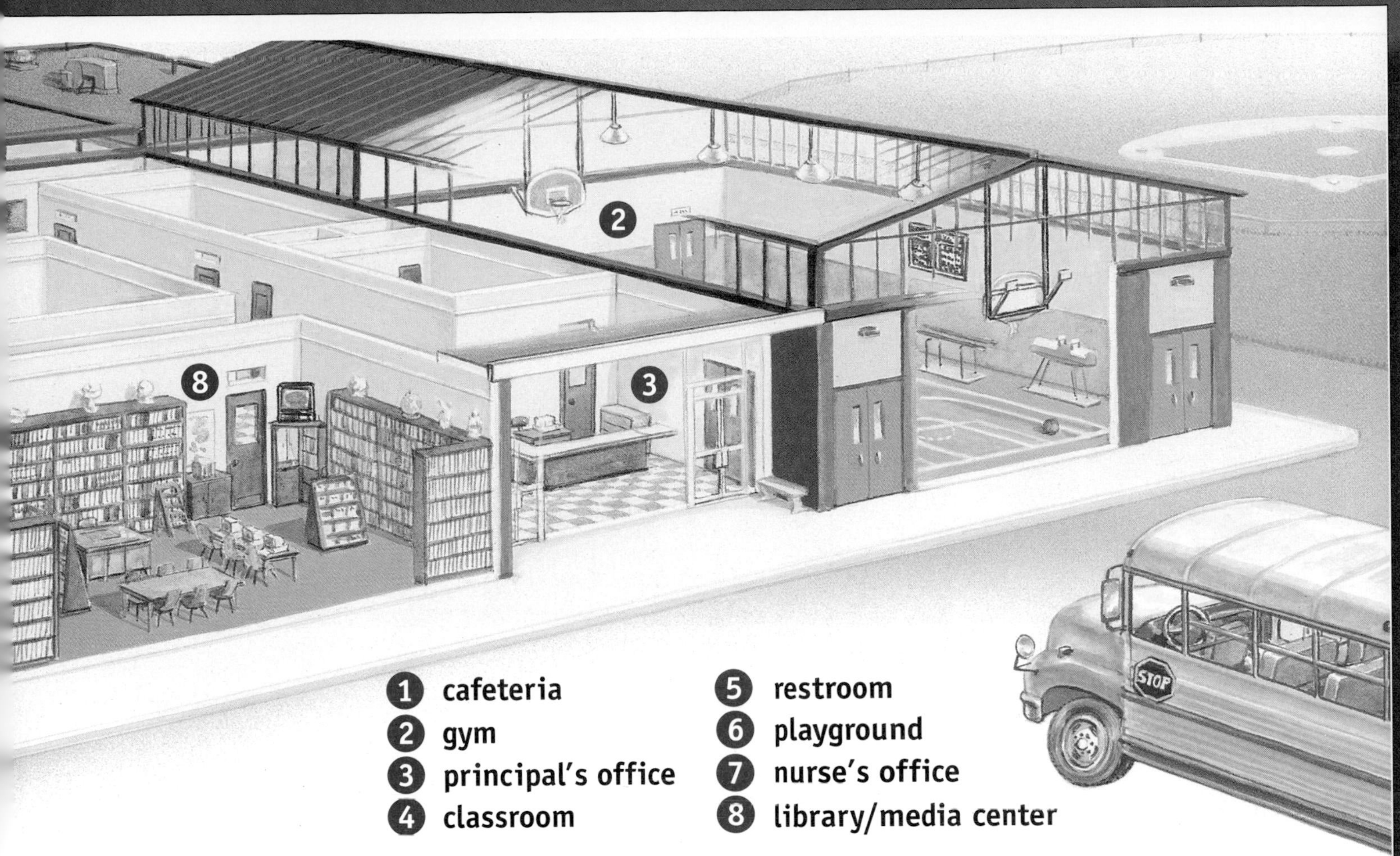

1 cafeteria
2 gym
3 principal's office
4 classroom
5 restroom
6 playground
7 nurse's office
8 library/media center

School Workers

librarian

principal

cafeteria workers

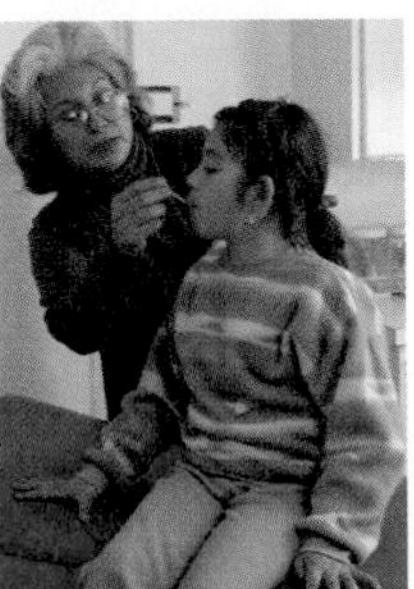
nurse

custodian

teacher

parent volunteer

secretary

School Supplies

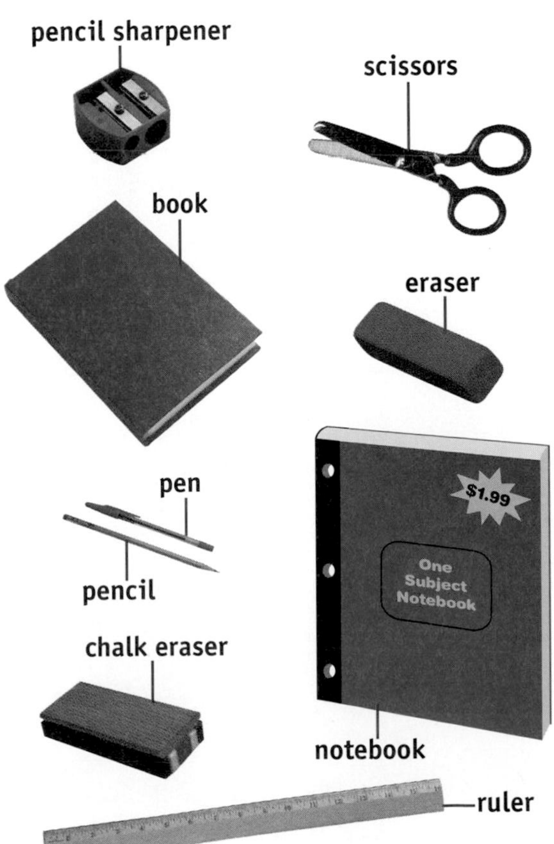

Things to Do

carry backpacks

raise your hand

read

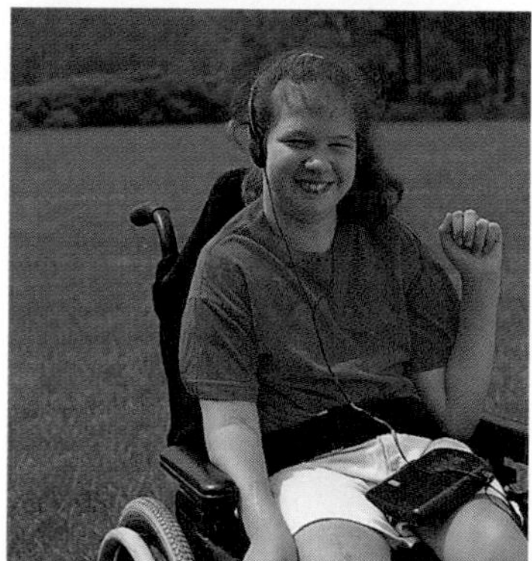
listen

laugh

give

play the clarinet

write

pull

swim

play ball

type

stand

sit

drink

show

do gymnastics

hold

push

talk

go

paint

jump rope

eat

Time

one o'clock

two o'clock

three o'clock

four o'clock

five o'clock

six o'clock

seven o'clock

eight o'clock

nine o'clock

ten o'clock

eleven o'clock

twelve o'clock

one fifteen
quarter past one

one thirty
half past one

one forty-five
quarter to two

morning
A.M.

afternoon
P.M.

evening
P.M.

night
P.M.

yesterday today tomorrow

August

SUNDAY	MONDAY	TUESDAY	WEDNESDAY	THURSDAY	FRIDAY	SATURDAY
	1 Bike With Fred.	2 Play Soccer	3 Mom's Birthday!	4	5	6
7	8	9	10	11		
14	15	16	17	18		
21	22	23	24	25	26	
28						

Index

Pronunciation Key

Symbols for Consonant Sounds

b	box
ch	chick
d	dog
f	fish
g	girl
h	hat
j	jar
k	cake
ks	box
kw	queen
l	bell
m	mouse
n	pan
ng	ring
p	pan
r	ring
s	bus
sh	fish
t	hat
th	Earth
th	father
v	vase
w	window
wh	whale
y	yarn
z	zipper
zh	treasure

Symbols for Short Vowel Sounds

a	hat
e	bell
i	chick
o	box
u	bus

Symbols for Long Vowel Sounds

ā	cake
ē	key
ī	bike
ō	goat
ū	fruit
yū	mule

Symbols for R-controlled Sounds

ar	barn
air	chair
or	corn
ur	girl
īr	fire

Symbols for Variant Vowel Sounds

ah	father
aw	ball
oi	boy
ow	mouse
oo	book

Miscellaneous Symbols

shun	fraction	$\frac{1}{2}$
chun	question	?
zhun	division	$2\overline{)100}$ = 50

Aa

A.M. (ā-em) 143
ab•do•men (**ab**-du-mun) 8, 12, 52, 104
a•bove (u-**buv**) 137
a•bove the ground (u-**buv** thu grownd) 137
A•bra•ham Lin•coln (ā-bru-**ham** **link**-un) 11, 88
ac•cept (ak-**sept**) 5
a•cross (u-**kros**) 137
a•cross the bars (u-**kros** thu barz) .137
act (akt) 5
ac•tion (**ak**-shun) 87
ac•tive vol•ca•noes (**ak**-tiv vol-**kā**-nōz) 59
ac•tor (**ak**-tur) 5
ad (ad) 5
a•dapt (u-**dapt**) 7
add (ad) 75
ad•dends (**ad**-endz) 5
ad•di•tion (u-**dish**-un) 5, 8
ad•dress (1. **ad**-res 2. u-**dres**) . .5, 60
ad•jec•tive (**aj**-ik-tiv) 5
a•dult (u-**dult**) 27, 61, 66
a•dult frog (u-**dult** frawg) 61
a•dult lu•na moth (u-**dult** **lū**-nu moth) 66
ad•verb (**ad**-vurb) 5
ad•ver•tise (**ad**-vur-tīz) 5
Af•ri•ca (**Af**-ri-ku) .25, 34, 56, 64, 100
af•ter (**af**-tur) 84
af•ter•noon (af-tur-**nūn**) 143
a•gree (u-**grē**) 5
ag•ri•cul•ture (**ag**-ru-**kul**-chur) . .5
air (air) 7, 32
air cur•rent (air **kur**-unt) 25
air pol•lu•tion (air pu-**lū**-shun) . .32
air•plane (**air**-plān) 108
Al•a•bam•a (al-u-**bam**-u) 64, 69, 89, 113
Al•a•mo (**al**-u-mō) 88
A•las•ka (u-**las**-ku) 42, 64, 68, 69, 113
al•li•ga•tors (**al**-u-**gā**-turz) . . .106
al•ways (**awl**-wāz) 5
a•maz•ing 49•ers (u-**māz**-ing for-tē-**nīn**-urz) 49
am•bu•lance (**am**-byu-luns) . . .134
A•mer•i•ca (u-**me**-ri-ku) . .6, 21, 58, 80, 100
A•mer•i•can (u-**me**-ri-kun) 6
A•mer•i•can fron•tier (u-**me**-ri-kun frunt-**tēr**) 96
A•mer•i•can mon•ey (u-**me**-ri-kun mun-e) 67
A•mer•i•cans (u-**me**-ri-kunz) . . .89
a•mount (u-**mownt**) 13
am•phi•bi•ans (am-**fib**-ē-unz) . . .7
an•ces•tor (**an**-ses-tur) 6
an•ces•tors (**an**-ses-turz) 20
an•gry (**ang**-rē) 129
an•i•mal (**an**-u-mul) 6, 39, 82
an•i•mal plank•ton (**an**-u-mul **plangk**-tun) 39
an•i•mals (**an**-u-mulz) 7, 21
an•kle (**ang**-kul) 122
an•nu•al (**an**-yū-ul) 8
●**an•swer** (**an**-sur) 8, 99
Ant•arc•ti•ca (ant-**ark**-ti-ku) . . .64
an•ten•na (an-**ten**-u) 12, 52
a•part•ment (u-**part**-munt) 132
a•part•ment build•ing (u-**part**-munt **bild**-ing) 132
a•pos•tro•phe (u-**pos**-tru-fē) . . .25
ap•ple (**ap**-ul) 130
A•pril (**ā**-prul) 124
a•pron (**ā**-prin) 81
a•rach•nid (u-**rak**-nid) 8
Arc•tic O•cean (**ark**-tik **ō**-shun) . .64
ar•e•a (**air**-e-u) 8
Ar•i•zo•na (A-ru-**zō**-nu) .15, 64, 69, 88, 113
Ar•kan•sas (**ar**-kun-**saw**) . . .64, 69, 88, 113
arm (arm) 122
arm•chair (**arm** chair) 133
ar•mor (**ar**-mur) 56
ar•ter•y (**ar**-tur-ē) 14
ar•ti•cle (**ar**-ti-kul) 71
art•ist (**ar**-tist) 8
ash (ash) 115
ash and smoke (ash an smōk) . . .115
A•sia (**ā**-zhu) 35, 64
as•ter•oid (**ast**-tu-**roid**) 103
as•ter•oid belt (**as**-tu-**roid** belt) .103
as•tro•naut (**as**-tru-nawt) 8
At•lan•tic O•cean (at-**lan**-tik **ō**-shun) 34, 64, 80, 97, 113
at•tor•ney (u-**tur**-nē) 55

Expanded entries appear in color.

● Indicates a multiple-meaning entry.

Bb

Index

Cc

Dd

Index

Ee

Ff

Gg

Index

Hh

Ii

Jj

Kk

Ll

Index

Mm

Nn

Oo

Pp

Index

Qq

Rr

Ss

Index

Tt

Index

Uu

Vv

Ww

Xx

Yy

Zz

Index of Idioms

Illustrations*

All illustrations by Roni Shepherd except for:
Doug Bekke, pp. 17 (3), 20 (2,9), 24 (9,10), 30 (3,5), 31 (3), 42 (2), 43 (3), 46 (4), 55 (2), 56 (10a,b), 56 (10c), 61 (1–8,10), 62 (1b), 63 (12), 66 (10), 70 (1a–j), 76 (1a,b), 79 (3), 82 (11), 86 (7), 87 (7), 92 (1a,b;8), 94 (4), 98 (9), 99 (5), 103 (1), 105 (1,8), 107 (3), 115 (3), 118 (10), 119 (1a,b); **Ka Botzis,** pp. 12 (4,5,7), 14 (1;4a–c), 15 (3), 18 (3), 20 (8), 28 (1), 36 (3), 39 (1,6,10), 42 (9), 46 (1,9), 57 (10), 65 (9), 66 (6), 71 (5), 76 (9), 79 (5), 82 (12), 83 (1), 94 (5), 95 (11a,b), 110 (9), 114 (10); **Ann Boyajian,** pp. 50 (10), 90 (5,6), 92 (9,12), 98 (6,10,11), 105 (7), 106 (10), 108 (5a,b), 110 (6), 112 (4,9), 120 (11), 124 (9–12), 138 (1,2), 142 (3,4,5,6); **Sue Carlson,** pp. 10 (2), 15 (4), 17 (9), 18 (7), 21 (9a,b), 25 (1,7), 29 (9), 56 (3), 68 (2,5), 69 (1,–11), 88 (1), 105 (4), **Chi Chung,** pp. 133 (1a,b; 2a,b); **Alexander Farquharson,** pp. 22 (5,6,7), 34 (1), 35 (9a,b,c,d); **Ray Godfrey,** pp. 124 (1), 125 (1), 142 (1,2); **Gershom Griffith,** pp. 10 (3), 11 (4), 40 (1,2); **Susan Johnston,** pp. 64 (1–3); **Doug Knutson,** pp. 96 (1), 100 (1); **Tim McGarvey,** pp. 104 (2), 125 (2); **Karen Minot,** pp. 46 (2), 50 (6), 52 (3), 58 (1), 60 (1), 65 (6), 116 (1); **Yoshi Miyake,** pp. 74 (all), 75 (all), 111 (1,3–5); **Pat Rossi,** pp. 51 (2), 63 (7), 67 (2); **Sandra T. Sevigny,** pp. 67 (7,10), 99 (9), 104 (5); **Rose Zgodzinski,** pp. 24 (7), 25 (6b), 27 (12), 44 (8), 77 (9), 86 (4), 108 (9,10).

Photography*

American Museum of Natural History, Library Services: p. 68 (8). **Animals, Animals:** Breck P. Kent, pp. 48 (12), 139 (6). **AP/Wide World:** pp. 43 (9); 45 (3). **Art Resource:** Erich Lessing, p. 92 (11). **Artville:** pp. 13 (3), 39 (5–b), 54 (3a), 66 (5), 67 (3a–d), 99 (3a,b), 112 (11a,b), 118 (9), 130 (6,7,9–16,18), 131 (2,3,5,6,9,12,18), 136 (1–3,5–9), 139 (1,3,7).**Joe Atlas:** p. 15 (7). **Batista Moon Studio:** p. 66 (12). **Cathy Blake:** pp. 6 (4a,b), 20 (6a,b). **Carnegie Museum of Natural History:** p. 68 (6). **Ed Carreon:** p. 53 (12). **Colorado, The State Historical Society Library of:** p. 97 (9a). **Stephen W. Conant:** p. 91 (5). **Corbis-Bettmann:** pp. 11 (9;10;11a,b;12), 22 (4,8,11,12), 23 (1), 41 (2a,b), 51 (11,12), 55 (3b), 85 (3,8), 88 (6), 95 (5), 115 (9); Reuters, p. 44 (6); Baldwin H. Ward. p. 55 (3a). **Corel:** p. 6 (10,12), 7 (4a,d).**Richard & Susan Day:** p. 88 (4). **E.R. Degginget:** p. 117 (4). **Digital Stock:** pp. 8 (8), 13 (6d), 16 (11), 17 (4,8), 18 (10a), 26 (12), 30 (7), 43 (12), 50 (7c), 60 (3,6), 67 (4), 73 (5), 77 (10), 85 (2), 104 (7a,b), 107 (4), 114 (1), 115 (1), 118 (12), 123 (3), 140 (4,8,10,11), 141 (4,5). **John Foster:** A Map of New England: p. 107 (8). **Free Library of Philadelphia, Print and Picture Collection:** p. 23 (3). **Gettysburg National Military Park:** p. 10 (1). **Gibbes Museum of Art/Carolina Art Association:** p. 101 (9a). **Glenbow Foundation, Calgary, Alberta:** p. 101 (9b). **Trelawney Goodell:** p. 91 (3,4,6,7). **Grant Heilman:** Runk/Schoenberger, pp. 17 (11), 27 (1), 29 (12). **Hampton-Brown Books:** p. 36 (7), 107 (5). **Image Club:** pp. 16 (1b), 26 (10a), 29 (6a,b,c), 33 (8b), 37 (3), 48 (2a,b;5a,c–f;6b), 54 (3c), 55 (11), 62 (9b), 63 (6a–d), 104 (11), 107 (1a–c), 115 (11), 136 (4), 139 (2,4,5). **The Image Works:** pp. 49 (1–04), 83 (11), 102 (5), 110 (3); Mark Antman, pp. 15 (8), 98 (12a); Tony Arruza, pp. 105 (11), 110 (5); Bachmann, p. 50 (12); M. Bernsau, p. 66 (9); Alan Carey, p. 42 (8); Joe Carini, p. 99 (2); Crandall, p. 88 (1); Elizabeth Crews, p. 78 (8); Bob Daemmrich, pp. 33 (1,06), 42 (6), 48 (3), 50 (5), 51 (5), 54 (10), 60 (2), 63 (3), 67 (11), 72 (7), 85 (7), 95 (12), 112 (8), 114 (6), 139 (12); Sondra Dawes, p. 110 (1); Townsend P. Dickinson, p. 47 (1); John Eastcott, pp. 38 (8), 110 (2); John Eastcott/Yva Momatiuk, pp. 84 (1–02), 94 (7c), 114 (12); Edrington, p. 87 (11a); Esbin-Anderson, p. 15 (5); Macduff Everton, pp. 5 (9), 57 (5); Alex Farnsworth, p. 98 (2); Myrleen Ferguson, p. 95 (10); S. Gazin, pp. 31 (1a), 108 (7); M. Granitsas, pp. 8 (6b), 50 (7b), 77 (6); Jeff Greenberg, pp. 46 (12), 115 (12a); John Griffin, p. 36 (4); Keystone, p. 59 (9); David Lassman, p. 38 (2); R. Lord, p. 71 (3); L. Mulvehill, p. 89 (3); J. Nordell, p. 90 (11); F. Pedrick, p. 13 (12); Tim Reese, p. 13 (9); N. Richmond, p. 112 (7); Loraine Rorke, p. 41 (6); Savino, p. 105 (9); R. Sidney, p. 94 (7d); Elen Senis, p. 90 (1); J. Spratt, p. 94 (7a); Syracuse Newspapers/Randi Anglin, p. 9 (10b); Topham, p. 98 (7a); David Wells, pp. 15 (9), 23 (4); D. Wray, p. 108 (3); Alison Wright, p. 50 (7a). **Index Stock:** p. 15 (10). **International Stock:** pp. 115 (4); Ron Behrmann, p. 82 (7); Gary Bigham, p. 17 (12); Mark Bolster, p. 46 (8); Chuck Mason, p. 120 (3); Buddy Mays, p. 17 (2); Patrick Ramsey, p. 18 (1–2); Stan Reis, p. 114 (2), Noble Stock, p. 36 (8a). **Bonnie Kamin:** pp. 31 (7), 56 (9), 99 (4). **R. Kolar:** p. 117 (5). **Zig Lesszczynski:** p. 43 (6). **Library Company of Philadelphia:** Peter Cooper, p. 23 (2). **Library of Congress:** pp. 51 (9), 87 (6), 91 (1,2), 101 (9c). **Christopher Little:** p. 53 (4). **Diana Maloney:** pp. 27 (9a–f). **Joe McDonald:** p. 7 (2). **Metaphoto:** pp. 7 (4c;5), 8 (1a,b), 12 (10a,b), 38 (10), 87 (1), 90 (10b), 130 (5). **Lawrence Migdale:** pp. 5 (3), 65 (4), 77 (5), 108 (8), 119 (3). **Missouri Historical Society:** p. 55 (1,02). **Monkmeyer:** Capece, p. 77 (2); Clay, p. 52 (1); Conklin, p. 89 (6); David Forbert, p. 119 (9); Dollarhide, p. 41 (7b), (9); Goodwin, p. 56 (8), 118 (6); Heron, p. 106 (11); Kerbs, p. 52 (2); Merrim, p. 90 (12); Press/Sidney, p. 120 (6); Rogers, p. 92 (10); Rue, p. 93 (10); Siteman, p. 87 (3); Ullmann, p. 52 (10), 73 (11); Yin, p. 73 (7). **Montana Historical Society, Helena:** p. 82 (3), 97 (9b). **NASA:** p. 13 (5), 93 (4). **National Museum of the American Indian:** p. 68 (9,10). **New York Public Library, Special Collections:** p. 111 (2). **North Wind Pictures:** p. 82 (2). **R. Packwood:** p. 70 (4). **Ilene Perlman:** p. 62 (9a). **Photo Edit:** pp. 84 (4); Bill Aron, p. 73 (12); Bill Bachmann, p. 57 (12); Vic Bider, p. 112 (12); Leslye Borden, p. 46 (7); Phil Borden, p. 46 (6); Robert Brenner, pp. 42 (3), 99 (7b); Michelle Bridwell, p. 90 (4); Cindy Charles, p. 26 (2); Paul Conklin, p. 57 (3); Deborah Davis, pp. 8 (6c), 20 (5a,b), 73 (4); Kate Deany, p. 42 (4); Mary Kay Denny, pp. 8 (2), 33 (5), 86 (8), 139 (15); Amy C. Etra, p. 52 (5), 112 (3); Myrleen Ferguson, pp. 5 (2,12), 20 (7), 31 (11), 37 (10), 79 (11b), 95 (7), 114 (3), 115 (8), 118 (2,4), 123 (7); Tony Freeman, pp. 19 (12), 21 (3), 33 (8a), 37 (9), 41 (12), 42 (1a), 48 (6a), 63 (10), 76 (2), 84 (3), 94 (1,7e), 102 (2), 108 (2), 115 (2,7), 119 (4), 139 (13); Robert Ginn, p. 85 (6); Spencer Grant, p. 85 (4); Jeff Greenberg, pp. 86 (11), 88 (3); Jack Grove, p. 62 (7); Richard Hutchings, pp. 22 (9), 102 (4); Bonnie Kamin, pp. 8 (6a), 25 (9); Dennis MacDonald, pp. 21 (5), 78 (10); Felicia Martinez, pp. 95 (9), 114 (7); Stephen McBrady, pp. 27 (7), 32 (6); McCarthy, p. 107 (6); John Neubauer, p. 22 (1); Michael Newman, pp. 19 (11), 62 (4), 63 (2), 78 (11), 105 (3), 109 (3), 110 (8), 115 (10), 119 (6), 139 (14), 140 (12); Jonathan Nourok, pp. 48 (9), 57 (4), 60 (4), 93 (11); Novastock, p. 118 (5); Alan Oddie, p. 93 (7); A. Ramey, p. 57 (8); Mark Richards, pp. 56 (2), 70 (12); Nancy Sheehan, pp. 79 (8), 98 (1); Frank Siteman, p. 41 (11); Gary Spencer, p. 45 (2); Rudi Von Briel, p. 106 (5); Dana White, p. 93 (9); David Young-Wolff, pp. 16 (2), 19 (6), 26 (8), 33 (11), 38 (4,5), 56 (12), 57 (11), 60 (12), 62 (5), 71 (10), 73 (2), 77 (11), 99 (7a), 102 (12), 105 (12), 120 (7), 137 (6). **Photo Researchers:** p. 118 (1); B&C Alexander, p. 110 (4); James L. Amos, p. 29 (2); Frederick Ayer, p. 117 (3); Bachmann, p. 88 (5); D.P. Burnside, p. 27 (5); Alan & Sandy Carey, p. 31 (8); Ken Cavanagh, p. 29 (5); Martyn F. Chillmaid/Science Photo Library, p. 29 (8); CNES, p. 59 (3); Suzanne L. Collins & Joseph T. Collins, p. 7 (10); Herminia Dosal, p. 89 (4); John Eastcott/YVA Momatiuk, p. 55 (10); Douglas Faulkner, p. 73 (6); David Frazier, p. 55 (4); Spencer Grant, p. 109 (1); Jan Halaska, p. 89 (2); Eunice Harris, p. 63 (9); Bruce M. Herman, p. 110 (12); Tom Hollyman, p. 79 (6); George Holton, pp. 16 (5), 51 (6); David Hosking, p. 26 (6b); Richard Hutchings, pp. 6 (1), 41 (1); Varin-Visage Jacana, p. 13 (6g), George B. Jones III, p. 20 (4); Joyce Photographics, p. 92 (6); Peter B. Kaplan, p. 13 (6c); Keith Kent/Science Photo Library, p. 117 (1); Franz Lanting, p. 16 (7); Ken Lax, p. 38 (9); Tom & Pat Leeson, p. 7 (1); 13 (6f);Rafael Macia, pp. 26 (9), 65 (3), 90 (9), 105 (5); Andrew J. Martinez, p. 107 (7a,b); Oliver Meckes, p. 71 (7); Lawrence Migdale, pp. 68 (3), 76 (10), 86 (10); Margaret Miller, p. 27 (6); Hank Morgan, p. 87 (11b,c); Emil Muench, p. 39 (10a); Joseph Nettis, p. 39 (4); Rod Planck, p. 89 (1); Doug Plummer, p. 59 (10); Gary Retherford, p. 13 (6i); Shirley Richards, p. 88 (2); Leonard Lee Rue, Jr, p. 47 (3); Blair Seitz, p. 109 (2); Chris Sharp, p. 73 (10); Peter Skinner, p. 38 (7); Steve Skloot, p. 120 (4); Jim Steinberg, p. 99 (1); Norm Thomas, p. 92 (5); Gerard Vandystadt, p. 43 (10); Elisabeth Weiland, p. 48 (4); Charles D. Winters, p. 15 (2). **PhotoDisc:** pp. 5 (10a,b), 5 (11), 7 (6,9), 8 (4), 9 (2,4,12), 13 (6b,e,h), 15 (1), 17 (7), 18 (9a,10b), 19 (8), 20 (11), 24 (3), 26 (10b,11), 30 (11), 32 (1,2,3), 33 (3), 37 (5a,b;12), 38 (10b), 39 (12), 41 (8), 42 (9a), 43 (7), 45 (5), 47 (1a,2a,4), 50 (3), 51 (3), 54 (1,2a), 56 (1), 62 (11,12), 66 (2), 67 (5,12), 68 (4), 71 (8), 73 (3,8), 78 (2,7), 87 (8), 90 (10a,c), 102 (7), 104 (1,4,10), 119 (5), 122 (2a,b), 128 (4,9), 129 (1,4,7), 130 (2,3,19), 131 (8,10,11,14), 137 (12), 139 (9,10,16), 140 (1–3,6,7,9,10), 141 (1–3,8,9,11). **Picture Perfect:** p. 15 (11). **Plimoth Plantation, Inc.:** pp. 80 (4), 81 (3); Gary Andrashko, p. 80 (3), 81 (1,4); Ted Curtin, p. 80 (2), 81 (2,5). **Fritz Prenzel:** p. 32 (4). **Private Collection:** p. 68 (11). **Richard C. Owen Publishing, Inc., Katonah, NY.:** Gerry Perrin/Paul Goble, p. 8 (9,10). **James Robinson:** H., p. 88 (7). **Sentinel & Enterprise:** Amanda Bicknell, p. 48 (10). **Stock Boston:** Bob Daemmrich, p. 83 (10). **The Stock Market:** Richard Berenholtz, p. 89 (4). **Stockbyte:** pp. 16 (1a,c), 42 (1b), 52 (7,8), 54 (3b), 55 (12), 57 (7), 62 (1a), 72 (8), 92 (3), 106 (12a), 118 (7b,c), 119 (8), 141 (12). **SuperStock:** pp. 7 (4b), 13 (6a), 15 (6,12), 16 (3), 23 (5), 24 (11), 26 (1), 31 (6), 33 (2), 37 (8), 47 (2), 48 (7), 49 (2), 59 (1), 63 (5), 66 (10), 76 (3), 79 (11c), 82 (4,8), 86 (6), 89 (10), 93 (8), 102 (1), 104 (9), 106 (1,3,6); Richard Heinz, p. 9 (5); University of Miami, Lowe Art Museum, p. 68 (7); John W. Warden, p. 66 (8), 78 (12). **Ned Taft:** p. 26 (6a), 42 (11), (2), 59 (11). **Tony Stone Images:** Lori Adamski Peek, p. 12 (12); Bruce Ayres, p. 112 (6); Brian Bailey, p. 120 (12); Tom Bean, p. 58 (1), Dugald Bremner, p. 84 (6); Paul Chesley, p. 59 (2); Peter Correz, p. 85 (1); Chip Henderson, p. 93 (5); Kalunzy/Thatch, p. 65 (2); Charles Krebs, p. 59 (6); Alan Levenson, p. 84 (5); John Marshall, p. 98 (7b); Cathlyn Melloan, pp. 21 (4), 112 (10); Kevin Miller, p. 59 (12); Dennis O'Clair, p. 44 (3); Jon Ortner, p. 44 (5); Jake Rajs, p. 58 (3); Andy Sacks, p. 43 (1); Richard Shock, p. 95 (8); Frank Siteman, p. 95 (2); Chad Slattery, p. 114 (4); Don Smetzer, pp. 9 (3), 94 (7b), 114 (8), 141 (7); Philip & Karen Smith, p. 98 (12b); James Strachan, p. 98 (7c); Bob Thomas, p. 118 (7a); Gre Vaughn, p. 82 (1); Terry Vine, p. 54 (7); Randy Wells, p. 44 (1); David Young-Wolff, pp. 110 (7), 119 (2), 139 (11). **Uniphoto:** pp. 12 (3), 59 (4), 63 (11), (9), 105 (2), 120 (2); Daniel Anderson, 1985, p. 41 (10); Robert Anderson, p. 21 (7); Bachmann, p. 105 (10); Peter Beck, p. 9 (9); Chromosohm/Sohm, p. 89 (5); Paul Conklin, pp. 31 (12), 44 (3); Bob Daemmrich, pp. 45 (1,4), 89 (11); Everett C. Johnson, p. 31 (1b); James Kay, p. 99 (11); Lew Lause, p. 38 (3); Jeffrey W. Myers, p. 25 (4); Carl Purcell, p. 21 (6); Mark Reinstein, p. 44 (2); Siteman, p. 25 (3). **Wenham Doll Museum:** p. 119 (7). **Whatcom Museum of History and Art:** p. 97 (9c). **Tracy Wheeler** pp. 123, 126, 127, 129 (2,3,6,8), 134, 135, 137 (1–5,7–11), 140 (2), 141 (6), 143 (1). **Beth Whitney:** pp. 16 (4), 50 (7d), 65 (1). **J. R. Williams:** p. 117 (2). **Liz Garza Williams:** p. 129 (5).

***Credits:** Illustrations and photo credits are identified by cell number (1–12) and positioned within the cell (a–z), in top to bottom order.

1	5	9
2	6	10
3	7	11
4	8	12